Pra...

Doing a 360: Turning Your Life Around to Follow Soul's Purpose

"This spherical or all-encompassing "three-sixty" philosophy has spiraled to the surface at a crucial time in history. Reverend Ash, a heart-centered teacher of heroic transformation through journey of the Soul, emerges in a fresh voice to help midwife the birth of our next paradigm shift, a shift from the illusion of separation to a world of Oneness."

— **Steve Farrell**, Worldwide Director, *Humanitysteam.org*

"Nancy Ash exemplifies the best of the yogic and mind enhancement qualities. Her book, *Doing a 360*, is an invaluable contribution to the field of self-liberation."

— **Joan Kaye, Ph.D.**, President, *Skydancerpress.com*

"Rev. Dr. Nancy Ash asks you to ascend with her through deep reflection, spiritual practices, meditations and inspirational writings to do a complete 360-degree transformation. She offers up the invitation for 'turning your life around completely' in an all-encompassing, multidimensional, circular experience... and to enter the 'sacred spin zone.' Accept Nancy's invitation to 360 and your life will never be the same."

— **Cathy Haven Howard**, Author of *Spirit Expression for Everyone*

"My esteemed colleague and friend, Nancy Ash, embodies the message of her book, *Doing a 360*, and compassionately inspires others to fully self-actualize."

— **Rev. Dr. Linda Marie Nelson**, *ADL, OFJ*

"I implore you to be present and available to this work of art, *Doing a 360: Turning Your Life Around to Follow Soul's Purpose*. My dear, Spirit Sister Friend has orchestrated a divine treasure for all who hear the call to return home."

— **Tracey Burrell**, *Oneness Advocate*

Doing a 360

Turning Your Life Around

to

Follow Soul's Purpose

Doing a 360

Turning Your Life Around

to

Follow Soul's Purpose

Reverend Dr. Nancy Ash

Copyright © 2012 Reverend Dr. Nancy Ash

www.Doinga360.com
Doinga360@aol.com

Published by 360 Publishing

Cover Design by Dawn Sebti
Cover Photo by Jonathan Ash

Notes to You: This book is true. The names of students and clients mentioned herein have been changed to protect their privacy. In many cases details related to individuals have been altered. The strategies described herein are lovingly offered as general information. The author of this book does not dispense any medical advice or prescribe the use of any strategies or techniques as a form of treatment for physical, emotional or medical problems without the advice of a physician. No part of this publication is intended to substitute for a competent medical diagnosis undertaken in consultation with a professional practitioner. The author and publisher assume no liability for your actions.

All rights reserved. No part of this book may be used or reproduced in any way whatsoever, electronic or mechanical, including photocopying, recording, or by any information storage and retrieval system, or otherwise copied for public or private use—except in the instance of "fair use" as brief quotations embodied in blogs, articles and reviews—without prior written permission of the publisher. Thank you for respecting the joyful efforts of this author. May all sentient beings benefit from this auspicious activity!

Grateful acknowledgement is made to Humanitysteam.org for permission to quote "Oneness" (Global Council Meeting, Greece), 2011.

Scripture quotations from The Bible: Authorized King James Version, Public Domain, 1611.

ISBN: 978-0-9883674-1-8
Digital ISBN: 978-0-988-3674-0-1

1st EDITION, November 2012

Printed in the United States of America

To

~ Jonathan ~

Joseph Campbell

and You

SPHERICAL CONTENTS

2nd QUADRANT of Going Deep: *Weaving and Healing*

3rd QUADRANT of 360 Change: *Spirit in Action*

Gratitude in Grace

To my Divine Source of Oneness…

or all my mentors, teachers, allies and students of the three times: past, present and future, I pay homage to these spiritual evolutionary collaborators. In particular, I'm greatly indebted to the integral musings of a keen mind, Dr. Joan Kaye, a 360 mentor and lifelong *yogini* sister friend. As with many of the rich blessings in life she introduced me to some of the greatest minds of our time: Jean Houston, Thomas Berry, and the incomparable mythologist, Joseph Campbell, whom I learned from as a teenager. Little did I know then that his brilliant award-winning work, *The Hero with a Thousand Faces* [1] would be full-circle pith initiation to inspire a life of service that I now call: "Doing a 360" (three-sixty).

Years later, on an auspicious day which is a rite-of-passage for any western young woman (my thirtieth birthday), through her loving introduction I met another glorious, exceptional man that would influence my thinking forever. He was my spiritual father and heart-friend, the renowned Dzogchen Master, Venerable Khenchen Palden Sherab Rinpoche.

A momentous scholar and author of many books, Khenchen Palden Sherab Rinpoche was a profound Lama in the Nyingma Lineage of Tibetan Buddhism. He was a rare enlightened being, an extraordinary humble man that walked his talk. Ven. Khenchen Rinpoche was revered on this fragile planet as one of a handful remaining authentic Dzogchen Masters from Tibet. (*Khenchen* is a Tibetan word that means great teacher, or senior abbot; *Rinpoche* in the Tibetan language is an honorific title that literally translates as "precious one.")

Tibet was his beloved homeland known as the mysterious "roof of the world" and remote "land of snows." Khenchen's stainless reputation worldwide went hand-in-hand with reverence. It was an agonizing, painful heartache when he passed away in 2010, shortly before I finished a draft of this manuscript. Sadly, his butter lamp has gone out... for now. As a senior devotee for twenty-plus years, I trained closely under his tutelage (and his younger brother, Venerable Khenpo Tsewang Dongyal Rinpoche). These loving siblings were inseparable. Rarely apart, these two Lamas uplifted humanity by spreading the precious Dharma (teachings of the Buddha) to every corner of the globe. Please consider visiting their comprehensive cyber home online at www.padmasambhava.org.[2]

Fortune graced me as I sat at the lotus feet of these masters learning to live mindfully toward liberation. May Ven. Khenchen Palden Sherab Rinpoche return swiftly for the sake of all sentient beings. May we enjoy boundless eons together. *Emaho!* [The Sanskrit word *emaho* (pronounced ay-mah-ho) is an expression of joy and wonder, and an invocation for auspiciousness.]

There are many others throughout the years that have contributed significantly to the ideas put forth here in this book, planting seeds in my consciousness with their profound knowledge, love, and encouragement. In that regard, I am so grateful for the continued loving guidance from a powerful Raja Yoga Master and philosopher, my dearest heart-friend and mentor, Chandra Shekhar Robinson, whom I met in his yoga class at the University of Maryland (student union) in October of 1977. Among the immeasurable blessings in this life he is undoubtedly a luminary, a bright light among men and women.

I wish to acknowledge a cherished longtime mentor, The Reverend Dr. Michelle Lusson (founder of the Creative Wellness Programs), and the late Reverend Dr. Barbara Hanshaw, as exceptional teachers influencing my growth as an integral "360" being. It was an honor to study closely and be personally ordained by both of these mighty women in the trans-denominational and interspiritual ministries that they each established with faithful dedication to advance Oneness.[3] [4]

I so appreciate the vision of longtime colleague and SSF (spiritual sister friend) Reverend Dr. Linda Marie Nelson, who boldly encouraged publishing this work with splendid support.

Upon her invitation to further join forces in 2010 as radio producers and co-hosts, we launched a global talk show called *"Consider This… with Linda Marie and Nancy."* Our online program is dedicated to the promotion of Oneness through an inclusive "360" dialogue with the leading and emerging voices of sacred activism for unifying spiritual evolution. Related to each show's weekly topic/theme my 360 Re-calibrations are guided healing meditations with music, sagely designed to raise the vibratory frequency of listeners. If you have been one of them, accept my heartfelt thanks for the support of this program on (TAO) The Art of Living Well Network at Blogtalkradio.com[5]

I have been privileged to share in this beneficial endeavor providing an all-inclusive and thought-provoking forum for deep discussion. Like this book, *Doing a 360*, we ask our audience to consider opening their heart to a spherical or three hundred and sixty-degree "both and" perspective, rather than a narrow, limiting "either or" dualistic point of view.

To all dear friends, old and new, and to family who support me while offering grist for the mill—thank you. Thank you so very much. I love you. I love you all. Especially I give gratitude to my parents: My mother, whose orb surrounds me since her death way too many years ago when I was nineteen; and to my Father who gave precious life.

I wish to distinguish two lifelong, dear friends that I consider to be extraordinary women: Dawn Sebti, the incomparable artist I met (sitting side-by-side) the first day of art school in New York City. Her most exceptional talent as designer and art director ornamented this book with a beautiful cover; and Tracey Burrell, who encouraged and supported me as a midwife to birth this work. She tirelessly proofed the manuscript with unconditional loving care, patience, and spherical insight.

Also, heartfelt appreciation is in order to book agent Susan Setteducato for her wise council years ago. The scope of her generous, encouraging editorial suggestions very early in this project fueled my passion to bring this book forward.

In the spirit of a circle which has no beginning and no end: Last, but not least, I dedicate this work to my lifelong love, dharma brother, and "three-sixty" buddy, my husband of thirty-plus awesome years, Jonathan. With joyful effort and clarity he read and then re-read this book offering excellent advice. His compassionate ear listened to my ruminations over and over again, *ad nauseam*. Jonathan is my Soul friend. He is an amazing man of integrity. A true love into all eternity that chose me (as I chose him again) on this incredible, wonderful journey of spiritual ascension that we call life.

I express gratitude daily from my "heart-of-hearts" (a term I use for the Soul) for abundant favor and protection of guidance that deepens with every moment. With prayerful palms together in the *yogic mudra* at my heart-space, I offer a traditional *Namaste* to celestial hosts encircling with divine love.

In every golden, shimmering breath I take into the trillions of cells in my body, I respectfully step aside to allow The Collective Presence of The One manifest these sacred spherical strategies into what I theurgically call, *Doing a 360*. (*Theurgy* is a Greek word meaning, "divine-work" or supernatural intervention.)

May this heroic, circular presentation of spirit in action assist individuals to re-calibrate their lives for personal and planetary transformation. During this most exciting, critical, and spiritual evolutionary nexus in history—this new age of a new Earth—may all beings be happy. *Lha Gyalo!* [The Tibetan phrase *'lha gyalo'* (pronounced la-jahl-lo) is an exuberant expression of joyful victory to the deities.][6]

With Love and Gratitude in Grace,

Reverend Dr. Nancy Ash
From snow-capped mountains in a land of enchantment,
New Mexico
New Years Day 2012

Preface

"You must do the thing you think you cannot do."

— Eleanor Roosevelt

elcome new friend, seeker of Oneness beginning a book with fresh wonder and curiosity. I salute you in this moment: A time of pause with some questioning and discernment as to whether you wish to consider reading further. Could this be a luminous portal to help turn your life around—completely?

These are indeed challenging times that we are going through. Dear reader, I am here in words to invite you on a journey. It is my utmost caring wish that these pages inspire change to re-calibrate your life. A "360" life: A lifecycle of radiant, deep sacred meaning and purpose—unquestionably, a Soul purpose.

After reading and re-reading, editing, and then re-editing this manuscript like a sculptor chiseling, sanding, and polishing, I discovered in circular reflection that a Preface is a *request* to the reader. This is your prelude, a divine clarion call to a new conscious life. Here within are the Soul stirrings of an encoded evolutionary urge for personal transformation that just may lead to our healed humanity. Book prefaces, though placed at the beginning, are written last. They are vigilant confessions of sorts: Revelations of work lovingly prepared. So the cool thing is, that the more I read these pages… genuine empowerment ensued for me, too.

Sifting through this material I raised my vibration spiraling upwards in subtle ways. Sometimes these adjustments alchemically altered into passionately deeper grottos of heart-awareness and subsequent bliss. Like the ubiquitous message from Joe Campbell to "follow your bliss" I was taking heed of his marvelous advice. If you are not familiar with the esteemed professor and most preeminent mythologist, the late Joseph Campbell, then I am so very honored and thrilled to introduce you to one of the greatest luminaries of our time. Simply sparking interest to study his transformative body of work will suffice in the worthiness of publishing this book. Please visit the wonderful Joseph Campbell Foundation online at http://www.jcf.org[1]

Like the vibrant, imaginative mind of Joe (I know he's smiling!) I was an open-minded and eager reader rather than just an author editing words. This sacred shift generated excitement to the healing power of *Doing a 360: Turning Your Life Around to Follow Soul's Purpose* for quickening the Soul into elegant, spiritual evolutionary collaboration. Quite frankly, at this nexus in history we all could use an upgrade. If each one of us do not re-calibrate to the powerful spiritual beings that we are potentiated to be, our general survival as a human species is dubious. You have probably heard that doom and gloom message before. Yet, I wish to be clear here for the record: I am compassionately optimistic about our collective future no matter how terribly abysmal it may appear at times.

During the six years that it took to write this book so much has changed in me, as in our world. I'm not the same person that I was. I am not the same as last year, last month, or even yesterday.

Minute-by-minute, as in the healing process of autopoeisis,[2] I alter and self-correct. That is part and parcel of spiritual evolution: Every moment we are growing spontaneously and organically. You are evolving too, even if not *consciously* aware of this sacred process—yet. Individually and collectively our species as a human family is spiraling up the proverbial ladder of ascension. We are ascending step-by-step to a world of Oneness, to a new world of integral awareness, or what I simply call "360" (three-sixty).

When an artist puts a last stroke of paint on a canvas and stands back to affirm that his or her work is finished, wow—what a moment! Similarly, on this printed page I asked myself: "What does *Doing a 360* convey? What does it really say?" This book is spherical. What do I mean by that? Well, it is not linear. Writing about three hundred and sixty-degrees of personal, complete, spiritual evolutionary change has got to be spherical. Its nature is a heroic, cyclical design.[3]

Turning your life around completely is an all-encompassing, multidimensional, circular experience. Therefore, you will notice (intentional) repetition throughout this entire book. In the experience of all life, here and in the mystic "after," we re-cycle ourselves over and over again. Life is just a magical display of all phenomena (as dear teacher Khenchen Rinpoche used to say). It's a dynamic, inexorable movement into the Absolute: Into a Source of All Being; into emptiness, or *shunyata,* as Buddhists term it; or Oneness, Presence, Allah, Great Spirit, the Tao, Christ Consciousness, Jesus, Goddess or GOD. (Whatever sacred name helps you feel comfortable on this excursion to wholeness.)

It is not by chance, happenstance or coincidence that you are in the presence of holding this book in your hands. By immutable universal laws and grace you have come to visit with me as a conscious, spiritual being. If these words resonate in your heart then know you have been led here deliberately by Soul, your Higher Consciousness, which is "self" with a capital (S)elf. Realizing (S)elf and knowing your own truth is the key to liberation and salvation. This means knowing (with what the Buddha called "certainty wisdom") that you are a spiritual creation *in* and *of* all that is Source. (However you wish to term it—The Creator or

The Divine One, etc.) You are a beautiful, individuated Spirit having an essential and most significant human experience. "Doing a three-sixty" is a sacred spherical matrix as well as a process or journey. Think of this as a circular roadmap for turning yourself completely around or perhaps even upside down, inside out!, offering a fresh perspective to engender a new way of being. That new way is your Soul being awake, AWARE every day of life… driving the bus, so-to-speak, everywhere you go.

As you'll read later, I've compiled decades of lively theurgical experiences into this book (theurgical means, divine intervention). They are shared not only as a Soul experiencing ITSELF in the creative function of writing, but for *your* inspiration as you make a commitment to self-realization on a journey to wholeness. "Doing a 360," as I found out turning my life around three hundred and sixty-degrees, is choosing to create a mature reality. That means, accepting responsibility for all of your life. That means, the whole enchilada: ALL actions in every experience of body, mind, emotions, and spirit. A mature, seasoned reality includes awareness of Soul's natural impulse to *create life consciously* as it is being experienced in the present moment.

My storytelling as a yogini (female adept in the art of yoga) began early at seventeen. I was invited to give a lecture on yoga philosophy with demonstration of yoga asanas (poses) to a group of my mother's colleagues at the Nassau County Homemaker's Council of New York. A beneficial and rewarding adventure, it was obvious that I had a natural inclination for this gift. During that time frame as a young seeker I encountered a heroic man who set me on the "360" ceremonial path of the heroine, the universal, circular *monomyth* of a quest for self-actualization. His name was Joseph Campbell, the one and only greatest storyteller of our age, and the rest as they say is history, or *her*story.[4]

My spiritual pursuits for thirty-plus years involve learning and teaching in multi-disciplinary ways. I was ordained in 1985, and trained further taking vows again in 1998 with a federally recognized ministry. It is trans-denominational and interspiritual, honoring and celebrating *all* faiths by weaving different sacred traditions into an interconnected, cohesive practice of Oneness.

My inspiration and intention has been to flourish, evolving into a better person: to live fully aware with mindfulness, inner peace, joy, gratitude and love. I've chosen a life with service to humanity at its forefront. It is my Soul purpose for living. Yet, with a list of shortcomings, faults, and foibles, I have made mistakes on this journey causing discomfort for many—of that I am sure. The inimitable poet Maya Angelou has empathetically declared: "If you live, you will make mistakes—it is inevitable. But once you do and see the mistake, then you forgive yourself and say, 'Well, if I'd known better I'd have done better.'"[5] With a clear sky of awareness in the all-encompassing "Five Wisdoms" from the Tantric Buddhist tradition, those experiences were part of a life that I chose to create.[6]

We all have choice. I whole-heartedly believe in our free will. Everything I have done or said in the past though ostensibly regrettable in part, is really perfect in the bigger "360" vision. Though I've experienced tremendous suffering at times I would not change a thing. Life is absolutely perfect in this moment. It all led me to you, right here and now—which is picture-perfect. From a grand 360-degree View, which is aligned in my beloved roots of the sacred, ancient Tibetan teachings of Dzogchen: *"It is, as it is."*

If this book helps you to become a better person as it did for me, then your joy will be mine: What goes around... comes around. Individually and collectively, we *will* raise consciousness for a brighter future of peace and harmony on precious planet Earth. It is my belief that IN this unity is where our real power as individuals rests. "Being" in an awakened awareness of this belief leads to the "Doing." Creating a new Mythology of Oneness is what we must DO. If we really are all "one" human family (the seven billion of us), then know without a shadow of a doubt that it is *your individual truth* that makes it so.

Introduction

"The Soul should always stand ajar, ready to welcome the ecstatic experience."

— Emily Dickinson

ou are about to enter a *sacred* spin zone. By the time you finish this book you will be thinking outside the box and around a circle: *Your circle.* I am not here to re-invent the wheel. My intention is to inspire you to re-calibrate your sphere of influence. You are not going to turn around only to face the other way... running from problems, which would be doing a "180"... but you will keep rotating until you do a complete three hundred and sixty-degrees. In doing so, you shall view existence with an all-encompassing, integral insight: You *consciously* create the life you choose from Soul's blueprint. This is a fundamental, sacred awareness of 360 Philosophy. I invite you on this journey to wholeness.

The vast, infinite, mythological mind of the late Professor Joseph Campbell produced the great classic text, *The Hero with a Thousand Faces.* He wrote of a universal rite-of-passage, a hero's journey going full-circle in life:

"The hero ventures forth from the world of common day into a region of supernatural wonder: fabulous forces are there encountered and a decisive victory is won: the hero comes back from this mysterious adventure with the power to bestow boons on his fellow man." [1]

Based on scholar Joe Campbell's archetypal, circular theme of separation, initiation, and return in the hero's journey,[2] this book offers a step-by-step process using sacred spherical strategies and exercises to support heroic, life-changing work. I've walked this journey. Quite frankly, if I can do it… you can do it.

"Doing a 360" is used as a verb throughout this text as the action of completely turning your life around. "360" is also a noun. Not only is it the transitional process of leaving an outmoded way of being, 360 is an entity—the embodiment of a complete or integral view. What is this view? 360-degrees is all-inclusive like the full circumference around a circle. 360 is a spherical, holographic belief in the Oneness (interdependence) of all life. It is a spiritual matrix or magnificent palace of existence—a great mandala.[3]

After studying, contemplating, and practicing the concepts in this book I envision you may say: *"I did a three-sixty. I changed my life* completely *to follow Soul's purpose."*

This publication presents you with deep, thought-provoking and cyclical concepts of God, your Soul/Spirit, consciousness, the universe, and your participatory role *in* and *of* them through user-friendly language via an underpinning of Oneness. With a multi-disciplinary approach to ancient wisdom spiritual traditions, a view of Tibetan Dzogchen[4] provides the rich and colorful, yet profound backdrop to this spherical revelation. Sprinkled with metaphor, myth, and true stories shared through gentle humor, this book provides a heartfelt compassionate undertone amidst a compendium of reality-check guidance. *Doing a 360: Turning Your Life Around to Follow Soul's Purpose* states that you create life—*all of it*—from Soul's intention to fulfill ITS purpose while in physical form. When you let Soul drive the bus, life flows more effortlessly. I prefer easy street. And *your* life does not have to be a struggle.

For some, this spherical voyage may be entirely foreign to a current way of thinking. For others, a 360 Philosophy of Oneness may be a resonant, friendly blend of what is already perceived as truth. For all of us, we share a heroic journey called the circle of life—in *that* we are sure. So, consider savoring this teaching as a favorite fruit smoothie quenching your thirst on a sweltering summer day, delighting the senses while soothing your Soul. During this vision quest you search for true love, inner peace, joy, and contentment. When completing "the return" (as Campbell wrote and taught about during his entire career),[5] you discover that these divine heroic qualities inherently exist within your true nature. As His Holiness The Dalai Lama has said, "We are all equal in wishing to be happy and to overcome our suffering, and I believe that we all share the right to fulfill this aspiration.[6] I believe that the very purpose of our life is to seek happiness."[7]

Message from the Author

"How wonderful it is that nobody need wait a single moment before starting to improve the world."

— Anne Frank

About this book…

have prepared this manuscript in a cyclical order to help facilitate understanding the 360 (three-sixty) concepts. Please feel free to roam around since the intention for you is to use this book often as a reference guide.

It is helpful—but not necessary—to have someone read the various exercises to you, or record them, which can be a lot of fun. Many longtime students participated in all the experiences described in this book. Their subsequent abundant challenges, questions, inspirations, responses, and suggestions helped weave my work into this form. Therefore, I am greatly indebted to them for what they shared. In the spirit of rotation, regular practice will re-habituate your belief patterns, so please keep upgrading or re-calibrating every day.

You'll observe that there are twelve chapters corresponding to the twelve months in a year. They are spherically divided into four sections designed as the quadrants of a healing circle, representing stages of your journey to wholeness:

1) Sacred Ground: *Inspiration and Intention*, (the two "I's" or "eyes" seeing clearly in all directions or three hundred and sixty-degrees, i.e., seeing the big picture)

2) Going Deep: *Weaving and Healing*

3) Changing: *Spirit in Action*

4) Actualization: *Transformation 360*

In one year, after working consistently with these spherical strategies, doing the exercises, walking the talk, etc., you will turn your life around completely towards Oneness. In doing so you begin to clarify Soul's purpose. In *Quadrant One*, three chapters represent the sacred ground, the first 90 days of 360 Training that unveils the philosophic foundation for a new you. This is the heart and essence of your inspiration and intention to journey to heroic wholeness in which you consider and embrace the fact: You ARE Spirit, and therefore *consciously create reality*.

Chapters 4, 5, and 6 in the *2nd Quadrant of Going Deep*, will dig down into the dark, nitty-gritty… revealing a crucial concept of belief patterns, and how they weave the fabric of your life. This section represents the next three months of deep, self-examination in the levels of your consciousness, emphasizing compassionate transparency in healing all of your relationships. It aligns with Campbell's fierce stage in the hero's journey: Battling your inner demons. I offer healing spherical strategies: Cleaning things up physically, mentally, emotionally, and spiritually.

Like a woman carrying her precious baby in the womb, after nine months you are ready to breakout and birth major changes in an empowered, new life. You are taking action by doing the exercises to effect change. Please remember that the "doing" only springs forth from "being." Chapters 7, 8, and 9 address innovative, spiritual life-coping skills encapsulating them into your essential 360 Daily Practice.

The *4th Quadrant of Actualization,* (which symbolizes Joseph Campbell's vital "return" in the mythic hero's story) offers some guidance and maintenance strategies to continue and support the transformative, integral lifestyle that you have created. Passionate, heroic action is now your *modus operandi* 24/7 with an expanded, sacred view of Oneness. 360 = One. You have gone full-circle: That is "Doing a three-sixty."

Okay. Let's get started...

1ˢᵗ QUADRANT of SACRED GROUND

Intention and Inspiration

Chapter 1

"Doing a 360"

*"The curious paradox is that when I accept myself just as I am,
then I change."*

— Carl Rogers

onsider this: Have you ever driven a vehicle on a wet or an icy road (black ice) when it started to hydroplane? (If not, just imagine that scene in your mind.) You begin to slide, losing control. It's scary, huh? Your heart is pounding as trembling hands grip the wheel. Your instinct is to STOP! So you hit the brakes and quickly spin around. Doing a full-circle (360-degrees) you land just perfectly, facing in the *right* direction *with* the flow of traffic.

Whew! Unharmed, you take a deep breath and sigh with relief. A feeling of profound gratitude overwhelms. Thanking God with a smile on your face you know in your heart that this experience was a very, very close call. Driving on courageously you acknowledge being spared from serious injury. When arriving at your destination you share what happened on this journey: How you faced the crisis and stressful danger of it all, making it through miraculously unscathed with a fresh opportunity to be whole and healthy. That little story I've spun (as a spider weaves her web) is a metaphor. You have just experienced what I call "Doing a three-sixty."

This book is about change. It's about "Doing a 360" with your life. If you want serious, radical, and heroic change, which is what I call a life re-calibration, then please read on for your own sake. From thousands of publications you chose this one. If you are like me (and we *are* as you'll realize), I read what I *feel* guided to. You see, I've done a complete three-sixty with my life and you can, too. If you are yearning for a more meaningful lifestyle, a more authentic, happy, and contented way of living to serve humanity, then the following pages offer a template to a new way of being. If you are willing to change your limited perception, accept this guidance based on my own experiences and some help from the "other" side. (I will get into all of *that* later.)

If I Can Do It... You Can Do It

Feeling dull, depressed, stuck or just plain stressed-out in a rut? Whether broke or rich, is your lifestyle boring you to death? At one time it was for me so I know how that feels. Do you perceive that life has no real deep meaning, no purpose? Are you just going through the motions of every day feeling exhausted, maybe even disgusted, frustrated or sick? Perhaps you have been walking a spiritual path but still feel stifled with a strange evolutionary urge or divine impulse to do more—much more. In a nutshell, that was me.

Consider that the teachings in this book may help no matter what level of spiritual development you are at now. How? Why? Basically, if I can do it... you can do it, too. Though working as a spiritual coach, I am not anyone particularly special. I am not a world renowned scientist or famous movie star, and I don't have my own television talk show—well, not yet, anyway. In high school I wasn't popular. I don't live in some exotic place like Bali, and this manuscript was not written while vacationing summers at a fancy Swiss chalet in the Alps. I am a normal, regular person living in an ordinary suburban community in a typical, small city in America. Yes, I was tired and stuck. My lifestyle was not a reflection of my higher calling, my purpose for being on Earth. Deep down into my bones I needed a major change, a serious download into my DNA. Perhaps this heroic message of re-calibration speaks to your heart, too?

Like a weary hiker lost from the trail into hazardous thick shrub could this be a welcomed signpost to get you back on track? Dear reader, you have entered a *sacred* spin zone. I share in this book the signs that helped me. In a timeless metaphorical "now" your hands tightly squeeze the wheel. Perhaps you are ready to brake—STOP!—and take responsibility for your entire life to a new way of being. You want to do more. You need to *be* more. In my opinion, "being" is THE foundation of "doing." You now wish to live and serve consciously, deliberately, and spiritually. You long for immeasurable joy. You desire balance in your life; and you need to feel empowered and fulfilled. With discernment, what may have truly led you to read these pages? Is it a coincidence?

Consider that there's absolutely no such thing as happenstance. You will recognize this in an insightful concept of the *monomyth* of a "hero's journey" which is a circular, 360-degree story of self-actualization.[1] Monomyth is what Joseph Campbell called this myth comprising the processes of separation, initiation, and return. Professor Campbell's teaching on this universal theme in all cultures and traditions throughout history is the ground of my own journey. Now it is yours if you choose its circular quest to Oneness. Dear reader, did you know that 360 = 1? (Oneness) Yes, this is our new evolutionary math, which I propose in this book. (360-degrees is the circumference of one circle.)

Before becoming aware of this Oneness or 360 Paradigm, I always had faith in divine guidance. I was no stranger to mystical realms or a concept of awakening. Yet, I wound up at midlife in a serious murky rut. As John Lennon's lyrics caution: "Life is what happens to you while you're busy making other plans..."[2] I needed to transmute my life in a very big way. I just could not articulate what that meant in the practical sense, you know, in the real world of day-to-day living, doing laundry, paying bills, etc. Even with my experience in the human potential movement for thirty years, the markers were obvious: restlessness, boredom, and a yearning deep inside for transformation with clear purpose from the Soul-level. Already ordained a minister in my twenties, I was definitely on a spiritual path. A longtime, traditional meditation practice was core to my daily experience. As a *yogini* I taught many throughout the years in 14,000-plus! classes, so blessed to help others through the ancient art and sciences of hatha yoga and meditation. Essentially, I was known as a "spiritual" person.

Having outgrown my stale job and old surroundings I felt a much deeper, passionate call from within. This was clearly a more urgent stirring than I had ever experienced before. Intrinsically, I *knew* my lifestyle was not supporting my purpose, and if I did not "do" something else my Soul would then make arrangements to check out (which means leave this embodiment, or die).

I was a classic case of burnout. Can you relate? After working so hard for so long, being all things to all people, I hungered for a joyful release like a song sung by Cyndi Lauper: *Girls Just Wanna Have Fun.*[3] It just kept dancing around in my head (playfully and sometimes a bit annoyingly). As you shall read in these pages, I found fun through a sacred journey from heartbreak to bliss. I moved my being, a re-calibrated Soul-driven life, to the corner of easy street and love. Here is more back storytelling to the journey.

Consciously Create What You Choose

What do people usually do when feeling stale? They go on vacation, right? They may choose to run away from it all—to refresh, renew, and rejuvenate for a week or two. You can relate to this, huh? So, I booked my very first trip to Hawaii. After reading Pila's fascinating, *The Secrets and Mysteries of Hawaii* that a friend recommended (as well as other historical books about the islands), my husband and I prepared to fly over the rich, blue Pacific. Ahead was a tranquil land of *aloha* steeped in a powerful infusion of the ancient Hawaiian shamanic teachings known as *Ho'oponopono.*[4]

BAM! We were robbed. Seventy-two hours before our trip, I came home to find our master bedroom window smashed with its thick blind-shades flapping their broken wings in hot Florida breezes from off Lake Clarke. Those creepy, out-of-place sounds punctuated an abnormal silence. "She" had finished her exploit just minutes before I arrived. (We later heard from the police that a woman robbed us for drug money.) Probably as I drove up our circular drive she heard the car engine and then made a quick get-away through that window.

All of our jewelry was emptied into a favorite, black leather backpack used in my travels on spiritual pilgrimage to India years earlier. How did I know? The night before I painstakingly packed it for hiking in Volcanoes National Park on Hawaii's Big Island. Much to my chagrin this favorite bag was now missing and its contents were strewn all over the floor. What a mess. She had dumped it out to conveniently fill it up again with our valuables: Cherished heirlooms from my mother, grandmothers' and great-grandmothers' were gone. My husband's stuff was missing as well. Even inexpensive but memorable and treasured gifts from friends and students throughout the years had vanished—all wiped out.

There was, however, something lying face down in the bedroom corner. I wondered what "gift" the perpetrator had left. As I stooped to pick it up I lost my breath. I was heartened to hold a powerful sight: Padmasambhava, the founder of Tibetan Buddhism.[5] The large pendant was dangling from a silky smooth, red protection cord given to me by my teacher, Ven. Khenchen Rinpoche, during an empowerment ceremony.

I then rushed to a small ornamented furniture piece that held all my *malas* (prayer beads) and sighed to see them hanging in full glorious view—even those made of semi-precious stones. Plane tickets were also still there. So was two thousand dollars (cash) in a desk drawer of our office—a room ransacked, too! Like the rare necklace of Guru Rinpoche, (a name which is often used for Padmasambhava)[6] they were miraculously untouched.

It was an inconvenient, disconcerting violation but I did not get too upset or angry. In fact, I did not react much at all. Fairly calm, I felt numb; it all seemed mysteriously interesting in a weird kind of way. My husband was relieved I was safe, and said that I handled the situation really well. I have to admit that I surprised myself. All things happen for a reason. I *knew* that. I had been preaching this philosophy for years. Yes, it was a little sad to lose those things, but they are only material. Memories are rich in the heart. This was a rather reasonable lesson in non-attachment, which could have been much worse. I hoped whomever wound up with our stuff was happy.

What I was left with was an enormous message, perhaps *the* message of life, as you'll explore. However, as we scrambled to replace window glass, dealing with police hovering compassionately just hours before our plane departed for Oahu, I sensed a sacred proclamation encircling life: It was time to move on. Somebody was trying to tell me something and they certainly had my attention.

By the way, (this is really true and very cool) this concept of "360" as a spherical healing process with a catchy phrase was envisioned *exactly* three hundred and sixty days after "Doing a 360" with my life. Well, if *that* was not a divine message from Great Spirit, I don't know what is. I happened to glance at the calendar to confirm an appointment when I noticed it was almost a full year since I moved to change my life. Prompted by strong, intuitive curiosity I actually counted back the days. Yes, you guessed it: three hundred and sixty. I thought nothing significant or special about this particular number. However, that night I saw a potent vision of a big, beautiful circle with the numbers "3-6-0" making a complete rotation, then transforming into a translucent, milky-white sphere. Now it became more than an inkling. It was a *knowing.* And I was listening.

Inspired, I wrote rapidly with vigor, barely keeping up with what poured out. The process was not exactly channeling in an auto-writing style, but it was close to that experience. The *context* of 360 and its sacred *content* you will read in these pages flowed effortlessly. Divine musings were as puffy white clouds drifting swiftly in the wind, high above in the cobalt blue skies of an enchanting, new refuge of New Mexico. It was not a question of local "self" dictating, "*Oh, how nice. Maybe I will write a lovely little book someday about circles.*" No—this was powerful. There wasn't any guesswork. The universe was moving me quickly as God orchestrated this project. Guidance came as a decree, and swiftly at that:

> *"Golden Daughter, this book is part of your job on the Earth plane. For forty years you have been wondering how to manifest your Soul's purpose for being here. Well, this is the beginning gift. Yet, as in a circle there's no beginning... and no end. You've been preparing—gathering information and experiences to teach The Higher Principles, and then present them in this written form to help raise your consciousness and uplift humanity to Oneness. 360 equals One. (360 = 1). Get to work Higher (S)elf... there is so much for us to do."* [7]

You know the old adage: Be careful what you wish for because you are going to get it. Well, it is a true perspective: What you think becomes real. What you dream, you become. What goes around... comes around. This is universal law, which I spin as the 360-boomerang principle coming soon in this chapter.

Turn Around—Completely

So what does "Doing a 360" really mean? It means turning around your life—completely. I am going to help you do that, but in your own way and at your pace. This book is sincerely crafted to help empower and cultivate a new YOU.

Responses from friends and family were interesting to digest while transitioning into a new 360 Lifestyle. I warn you because you may experience their varied paranoia, which are knee-jerk reactions from deep, fear-based judgments.

If you do wind up moving very far away as I did, the typical sadness of losing closeness with a loved one is going to be an issue. Moving may be a challenge with family and friends. It is noteworthy how everyone handles it differently. Just watch it all as a magical display. Some will back off from friendship when they discover you are leaving. It is hard for some; they are dealing with their own abandonment issues. Some will surprisingly come out of the woodwork spending quality time with you—even helping you to pack. Others may react grumpily or make excuses that they cannot see you before leaving. Everyone is different. Remember, they have their own issues. I will address an effective strategy and exercise for handling this when you enter the *2ⁿᵈ Quadrant*, teaching a 360-degree coping skill-set of weaving and healing life patterns.

Reactions to the process of "Doing a 360" will also be so supremely empowering. Expect the best. A few statements were, "I wish I could do what you are doing. You have courage. Wow, you just quit everything? I wish I had the gumption to do it!" At my husband's farewell office party one of his friends said, "When I grow up I want to be like you. I just don't have the guts to do what you guys are doing."

You see, at mid-life, I quit a cushy 401k job and a private practice, sold our home quickly, left behind dear disappointed friends, aging family, and a beloved *sangha* or spiritual community. I moved two thousand miles away to a place I'd *never visited* (except in cyberspace on the Internet). I had absolutely no employment prospects, close friends or relatives waiting there—nothing.

Let me back-up a little to explain: A few months earlier at a dinner party my husband and I met a couple visiting from New Mexico urging us to go there some day. We had never been but heard good things about it. "The Land of Enchantment" is this Southwest state's alluring motto. Hmm. I thought… intriguing. Jogging my memory, an old friend had vacationed in Santa Fe years ago. I remembered she had stated emphatically but with unknowing prophecy, "Oh Nancy, you would really flourish out there." Now our dinner partners advised, "If you are thinking of relocating, consider moving near us. It's really an awesome place to live." There was a Soul-to-Soul connection. After a memorable evening filled with laughter and good cheer our new acquaintance and her husband periodically sent packages of enticing photos, real estate magazines, and local news, etc. Though our meeting had been brief, I was delighted in this support from a new friend. Perusing her materials a strong impression formed that we would definitely meet again. The first package had featured a note saying that this was possibly the beginning of a journey for us. She had no idea how prophetic that was. Little did I know only fourteen weeks later I would quit my entire life and then stay with her briefly while purchasing a home.

Days after that fortuitous encounter at dinner, we took a long and tiresome trip prospecting houses for relocation in a different Southwest state. Upon returning from the airport my husband and I were deep in discussion. The dilemma was we wished to be near our two Godchildren; yet, we didn't feel particularly drawn to that area. So now what? Where would we go: Back to alluring Hawaii or the remote, high desert of New Mexico suggested by the new couple? During this perplexing conversation our doorbell rang. We weren't expecting anyone. No one knew we were back home in Florida yet. Suitcases were still unpacked flanking the front doorway like faithful Tibetan guard dogs.

"Hello…" a strange woman said, enthusiastically peeking her head into the door opening. She was a realtor. "Are you willing to sell your house? I have folks from Texas wanting to buy right now!" Well, quite frankly we were flabbergasted. Our house was not on the market. There was no "for-sale" sign blemishing the front lawn amongst the palm trees and a twenty-foot tall, bird-of-paradise plant that graced our entrance. How could this be? Who sent this lady to us? Astonished, we said that we had just returned from a vacation but would allow the unusual tour.

"Excellent!" she responded, "How about in an hour?" My husband and I rolled wearisome, jet-lagged eyes, shrugged our shoulders and said, "Well, okay."

I have this saying now: "Just get out of the way and let Spirit lead." First of all, the buyer loved the home and requested to bring her husband back in a few hours. During this unexpected afternoon we went for a nice long walk in the neighborhood to digest what was happening. The story gets bizarre: As we finished to stretch in the front yard, a different, younger woman with *another* couple drove by slowly looking at our house. They got out of a car and were lurking near the bushes. I sensed they were not lost but had a purpose. Sure enough, once we went inside our phone rang. This second realtor was an associate of the first, and also asked us if we would sell. Chuckling with wondrous delight, okay, now I really knew that Spirit was calling the shots for us to move. Remember the robbery? Yeah, I got the message—loud and clear.

Two contracts presented in a bidding war until ten o'clock that night yielded a good price. As this strange story goes, neither of those families bought our house! However, a few weeks later we caught our breath and sold it with grace in the smoothest, easiest real estate transaction of our lives. Doing a 360 (the start of the biggest sacred journey of my life) was well under way.

Some advice: Be prepared for people to be shocked by your actions when making a really big change to your lifestyle. "What if you don't like it there? You're crazy! Go visit first before you move so far away. I think you're being foolish," said one of our perturbed friends. Remember, you don't *have* to move away. I did, but that doesn't mean you have to. I wrote the book on it so my experience may be more intense. It was my calling and therefore I acted on it.

Please keep in mind that we are all so fabulously unique. You may choose not to quit your job either, at least not right away— or ever. Doing a three-sixty is your intimate, special journey to Oneness. I was called to experience this particular, dynamic shift of divine transformation. Your process may be much less or perhaps, more drastic. It really does not matter. Just be aware that people may think you are nuts to give up the old you, and birth a new and improved version.

Some thought we were surprisingly bold and brave. Shortly after settling into a home nestled in the beautiful foothills, an old chum called one night. I'll never forget what was said, "Wow, you are my hero. I wish I could do what you did: Just pack up, and leave everything behind and start fresh." After suggesting to him that he *could* absolutely do it too, there was that hesitation, that doubt and silent fear on the other end of the telephone. These prevent you from breaking-out, re-calibrating your life to a full three hundred and sixty-degrees of Oneness. Remember our new mathematical equation: $360 = 1$.

Consider this choice: You have to take the hero or heroine's journey—going full-circle. Realize that fundamentally *you really do create your own reality*. That's what this book will help you to see: A 360 Vision. This means, whatever you wish to do, you *can* do... you just may erroneously think you cannot. If you really desire major, radical, and passionate change in life then you have to be willing to do what it takes with a mature or seasoned understanding of your situation. Contemplate that you may have been asleep. Okay, maybe you've just been taking a nap, stuck unconsciously in a fear-based, ego-holding pattern. I'm here to help get you out.

Time and Space 360

When doing a 360-degree re-calibration, day-to-day reality will move very, very quickly. Things will unfold and shift so fast that your head will begin to spin. Stuart Wilde, the fascinating metaphysician, prolific author, entrepreneur, and millionaire at age nineteen, taught in his empowerment seminars: "You have to be fluid, flexible, and mobile. You have to be ready to just pick up and move in the morning."[8] I used to hear all that and think it was utter hogwash. Well, he wasn't kidding. And I am here to tell you: Yes, you can do that. I did it. You absolutely do not *have* to, but you may. You have choice.

When deep into this process my lifecycle was moving so fast that there was barely enough time in a day to get the laundry done. Every time my girlfriend came over bringing more boxes she commented in disbelief how quickly that I was really moving away. "Wow. This is all happening at lightning speed," she said while loading the car with some favorite plants I was gifting her.

Have you noticed the general "shift" in time? If not, you definitely will. I promise you that, and I do not make promises lightly. Time has accelerated during these challenging times and continues to do so as we (individually and collectively) evolve the consciousness of our human species. However, time (as we may know it in our limited perception) does not really move... *we* move *through* time. So, time is really only space that moves, as we perceive it. Let me repeat that for your consideration because it is a mind-bender: Time is space that moves. According to teachings of the Buddha, there are three times: past, present, and future.[9] They are happening at the same time. You could meditate on that for a while, huh?

Everyone is stressed for time and the lack thereof. Think of verbiage we use in business: I need it yesterday. ASAP! As an old friend, former dean and professor of literature at the University of Montana used to opine, "We are stressed-out-of-our-gizzards!" (Sadly he passed away before seeing this published.) Yes, I believe we have lost it, and yes, we must "find" time. To be in time is to be in the now—this moment. Finding time is no longer a luxury; it's a necessity. You've got to find the time to explore the inner landscape of your sacred heart. At this nexus in history, time is running out on the old paradigm and structures.

Downtime is an interesting term our culture has adopted. I remember my first big job after college working for a science corporation. Downtime was simply not good. We needed lots of "time-sold" on the weekly time sheets. Oh, if you had downtime then you were just slacking-off. Fill up those forty hours with more government contract numbers or else you were basically known as a slacker. Yet, downtime is so important for creativity. I don't mean spending all day on Twitter or Facebook, either. A little bit of that energy may be just fine, but watch out for the shadow side of it.

We need much more time for deep reflection. We need time to pause and re-calibrate ourselves. My 360-spin is this: I call it "uptime." Imagine it like a giant geyser gushing to the heavens. Even though the terms down and up are relative, the English language has a strange way of influencing our actions, doesn't it? We mistakenly think that downtime is unproductive or goofing-off. So I call it *uptime*. For example, puttering is a creative and sacred act of mindful uptime.

Today, more than ever, we need to adjust our frequency to a higher vibration in uptime. Uptime is walking in nature. Uptime is being relaxed. Uptime is puttering for the sake of just puttering. Uptime dwells in the domain of your Soul—it is powerful, yet, subtle energy.

A great experience of giving up my "former life" was taking a chunk of this uptime to start fresh. All was left behind in non-attachment. I went "off the grid" (exactly three hundred and sixty days) as a healing gift of time. In that stage of "separation" (as Campbell termed it in the hero's journey), I got an epic taste of freedom and emancipation to re-invent myself. That was massive uptime and I loved every minute of it. In retrospective release, I would not change a thing. It was absolutely perfect.

You may feel that you are not able to do this in your present circumstances. It's okay. All in divine timing. Have courage that you will be guided. Remember, my experience may be considerably more radical because this book was birthed through my total experience of "doing." I wrote the book on it. My Soul's job was to bring forth these spherical principles or an *entire* view—three hundred and sixty-degrees. You'll take a journey in your own way and at *your* pace. As legendary saxophone player Charlie "The Bird" Parker said, "If you don't live it, it won't come out of your horn."

We are all moving through time… experiencing this life at accelerated, frenetic levels. Your vibratory frequency is changing, being altered even in this moment. You are energy. Everything in the universe is energy and everything vibrates. This is just basic physics. Our culture is moving so fast because it is made up of millions of awakening individuals, like you and me.

As the space-time consciousness continuum is perceived to be moving faster, our lives fly by. Think of computers with their incredible speed. How about Tweeting, Facebook posts, e-mail, and DSL technology? By the time this book comes out DSL will be a dinosaur. It's dying now. The term "snail mail" didn't exist twenty years ago. Unfortunately few of us craft beautiful handwritten letters any more. They've become archaic works of art swallowed up into e-mail. Most of us have websites. (Mine is Doinga360.com.) Websites are definitely the new calling cards. If you don't have a web URL yet or a blog, etc., trust me, eventually you will.

Our children are reared with these lightning-fast technologies. It's their reality. Eight-year-olds use cell phones. Talk to your kids about life without their iPods, iPads, Mp3s, Kindles, texting, and computer games, and they will look at you as if you have just arrived from planet Mars. They cannot imagine that. It's like us envisioning life back in the fourteenth century without indoor plumbing and heat. Observe the news media. Stories come so fast that they are still developing as we watch them. Often the news has not fully happened so we unfortunately receive reportage of half-truths.

Corner of Easy Street and Love

In my former life before making a 360-turnaround it was challenging to deal with the busyness of subsistence. I was engaged in the framework of a typical, hectic lifestyle, not a consciously empowered, balanced style of living. I *perceived* experiences to be difficult.

Life is not a struggle unless you choose to make it so. Nature is spontaneous. There is no effort in the change of the seasons, in the flowers blooming in spring. Here I share another perspective, which is *experiencing life consciously*. Please meet me at the corner of easy street and love. I'm not suggesting that there aren't going to be challenging experiences in your life. At times I have suffered tremendously. I'm sharing that there is a choice you have: To see ALL experience as opportunity. To live effortlessly with divine flow, cultivating a fine art and practice of creating sacred space arising from mindfulness. Mindful that you are a part of all there is, which is Oneness.

Consider now that you may have already chosen to re-invent yourself from a life of default. That is why you seek a true, deeper meaning to life. You awaken to remember who you really are and why you are here in this physical form. Significant re-calibration comes when you are *consciously* authentic and therefore creative, healthy, happy, content, and abundant. As a sojourner you shall feel empowered to do whatever it is that your heart desires.

In this book I offer some effective spherical strategies and techniques used for many years with wonderful students: A blend of skills and practices, the sublime and simple, weaved together as a blanket of truth. Remember the little "blanky" you may have used as a child? That warm cover gave feelings of love, comfort, and a safe *feeling* of being home. Acknowledge coming home to yourself now. I narrate this to students during shavasana[10] (an essential yoga pose of deep relaxation discussed ahead in the 8th Chapter):

> *"Feel that you are coming home now… returning from a long journey. Remember the feeling deep in your Soul and experience love, comfort, safety, and joyful familiarity when you turn the corner… and see your home, sweet home."*

That is what I envisage for you also dear reader, to *remember* who you really are. You are going full-circle and therefore, coming home. Your new abode is located at that sacred corner of easy street and love.

I invite you to use these pages as a source for inspiration to effect powerful life-change. Allow this book to be your caring companion and guide on the greatest journey you will ever take: Making friends with and loving your (S)elf; and *knowing* deep in your heart-of-hearts or deep in Spirit… your Soul's purpose. Presented herein, is a creative, step-by-step approach to enrich your life. I cut my spiritual teeth with Joseph Campbell who said to me with great compassion, and is now famous for this advice: "Follow your bliss."[11]

What Goes Around… Comes Around

If you think that you are not ready (at this time) to make a complete three-sixty, well, I respectfully disagree. *Now* is the time. There is no other time than NOW. Each one of us is part of the spiritual evolutionary pulse or conscious urge to grow, to ascend inexorably to Oneness. Even if you are not aware of that fact in this present moment, eventually you will be.

I believe this is the most important and wonderfully exciting cornerstone in history. Our entire human species is involved, which means you, too. This is a most electrifying time because it is *your* time. No one has ever been you; no one *is* you; and no one will ever, *ever* be as wonderful, magnificent, and unique as you!

You have been guided to feel those words and hear this clarion call. If you inaccurately *think* that you are not ready—then okay, you won't be. All happens in its proper divine timing. I'm here to nudge gently, to prod, and inspire you to wake up. Dear reader, your nap is now over.

The 360-boomerang principle simply means this: What goes around… comes around. It is really nothing new, just a creative spin with a subject discussed quite a bit in recent years—like attracts like. From a more scientific point of view it is a law of attraction. You may have heard some buzz when an elementary movie and a subsequent book, *The Secret,* was released. The law of attraction has been taught for centuries with many different names, which definitely is not important here. What really matters now is this: It is universal law. It's what I call "walking your talk" or "spirit in action." If your fears kick up their ugly head, it is okay. This is normal for many. Hey, you may feel that it's safer to stay the same. I understand that change can be scary.

At this tipping point in our fragile world, if individually and collectively we don't wake up and change, then I am concerned things are really going to get scary. You want to see fear? This planet is going down fast. If we do not live through Oneness in our hearts with sustainability that we are ALL interconnected as islands under the sea, then we won't have much time left.

What goes around… comes around. Remember, theurgy (supernatural intervention) guided me to a far away friendly place. My fearful, local self (of the ego) was thinking with judgment:

> *"What the heck are you doing lady? Do you know how hard it is to get jobs with security at your age? How can you leave your family? They are getting older. How can you leave friends? Like a sand mandala, everything you have built is being blown away. Where are you going? What is your plan? Yikes! Are you nuts?"*

When reflecting, I must have been out of my mind. No wonder some people thought of us as fools. Yes, I was out of my mind—out of a mentally created, unconscious, complacent, safe life not following the blueprint of Soul. Actually, I was really in a state of ecstasy. Ecstasy's root is the Greek word, *ekstasis*. In the dictionary it means, a being that is out of its place; or, outside of itself. I did not know then (consciously) that I would write this book. Without radically changing my lifestyle I would not have given birth to "360." I made a heroic journey. "I did a 360." I am living a new mythology, a new story of Oneness for the sake of all sentient beings. You can, too.

360 Philosophy

Remember the metaphor of losing control of the vehicle to then hit the brakes? STOP and get quiet or you will never hear the message as your Soul speaks. Eventually, self-realizations will come from this material or another source. Have you heard the saying: When the student is ready a teacher shall appear? Let's face it; you are still reading because somewhere in this Higher Consciousness you know that change is imminent. Find *your* precise way. My exact way is not yours. I only hold a lamp on the path. The only thing that I can tell you, which is constant in this universe, is change. Every organism grows or dies. Seeds burst before they blossom; that is an immutable law of nature. All of your pain and anguish, anxiety, anger, doubts, hopes, and fears have prepared you for this moment—as grist for the mill. (Grist is grain that has been separated from its chaff in preparation for grinding. The proverbial metaphor 'grist for the mill' means that *everything* is useful.)

Crucial to 360 Philosophy is learning to identify, weave, and heal life patterns created from a limited belief system, which has previously shaped experience and molded you into a frozen being. Jean Houston, the prolific author and evolutionary philosopher demonstrates a marvelous, mythic life of "leaky margins." Like this leading thinker, learn to melt edges while promoting healthy boundaries. Cultivate a fine art of "P and A," an essential skill in the 360 Lifestyle you will read about in Chapter 3.

People generally comment how hard life is; and how so very tired and unhappy they are. Sometimes I hear one big collective sigh. Even after years of compassionate teaching I contemplated:

How can I help more effectively? Offering a divine palace of 360 Philosophy has some merit. This is a way out of the linear illusory world of an ordinary mind (the ego), and into the gratitude of grace in spherical awareness. Life does not have to be a struggle. Your signpost rests at the corner of easy street and love.

I have sat at the feet of the Masters. I've read the books, taken notes, and stood on my head. I have walked the ocean shoreline and hiked the hills. I have floated down the river Ganges at dawn, chanted with His Holiness The Dalai Lama, and lived happily in deep love and spiritual practice with the same amazing man for thirty-plus years. Though I most certainly do not have all the answers, I have been around the block a few times. I've heard the magical call of the Cuckoo bird during cool evenings of Russian spring, and maintained loving friendships with childhood pals. Teaching thousands of classes I have worn many hats. During this moment with you I evolve in a life of *conscious* service. Here is my humble honor championing your noble quest for wholeness.

"Doing a 360"

What will be the full-turnaround-time for a new impassioned you? Can you "Do a 360" in just one day, during the weekend attending a seminar or at a weeklong retreat? Maybe? But as I've observed in longtime students, growth depends on the individual and how deeply entrenched their imbalanced belief patterns are.

For me, (as explained before) this excursion was a few days shy of an all-encompassing year. Weekends by the sea and get away vacations to exotic places help, but only as the beginning catalysts for big change. Once you have the inspiration and the intention to wake up in the now and see with two "eyes" to change your perspective of life, they will provide a way to hit the brakes. STOP and go within where the divine dwells in your heart-of-hearts. STOP and listen as Soul takes the wheel.

When you start practicing and then living 360, you can do whatever you choose because Soul is totally in charge. Give up completely. Surrender unconditionally to The One, The Universe or Universal Intelligence, Divine Presence, Great Spirit, The Buddha, Jesus, and Allah, to God, Goddess or The Source. We humans of form are creatures of habit. So, you are going to re-habituate into a deliberate, conscious being to manifest whatever IT (Soul) chooses.

During many years of spiritual coaching, I've witnessed good folks returning from vacations, retreats, "spiritual" workshops, and conferences, etc. They are seemingly changed until the high vibration wears off in a few days or weeks. Elevated vibratory frequency or tonality lowers again as they cycle back into the old patterns because they are unaware of having patterns, and/or are severely addicted to them. People have spent a small fortune this way. They are excited and pumped up for a while; and then sure enough, there they go again, right back to where they were: angry in their relationships, stuck again in life's circumstances, broke again, bored again, and blah, blah, blah, again. They are ready for the subsequent book, guru, advanced yoga pose, workshop, or the next trendy thing out there to fix all of their misery. It is a vicious cycle, but certainly not a spherical view.

"Doing a 360" is an overarching, creative process of self-realization that leads to an empowered, 360-degree Lifestyle. But let's get real: It is *not* going to take a day. After you mindfully read this book, and work joyfully with the strategies and spherical exercises—continue to practice, practice, and practice. Trust me, dear reader, you shall have plenty to practice with. During our weekly, online talk-radio shows *"Consider This,"* I usually mention this aspect of spiritual development learned from a great yogi: "An ounce of practice is worth a ton of theory." You will meet this yoga master, Swami Vishnudevananda, in Chapter 11. He always quoted his own teacher (and also one of my guides), His Holiness Sri Swami Sivananda. The new you begins with living a real identity, which is a conscious awareness from your Soul. It is a seasoned or mature understanding to know that *you* create reality. It takes a patient plan of courageous, creative, and integral action to nourish new patterns, once you purge the old ones.

As a teacher and minister of the sacred ways, I've compiled tools of the trade in a simple, yet unique 360-language. I trust you ok like a fine, twenty-year tawny port reduction:

's boiled down to a thick, creamy, and delicious

... your life.

Doing a 360: Turning Your Life Around to Follow Soul's Purpose reveals an essential mandala: A 21st Century mythological matrix of practice skills and drills to support its philosophy. Think of me as your personal, spiritual stress management coach: a cosmic bag lady, a *dakini* or sky dancer[12] on the wind carrying priceless gems inside a mystical, rainbow-colored bag. Each cherished nugget of various sizes, shapes, and colors assists in changing your life to follow Soul's purpose. Hear laughter in your heart and the giggle of Soul as you reach in to grab all the treasures. It is time—raise your sacred chalice and drink the nectar of Oneness. You are worthy and deserve these precious gifts. Make the changes. There is nothing holding you back in this present moment except fear, stemming from ego-mind with its same old, same old, same old patterns that need recognition, understanding, honoring, healing, and release. It is time to retire the local self and empower your HIGHER SELF into the forefront of deliberate living.

In Chapter 2, you are invited to practice Sacred Imagery. Within this context is a core visualization to help you understand the perception of a "Higher Self." I learned this type of exercise from a co-founder of The Human Potential Movement, Jean Houston, while attending her Mystery School. If not familiar with this amazing luminary I implore you to read her books; and better yet, listen to her radically powerful, visionary voice. Google and YouTube to your hearts content to appreciate one of the most dynamic and brilliant women of our time. Visit a convenient list at the back of this book offering "must-know" global-change SEC's (spiritual evolutionary collaborators), luminaries like Joe Campbell—heroic beings of bright light.

To get started, you may wish to jump ahead to the very end of Chapter 2 for an exercise called The Throne, or maybe not yet; it's your choice. Feel your Soul… decide *consciously* what to do in this moment.

Chapter 2

I Don't "Want" to Be Spiritual

"Within you is the immortal Soul. Within you is the fountain of joy and happiness. Soar high always in the realms of spiritual knowledge, and realize the goal of life.

— His Holiness Sri Swami Sivananda Saraswati

Generally I've heard people mistakenly say that they want to be spiritual. "I want a 'spiritual' job like you have," they lament. "I wish I was spiritual like you," they longingly declare. Dear reader, I am asking you to consider that it is not a good idea to *want* to be spiritual. Does this sound a bit controversial? Do I have your attention? Perhaps you are thinking: *Really? What kind of a spiritual book is this anyway? Of course I want to be spiritual... what the heck is wrong with wanting to be spiritual?* Everything. Once you adopt and implement into the core of your being a 360 Philosophy of Oneness, you will never say that again—or think it.

There are three simple steps in this realization:

Step 1. You ARE a Spirit: 24/7

You *are* a Spirit with a Soul presently inhabiting a physical body. PERIOD. There is no *wanting* to be "spiritual"—you ARE Spirit. If you are breathing then you are a spiritual being of light. This sounds so simple and basic as a tenet of Spirituality 101, yet it concerns me how so many do not have this essential belief. Individually and collectively, the human species is evolving into an awakening of this truth. If the seven billion of us on planet Earth already had this awareness, then this book would not have to be written. I'm here to lovingly jolt all to their sacred heritage.

Consider that I certainly do not saunter around town saying, "Oh, I really *want* to be a woman." "Gee, I *wish* I was an American." Wouldn't that be absolutely ludicrous? I know that I'm female and possess a passport from the United States. These are truths I don't have to ponder, imagine, daydream or fantasize about. I know who I am. PERIOD. This sensible consideration applies to your divine nature and this 360 Philosophy. All humans, even the meanest of murderers, terrorists, and evildoers are IN and OF Spirit. Though some people may not comprehend it, all of us are spiritual beings, 24/7. We are all One.

My beloved, master teacher, Khenchen Rinpoche used to say jokingly during his Dzogchen retreats: "WHO are you?" We all laughed with him but he was really serious—dead serious. I ask you: Do you know who you are? If you do, then I am so very, very delighted for all awakening, divine beings. This is good news. What one person thinks and does affects the whole universe. This is not "airy-fairy woo-woo." The inter-connectedness of all life is validated by the science of physics.

As more of us have a vibrant, clear, and quick answer to Khenchen's question, my resolve strengthens that we *will* birth a consciousness of Oneness on this fragile planet to sustain all sentient (conscious) life for our future generations. Yet, many still think that they are only a solid physical body having *occasional* spiritual experiences, or some "energy" around them. They are not clear in "certainty wisdom" who they really are. Many more are intrigued openly with the prospect of selected "spiritual" experiences—even if only sporadically. Some may witness a miracle or strange phenomena that they don't quite understand or relate to. Most have felt a shift in their consciousness that they perceive as "weird, cool, unique, amazing, scary, eerie, awesome, wondrous or unexplainable." I've heard these descriptions from fabulous folks that do not quite completely understand their divine heritage or birthright. During this global awakening thank goodness so many are now seeking to engender a *grounded* sense of the "spiritual" in their lives.

If resonating to this, consider now that you must raise some expectations for yourself. ALL events, whether from the exterior landscape of life, or internally generated, are "spiritual." They are part and parcel of a steady flow of Godly awareness because you *are* Godly. You may not have been conscious of this priceless inheritance (until now). This is the great "planetary shift of awakening" that you may have heard about during these perplexing times. There are authentic phases of awakening for each Soul. That does not mean one person is more advanced than another. Soul awakens when IT needs to, and in the degree required for ITS specific or unique ascension plan.

A caveat: As you blossom like the flowers in spring with a fantastic "aha" in this transcendent realization, you may not *sustain* that fabulous feeling for very long. You need an in-depth, personal mythology of Oneness: This myth grounds you in the belief that you are truly a *Creator*, just like every other human being is a Creator, too. ALL are infinite architects of the divine. Some give lip service to the idea but they do not really own this core belief. Once you do, Soul drives the bus wherever you go. There is a popular saying: "Wherever you go, there you are."

Confidence that is manifested through Soul's blueprint is unshakable. You stand in grace and it feels oh, so very, very good. The great mystery of life is your sacred playground. Until this belief and profound realization is deeply encoded into the heart you will not discover Soul's purpose. Global strife during this bewildering time-period stems from individuals not knowing the truth that separation is an illusion. Divine awareness that you *are* an individuated Spirit must sink in 24/7 permeating every cell of your being on a practical, day-to-day, relative level.[1] 360 assists you in this heroic endeavor.

People may read religious and "spiritual" books, and talk about God and cool "spiritual" things, which is just great. Yet, are they really *living consciously* from Soul's direction every day? Do they know in "certainty wisdom" beyond a shadow of a doubt that divine nature dwells within? I hope so. During conversations with some students and clients throughout the years I discovered (much to my chagrin) that this was not the case. What I found disconcerting (with sparkling seekers in spiritual pursuits like yoga, meditation, healing, etc.) is that they were mesmerized by this idea, dazzled, as if it were some far away, romantic notion. Dubious faces began to cry when I matter-of-factly told them, eye-to-eye and Soul-to-Soul, how magnificently wonderful a divine being of light they were.

Honestly, what it may come down to (in my opinion) is an apprehension of the daunting realization: Total, 100% complete responsibility for ALL you do—24/7. Some find this a hard pill to swallow. I am here to articulate distinctly and clearly that your Soul is not a "temp" or a part-timer. This is the real, big gig. It's a matter of absorbing a panoramic view of three hundred and sixty-degrees to shift perception that EVERY human is a formless Spirit that is now in physical form. That is a beginning cognition of wakefulness or what is termed, awakening to enlightenment.

As much as I wish I didn't have to repeat this message, with loving kindness and compassion, I will: YOU ALREADY ARE A SPIRIT inhabiting a body, no matter what you do or say, no matter what you think, or how you act. The limiting belief of *wanting* to be spiritual must be reconciled. You may change that mindset starting right now. Like so many during this special period of transformation you may not have been conscious of the truth of who you really are. You were asleep taking a snooze. I appreciate you would like to get more shuteye but now it's time to WAKE UP. Affirm it is already so. YOU are a complete divine being. Amen. So be it. Period. When you start living this beautiful truth, when you *know* it as an irrefutable fact with every fine fiber of your divine essence, then life is going to change.

Keep in mind that arching boomerang: like attracts like. If you constantly think "wanting" you are only going to experience longing and more wanting. God, the God Force, the Christ Consciousness, the One Presence of All Being, etc., will deliver or actualize what you "want." As you come to re-cognize (know) Soul's awakening process, you begin to live consciously from that divine identity, manifesting what IT chooses. Affirm who you are with self-assurance. You are part of a divine matrix of ALL life— Oneness. Therefore, YOU are implicitly and explicitly divine, (which means, your inner landscape of being, and outside in the world). This divine scenery lives *within* your heart as well as "out there." It's the perfect, all-encompassing 360 View: as if you were standing on the citadel of the venerated Tibetan Mount Kailas seeing the entire, magnanimous world-sphere from 21,800 feet. The veil of separation vanishes. When you "see" life with this 360-degree and all-inclusive awareness, then ALL possibilities are your divine inheritance.

According to the teachings of Vajrayana Buddhism, which I was most fortunate to study for twenty-plus years under the tutelage of a holy man, we are *already* enlightened. We have the mind of enlightened activity but may not know it *consciously*. The Buddha taught the need for study, contemplation, and practice to reveal our true inner nature, which has the pure intrinsic qualities of love, compassion, and wisdom. These deep, illumined ancient teachings of Dzogchen, (which is the ninth *yana* or vehicle of Tibetan Buddhism) say that we are already perfect. (In the Tibetan language, Dzogchen translates as, The Great Completion.) To become enlightened, to attain Buddhahood, means essentially to "wake up" and see clearly the *rigpa* (pristine or pure awareness) that penetrates the great *shunyata* (emptiness) of all creation. (The Sanskrit word *Buddha* means, "awakened," it's a past participle of the root *Budh*, "to awaken.")

I recommend this practice: Recite while feeling a confidence of the truth in your heart-of-hearts: I AM SPIRIT. I am a Soul here to feel and to experience the gift of life. I AM DIVINE.

Affirm and believe it. This is a big, first step in walking the hero's journey and therefore changing your life. Believe in a benevolent, 360 = 1 vision of yourself (human), and YOURSELF (divine) as part of a beautiful, divine matrix of one inexorable existence. *That* is Oneness.

Okay. You may be fortunate to already know this as truth—great. Thank God. I beseech you to share that message within your sphere of influence. If you hear a voice in your head saying: "*Yadda, yadda, yadda. This is nothing new.*" Then I query you this way: Have you been taking action 24/7, CONSCIOUSLY following Soul's purpose? You have been? Awesome! I was not. I hadn't fully articulated what my passion was, and how to place it into action every day, every moment, and in every impassioned breath that I take for the sake of all sentient beings. We live on Earth to evolve consciousness. I believe the Soul creates human life to evolve in Spirit until happy with ITS progress. When the game is over, having finished a karmic cycle on this particular planet, Soul may choose to come back again... and again. Souls evolve further in The Great Plan (but I am jumping ahead; that is plenty to discuss in another book). Let us focus on *this* exquisite life and self-realization in the present moment.

Some planetary teachers have said that life is a school with lessons to learn. Well, I think a little differently: Life is a big playground and it's time for recess. We are the children of God; therefore, it is time to play. It's time to feel the joy of being. Time to "do" what we came here to do. There are many grand games and beneficial activities to do—so much fun. With total surrender let Soul *choose* which ones, and play to your heart's content. You are a miraculous spirit-being here to generate experience so your individuated Soul can FEEL the conscious creativity in the divine evolution of life.

I ask again: Are you choosing to take sacred action on a daily basis? Have you unconditionally surrendered to God's guidance? Have you been seeing deliberately through the eyes of Soul? Even as an interspiritual minister with all of my study and preparation, training and practice for decades, I will admit that I wasn't. Not until I did a full, three hundred and sixty-degrees-turnaround with my life. If you are not passionately happy, content, and peacefully doing heroic deeds with joyful effort, then you are not thriving from the depths of your Soul. It's time to let GOD control the wheel for a sacred spin around the playground of life. It is time to follow *your* bliss.

Step 2. Spiritual Development through Action: Joyful Effort

The next seasoned or mature awareness is taking action to whatever level is appropriate for your sacred blueprint. Another way of perceiving this: It is your karma, or, it is your script. What specifically works for one individual may not necessarily succeed for another. Find a blessed path that you resonate to with passion deep in your heart and STAY on it. Go within… seek from your source. Avoid scattering energy (this may be one of your patterns ahead in Chapter 4). Seekers flit from one psychic or healer to another, book after book, after another and another, without putting into practice what they are learning. You have got to shift from within. Focus on 360 Strategies and do the exercises. These will help actualize your journey to Oneness. Remember, the great poet Maya Angelou said it best: "You did what you knew how to do, and when you knew better, you did better."

People mistakenly believe that if they meditate for a couple of weeks, take some yoga classes, attend a symposium with a "spiritual" luminary, watch a video, (which are all really excellent choices) that they are instantly going to acquire financial freedom, and find their perfect life partner, or land a "spiritual" dream job. Once you surrender COMPLETELY you will take consistent, sacred action from your core belief of Oneness. Without it you are never going to fully change circumstances. You must act in accordance with your peak passion and highest purpose ALL the time—that means 24/7. This takes practice, and lots of it. Quick fixes do not work. It takes joyful effort grounded in certainty wisdom to make a complete-turnaround with your life. You are a divine work in progress, so please don't give up.

Masters lead by action. Heart-friend and mentor Khenchen Rinpoche was the most pro-active person I ever knew. He practiced meditation and prayers tirelessly for the benefit of all sentient beings. I assisted him with projects for many years during his "free" time between a very full teaching and lecturing schedule. In the tradition of Mahayana Buddhism, (the great vehicle) we learn of transcendental joyful effort, which is the fourth *paramita* (perfection) of the *Prajnaparamita*. I was blessed to help Venerable Khenchen Palden Sherab Rinpoche publish his teaching in the form of a book entitled, *Prajnaparamita: The Six Perfections.*[2] His essential instruction conveys great courage and commitment to do beneficial activities for the good of all. Joyful effort is the antidote to laziness, procrastination, and a lack of inspiration. If you live a life of transcendence in joyful effort then manifestation will arise in what you envisage. Effort is action, so as you move deeper in this heroic journey, the 360-template will inspire your joyful effort.

Ven. Khenchen Rinpoche was always building: planning and organizing the expansion of his Dharma centers worldwide. He translated ancient texts and wrote many scholarly books. During "uptimes" he and his younger brother blessed hundreds of ritual objects, hand-carved *mani* stones (sacred mantras engraved into rocks), helped devotees heal with Tibetan medicinal remedies, and gave countless individual interviews to members of their loving sangha. They traveled extensively to the four corners of Earth offering teachings and retreats with intricate empowerment ceremonies requiring much preparation. Khenchen Rinpoche took action in joyful effort. He led by example. I've been so blessed to travel around the world with this enlightened monk. During long plane rides, malas were huddled close to his heart in soft, joyful ease while chanting tenderly in prayer for the sake of all beings.

Life is precious—he did not waste one minute of it, and neither should you. Rinpoche privately shared during a time when I was directing one of his centers: "Nancy," he said endearingly with his strong Tibetan accent, "you must think big. Everything I do now is for the future of the Dharma. I am planning for two, three hundred years from now." I never forgot that: Think BIG.

We are asleep at least one third of our lifespan. Lamas teach how to meditate and practice *bodhichitta* with joyful effort—even while sleeping. (Bodhichitta is a Sanskrit word roughly translated as, awakening mind of enlightenment.)[3] According to the Tibetan Buddhist teachings, this is a distinct form of yoga called Dream Yoga, a sophisticated training of sacred techniques that lead to a realization that our life is a dream. Westerners may know of this experience as lucid dreaming, which is the skill of being aware of your dream *while you are having it,* and then expanding that ability to do whatever you choose during that dream.[4] Tibetan Buddhist practitioners are masters of Dream Yoga. Their ancient texts—earliest known from the eighth century AD—describe some fascinating methods for producing lucid states, asserting that the masters of this practice may visit any realm of existence and actually change waking consciousness with their intention. The beloved Tibetan Saint Padmasambhava said, "Don't waste time and sleep like an animal! Practice the profound Dharma while you sleep!"[5]

Everything arises from the intrinsic, clear awareness of pure consciousness whether you are dreaming or awake. Let's face it; life *is* like a dream, isn't it? (In Chapter 6, you will explore the realms of consciousness in more detail.) Khenchen Rinpoche always taught this contemplation: "Where is your mind? Mind is *everywhere.*" Spiritual development is really just (S)elf evolutionary development. It is confidently recognizing who you really are. That is what this book teaches. Without working persistently in joyful effort, you stagnate, wither, and wilt. I know because I've re-calibrated from a former life of dreary monotony. Thank God I am not the same person I was last year, last month, last week, or even yesterday. Perhaps you may already notice a vibratory shift in *your* warm heart since beginning this book?

Step 3. You Create Your Own Reality

Based on my experiences, this following step is usually the hardest for people to accept: It is the mature premise that YOU CREATE YOUR OWN REALITY. That means, not blaming your parents for everything that goes wrong. Not faulting them or others for every time you make wrong choices. Not impugning other people for your faults and foibles. You must accept total responsibility for your own stuff. Do not blame your spouse, your kids, the boss, co-workers, associates, teachers, etc. You have choice in life because you are divine—you create. Once you realize this fact, Stuart Wilde says, "The awareness is like a warm wind, a divine breeze that comes and stands next to you... to empower your being."[6]

Once during a stress management class an older participant got very upset when I taught him this philosophy. Scowling, he promptly closed his arms tight around his chest—body language revealing the heart-space is closed, restricted, and recalcitrant. It's an attitudinal stance of: "I have my beliefs; I don't want to change, and you can't make me!" Having taught and counseled extensively with active senior adults (long-term as case studies) this was a fairly common, typical response. However, you *can* teach new tricks—I have done it successfully. I had the greatest students for many years and their eager participation helped fuel the sacred fire for 360.

Here is the thing about your reality and that "hard" pill to swallow: You create ALL of it. When someone treats you poorly—it is your doing. Like Shakespeare said, "All the world is a stage." You co-created the drama (wrote the script) as a divine playwright. That behavior, along with your fellow actor(s) on the stage of life, is yours. Take responsibility fully for your actions. If you're broke because someone stole all of your money then you scripted that. Yes, you co-created that experience. Remember my personal story about being robbed? I fashioned that incident from the Soul-level, long before I was born. I wouldn't change it now. That was a noteworthy, catalyzing event.

Let's look at this "you create your reality stuff" from a more scientific perspective. The substantial law of attraction says that all energy draws like energy to it. Our thoughts and feelings arise from consciousness, from Spirit as energy. So, the most powerful essence in the universe is energy. Energy is God. Energy cannot be created or destroyed. *It is, as it is.* We know this from many experiments in quantum physics. One of the best global speakers in our midst is prolific author, Gregg Braden. He has an uncanny, easy way of bridging science and spirituality for the layperson. I encourage you to read his many books like *The Divine Matrix*, which provides a plethora of scientific experiments to help corroborate that we create reality. Our feelings and thoughts are real energies that attract like energy to them. So, if you feel crappy then you will draw more crap. It's a law of nature whether you believe it or not. If you feel happy and focus on good things using joyful effort in action, you invite more goodness and happiness.

Like the ancient, Aboriginal boomerang that swirls around, wherever your attention goes… manifestation follows. That is why there's an old saying, "be careful what you wish for because you are going to get it." I recycle this spherical view in subsequent chapters since it is vital in the hero's journey to wholeness, and therefore, in completely changing your life. Before manifesting a physical body, we chose life conditions—the majority of them. Yes, we do have choice (free will) in all situations; yet, a lifecycle has already been planned. We created a blueprint to evolve in the universe. That is the ONLY reason for Soul to take form: Create experience as a divine human being to follow ITS evolutionary impulse.

To assist in refining a spherical understanding, I love to use metaphors. (As you already know, my book title, *Doing a 360* is obviously a metaphor.)

Imagine a blueprint for a building—let's say it is your house. The architectural plan is already drawn out on paper; yet, you may make some modifications to this structure, yes? Maybe a wall has to move a little bit, or a window position can be shifted. As the project continues a realization may arise to change some electrical outlets. There are choices for building materials. Essentially, the blueprint is followed even though tweaked, slightly—it's still the same house envisioned. You choose the paint color and brand of cabinets, etc. Decisions help you to finish building with complete satisfaction. So, in the very same way Soul creates a life choosing the location and parents. Then a beautiful, divine Soul arrives in a tiny baby body ready to play the games on a playground of life, making powerful choices in ITS evolution of consciousness.

Fruit on the Tree

It may take time for all of this to sink in or you may already be on the same page with me. Metaphorically speaking (I do this a lot), if you observe the great tree of life, does every piece of delicious fruit ripen exactly at the same time? Of course not, all is perfect in divine timing—always and *all* ways.

Years ago, a charming student commented one afternoon after wellness class, "Uh, I'm not sure I get all of this. I mean, uh, I am going to have to think about it. How can I be responsible for *everything* that happens to me?" She had a point. Her reticent ideology represents the illusory belief of many. It is intense to realize this initially, I know. For some, it's very heavy. You may or may not feel a bit burdened at first; if you do, that is just ego validating its solid existence. It's okay. Eventually this magical, mystic maturation process yields liberating truth.

Remember that empowering, divine, warm wind blowing in to stand next to you? For me, it was a relief. As you live *consciously* in spherical knowledge that you are Spirit incarnate, perceptions transform. "Bad" things may happen but you realize that they are part of a chosen blueprint to grow with. How much growth have you had so far? If you are deliriously content and fulfilled then why change? Bad and good are relative terms. There really is no bad or good in our life, only a *perception* of what is bad or good. Perception is the king. If you felt low before... now you might perceive that you are up. This is duality thinking. In the world of God, the Absolute, Great Spirit, there is no hot or cold, clean or dirty, left or right—*it is, as it is*. Hey, but we do live in this third dimension "3D" so, unwisely we believe in the duality of "this and that" and "me" vs. "them."

Speaking of "bad" things: is it possible that the peaceful Tibetans of pure heart would have come to the West if it hadn't been for the devastating 1959 communist Chinese invasion, which almost destroyed their culture? Well, I don't know. Probably not, why would they want to come here? Yet, it happened; and was prophesied centuries ago by the Saint, Padmasambhava. In such a remote country of seven million inhabitants, about one million nonviolent Tibetans were killed. All but thirteen of the country's 6,254 ancient, holy monasteries were heartlessly, hideously, and severely damaged or completely razed in ruthless hatred to the cold, hard ground of Tibetan soil.[7] In the West, we are at least grateful for the silver lining of this horrendous diaspora: The Dharma has spread to the land of the red man.[8]

Having fled Tibet under gunfire, my mentor Ven. Khenchen Rinpoche (that you met earlier) sorrowfully lost his mother and both sisters due to illness as they reached exile in India. During this dreadful exodus more than 100,000 refugees also died at the hands of the brutal communists.[9] Was this tragic? Yes, of course it was horrible. I cannot fathom the horrifying conditions faced by Khenchen Rinpoche and his family: Mile after frozen mile of unforgiving tundra; being on the run, and starving so badly that they boiled leather bags in melted snow and drank the liquid to stay alive. Along with his father and younger brother, Khenchen Palden Sherab Rinpoche survived. Did it make him stronger? Yes, of course. Would the great Nyingma Master have left his sacred home and travel to America without this devastating heartbreak? I don't know—maybe or maybe not. It's really not my place to know. I am just a humble heart-student reminiscing many glorious evenings. We would sit around a table after feasting on scrumptious meals prepared by another devotee or myself, deliberating the arduous journey from his persecuted homeland.

Stories of conquered Tibet were so difficult to hear—the injustice and inhumaneness of it all. Yet, at times Khenchen would courageously laugh as he animatedly described bullets whizzing by his head: *"cheeeeng... cheeeeng... cheeeeng."* Once he was surrounded with guns pointing within inches from his face. He threatened the soldiers to go ahead and kill him because he really didn't care, either way. They felt power in divine presence and miraculously let him go. I share this to help you understand that we (all of us) create reality. It was part of an astonishing life of grace to do what he did: Live as an enlightened being for the sake of others. You see, dear reader, a realized Master doesn't live in the domain of duality. They don't say, "Oh, it's a very *nice* day, isn't it?" They know there is no nice or not nice. It's just another day. And so... *it is, as it is.*

Islands Under the Sea

We choose (before birth) what are known as "check out" or exit points. Many psychics parley this topic. These are events previously co-created so Soul can leave the embodiment if IT chooses. If Spirit feels finished with the lifespan—that IT has accomplished what was needed—then IT is ready to go back home. Soul checks out. Why do you think some people amazingly survive ghastly accidents and others do not? Luck? Nope. I don't think so. Can you reflect on a close call that you or a friend may have had? I have had a few but I'm still here. Soul had to get this 360-material out before moving on to other galactic encounters. If your Soul has not done what IT needs to for ITS creative spiritual evolution, IT won't transition, die, or check out.

Consider our lifespan metaphorically: Soul has checked in at birth staying at a hotel, which is the form or temple of the physical body. Some Souls stay longer than others, but they all *know* ahead of time how long they will be staying because they have already booked a reservation. Soul knows what kind of an establishment IT is staying in. IT knows how "fine" a hotel it is—the posh Ritz or a dumpy dive. Soul makes the choice. Just like vacationing at a resort, when you make your transition or die—you check out.

A lovely young woman that I hired years ago (I'll call her Devina) sadly lost her second child just thirty painful hours after giving birth. It was so awful, but in her own wise words Devina expressed a 360 View: "Although she was with us briefly, she has imprinted herself upon our hearts and changed our lives forever." The trauma was unbearable. How could God let a little innocent baby die like this? Devina was a fine Christian girl so how could this be? From Soul's view, this baby girl came in to her parents briefly, in just a whisper of time to help ITSELF in evolutionary development. Also, to help all those around IT grow from a tragic experience. This was scripted ahead of time. Was it dreadful for the family? Yes, of course. Yet, this loving mother dealt with it the best she could by dedicating herself to a cause for a cure, raising awareness of premature infant death. So, even now this infant (her progressive Soul that graced us all for a fleeting moment) teaches here through these words.[10]

Every year half a million babies in the United States are born prematurely. Premature birth is the leading cause of newborn death and numerous life-long disabilities. One out of every eight babies will dangerously enter the world before their time. This precious baby (a Soul that created a very short lifespan) is raising consciousness to help others, even though her physical life has passed on. If we gaze at this from a higher perspective—a 360-degree View—it makes some sense. Of course, Devina sustains the miserable pain of losing her sweet child. What suffering could be devastatingly more severe than burying your baby? With heart-felt prayers I feel an ocean of compassion. Some select life on Earth that is very, very difficult. Soul knows that the lifespan will be intense but also that the experience contributes greatly to ITS evolutionary plan. Eventually, we all return into the arms of our Source: Jesus, Allah, Divine Mother, or the Tao.

Devina's anecdote has a layered backstory: Her first daughter was born severely premature as well, but this child had lived. I remember holding her dearly in the palm of my hand since she was so very teeny-tiny, only weighing less than a pound. She was the miracle baby. Devina was only six months pregnant when this happened. A healthy and diligent worker, I felt very comfortable getting away before hiring a temporary replacement while she would be on maternity leave. My husband and I went on vacation by the sea to the Gulf of Mexico. In the middle of the night I violently swooped up in bed gasping for air. I was freaking out in panic like I was going to die. I could not breathe. After what seemed like an eternity I was ready to go to the nearest ER. Then, strangely the symptoms subsided, and we fell back to sleep.

I returned home the next evening to an urgent telephone machine message: Devina was at the hospital in premature labor. I rushed to her bedside, at which time I learned she had a lung embolism and almost died the night before (the same exact time of my nocturnal event). When I shared our psychic synchronicity her eyes widened like an eager child on Christmas morning. She was shocked; I wasn't. We are all connected interdependently as islands under the sea. I chose to bring this wonderful family into my life long before she walked into my office on a job interview. And her Soul chose me, too… way before she accepted a position.

John Walsh's beautiful son Adam was brutally and inhumanely murdered in 1981. You may have seen the wrenching, heartbreak film of this true story, *Adam*.[11] If you've ever watched television, John Walsh's face may be familiar from his program, *America's Most Wanted,* which has caught hundreds, perhaps thousands of criminals. Though his son's killing was a gruesome and horrific tragedy, John went on with his life to fight for justice, becoming a powerful victim rights advocate. His passion has saved countless people in the memory of his darling boy.

The U.S. Congress passed the Adam Walsh Child Protection and Safety Act in 2006. From a higher divine perspective, I believe Adam's Soul was very, very advanced in ITS journey through this universe. He came as a hero of heroes to raise consciousness, and in doing so, saving others from the torture that he suffered. Even his name—Adam—is divine. Had this sickening murder not occurred would Mr. Walsh have lived his life in the same way? I don't know. What do you think? I have never met John Walsh, but I hope one day our paths will cross so I may thank him with a big hug for his remarkable courage. Like his extraordinary son, he is also a hero.

The point here is that our life is *already planned out* as part of the beautiful tapestry of divine order woven within the spiritual matrix of all existence. And when we wake up fully to Higher Consciousness passionately fulfilling ITS purpose, then life is full of awe. Life is awesome. It may be brutally tough at times, but it's awesome. Courage is awesome. Heroes have courage. Consider that your Spirit *knew* you were going to read this book, just as I (my Soul) knew I was going to write it in the "future" which is now your present, courageous moment.

The Lemon

This material has been a bit deep. I know there is much to contemplate, so let's have a little bit of fun. Remember, life is just a big playground and it's recess. Trust me, we will get back to all of the nitty gritties later because this is the beginning of *completely* changing your life. I know change is a bit daunting. I have been through it. "Doing a three-sixty" does not have to be hard work unless you perceive it to be so.

Here's a game to play. I've shared this visualization exercise successfully for decades—it is simple but brilliant. I'm not sure of its actual origin, but I will say that my dear friend and superb 360 mentor Joan, taught it to me when I was around eighteen.

This is an introduction to the world of Sacred Imagery: I call it *The Lemon*. I suggest you get familiar with this visualization, so read through the exercise first, and then put this book down to play. Create a sacred space. Mute your phones, etc. If you don't know what "creating a sacred space" means, just generate calm in your surroundings, and then focus on this present moment. I shall clarify the art of creating sacred space in the next chapter.

Exercise: The Lemon Visualization

Practice Time: 5 minutes.

Practice: 2-3 times initially, until physical results are realized.

Read through this script slowly before you practice; record it and practice, or have someone read it aloud to you. Avoid rushing through the words; pause between sentences.

Create a sacred space.

Within the context of sacred space, sit or lie down. Get quiet. Close your eyes and breathe deeply a few times.

Relax. Find rhythm in your breath. Feel any tensions in your body dissolving. Relax completely. Feel very comfortable. Calm your breath. Long, slow, deep breaths flow in and out.

Repeat silently: I am relaxed; I feel relaxed; I am peaceful; I feel warm and relaxed.

Visualize the color yellow. See it take form into the shape of a lemon.

Place yourself into this visualization—in a kitchen. Take your time and relax as you develop this image of a lemon in your mind. Look at the shape, size and color of the lemon that you are now holding in your hand. *Feel* the weight, and see the texture of this lemon—explore any details. Relax and really go with it. Look at any markings or labels—anything that you see is okay.

Imagine you are holding a sharp knife and carefully cut this lemon open in half. See the juice running as you cut into it. This is a particularly rich and juicy lemon. It is very fresh so you can smell its strong fragrance. Study the inside of your lemon. See the pits and fiber in the sections of this fruit.

Feel and sense the entire experience. Smell it again; and now take a big, juicy bite out of your imaginary lemon. Yes… take a big bite.

Feel this experience. Taste the sourness. Suck on the lemon and notice what is happening to your physical body. Be in the presence of the moment.

Meditate on any sensations you feel. What do you notice? What has occurred?

When you are ready, let the visualization dissipate. Let it all fade with your next rich, complete breath. Slowly return to the awareness of your surroundings by gently opening your eyes.

If you are like most people, your lips puckered and you felt like swallowing. Perhaps you even swallowed urgently—more than once? You just experienced (in your mouth) the physical sensation of salivary glands producing saliva, which is the initial process of digestion—a physiological function. You perceived that you were *really, truly* tasting a lemon.

Basically this is what happens: Your 3-lb. brain, which is the physical organ of your mind, makes a telephone call down to the little glands below it and says:

> *"Hey guys. How are yah? Listen, I have been told by this person I work for (from the thoughts in their mind) that they are eating something. Hmm, it is actually a lemon.*

*Why anyone would want to eat a lemon? I don't know.
Anyway, it is their choice. I'm just doing my job up here.
Would you kindly do your thing and start digestion? Send
some saliva please. Thanks, I appreciate it."* So, the
fellow salivary glands respond, *"Hey, no problem
buddy, uh, I mean to say, Mr. Brain. That's what we do.
Tell the big boss that is what we are here for. Okay. Saliva
is now on the way..."*

Remember as a kid your parent(s) may have wisely admonished
you to "chew your food!" That is how we digest, initially—in the
mouth. 99% of those I've done this exercise with have had a strong
reaction physically, even to the point of excessive swallowing
because of so much saliva. On rare occasions, participants taking
medication for glandular health-related problems didn't do as well.
You may be thinking: *Okay, so what is the deal with this lemon thing?*

This basic, little mind-game is crucial and quite profound in
understanding that *you create your own reality.* You weren't really
eating a lemon were you? Of course not, you are sitting in your
comfortable chair reading this book. However, your body does
not know the difference between fact and fantasy, between the
real and unreal. No, it does not. How do I know? Because your
physical body (the brain and salivary glands) reacted to a stimulus
(visualization of eating a lemon). Please consider repeating the
exercise if you've not grasped the full understanding here. Having
been a teacher for many years I know that repeating things helps
to change entrenched belief patterns. This entire book, as in the
nature of a circle, will go around and around many times—which
is intentional.

Can you imagine how your poor heart and liver must feel
when you are screaming or yelling? Yikes, your whole immune
system temporarily shuts down when stressed-out. No wonder
we get sick. We are blasted with a damaging excess secretion of the
hormone cortisol, nicknamed "the stress hormone." So, if simply
thinking about a small piece of fruit for a few minutes can effect
palpable change in your physical body, imagine how constantly
thinking negative thoughts radically affects your health?

Cutting-edge mind coherence research from the organization HeartMath shows this, and so much more.[12] We now know that our heart is a powerful emotional organ, more so than our brain. Ever wonder why we draw hearts instead of brains for Valentine's Day? How about a chocolate brain for your loved one!?

In my assorted wellness groups, as well as with individual clients, Sacred Imagery of "The Lemon" is a game-changer. So many, possibly like yourself until now were unaware of this fact: You create reality. You tricked your body into thinking that you were actually eating a lemon. Your proof is the actual, physical change within the body—you cannot deny that this is a fact. Your perceptions, beliefs, and many thoughts of your mind do create reality. Here is tangible, quantitative, and immediate proof. It's just a truth: What you think about will manifest in your physical world. *It is, as it is.* When you "get" this: When that stunning self-realization really sinks in, it will be liberating. And for some it can be absolutely frightening because they can't blame their stuff on anything or anyone else, anymore.

Note: If you are not a very effective visualizer, you may need to repeat this exercise before really *feeling* the results—that's okay. Please just keep practicing. I had a woman comment surprisingly that she absolutely did not like lemons so she wasn't going to do it. Once I coached her, she "got it" and was glad. This Lemon exercise is so powerful that folks reported months later: massive changes in awareness, proving that you are what you "think."

Back in the 1980s I created an empowerment course called, *Spiritual Lotus 1-2-3*, which I taught mostly for advanced yoga students. One very intelligent yogi I was quite fond of alleged that The Lemon didn't work. He was puzzled, saying openly to the group: "I don't understand this." Instead, I suggested we all focus on popcorn. After visualizing himself buying fresh popcorn at the theatre, smelling this familiar snack and eating it, he had an "aha" moment in consciousness. I repeated The Lemon exercise for the entire group and then he was satisfied to "get it." Learning and applying 360 Philosophy on a day-to-day basis is like working on a Spiritual Ph.D. of sorts, or at least a fantastic, all-encompassing spherical education. So, let's summarize the 3 steps:

360 Recapitulation

1. Affirm you *are* Spirit. Using whatever concept you feel comfortable with and accept as truth in your own way: You are *in* and *of* Goddess, God, The Christ Energy, Christ Consciousness, the Buddha, Jesus, Great Spirit, The Source, Tao, The ONE, Allah, Presence, etc. Accept this with certainty wisdom—it is a *knowing* not a question. If you need more help then use the art of affirmation to change your engrained belief patterns. The ones below may be inspiring or you may be guided to affirmation books for others. Consider creating your own by genuinely listening to Spirit. Write them down as I did here for you:

> I affirm I am Pure Spirit
> I affirm I am of THE ONE
> I affirm I Creatively Live in the Light

2. Take action with joyful effort. Develop awareness as you are guided. Trust in YOUR OWN TRUTH. Do the exercises in this book. Create an action plan for the next year of your life. Ask for help from 360 mentors. Know who your allies are and weave healthy patterns. Practice journaling, paint, write, dance, walk a labyrinth, make a life-map or collage. Learn to listen, which helps develop your intuition skill-set. Research books, audio programs and videos; attend some lectures, go on retreats, concentrate and meditate, use sacred movement disciplines, say affirmations and prayer. Being is the sacred ground of doing.

Whatever Soul guides you to do—please just *do it*.

3. You create your own reality. Anything that happens, you have created it. Remember the boomerang encircling: What goes around... comes around. What you think, you are. Only *you* teach others how to treat you; so, take responsibility. You created the blueprint, now choose to decorate your world. Take the heroic journey with conscious knowledge from your Soul or Higher Self.

The Throne: Feeling Your Higher Self

Here is another providential experience, which has been very successful with divine aspirants to acknowledge and empower their Higher Self. This is Sacred Imagery to engender your real identity with Soul. I call this visualization exercise, The Throne. Read through the script slowly before you practice. Record it and practice, or have someone slowly read it aloud for you. Avoid rushing... pause... between sentences. You'll need a comfortable, straight-backed chair.

Exercise: The Throne

Practice Time: 5-30 minutes (as you feel guided).

Practice: 3x a week, or daily, if needed.

Create a sacred space.

Sit straight, upright, yet very comfortable in your chair.

Close your eyes. Feel the sacred space of your surroundings. Sense a beautiful quiet within.

Breathe very deeply, yet gently, a few times. Hear your sweet breath flowing in and out, rhythmically. You feel so very, very relaxed. You feel so present to this moment. Your calm breath is softening as you settle in to this experience. Feel peace within... flowing effortlessly.

Imagine that you are sitting on the most dazzling, beautiful throne in the universe. It's the most marvelous, majestic chair you have ever seen, and now you are honored and privileged to be sitting on it. The woodcarvings are intricate, inlayed with various shapes and sizes of precious and semi-precious gems of every color in the rainbow. There are gold and silver, bronze, and copper designs with gorgeous fabrics, and the finest brocade and silks. Study your throne... meditate on this amazing beauty. Let your throne be as creatively elaborate as you wish it to be. You feel comfortable with abundant joy in this great chair.

You are a king or queen—powerful—with an ocean of royal compassion. You are kind, but strong. Your word is your bond. There is a majestic quality to your posture. Feel empowered. You *are* royalty. You are the creator and ruler of your universe. You feel mighty and grand, which is your birthright!

Stay here for as long as you wish. Breathe. Infuse your (S)elf with divine majesty. When ready… be fully present and available to the conscious vibration of your surroundings, and gently open your eyes.

As you start to feel comfortable with the idea of being on a divine throne as a ruler in charge—mighty, potent, and grand—you will transmute physically. "Bear in mind"[13] your previous Lemon visualization exercise: When practicing The Throne, you actually *feel* taller as your spine elongates, lifting upwards to the heavens—physical proof that it works (like The Lemon). This majestic imaging-exercise empowers a sacred, new way of being. Let Soul have some fun feeling ITSELF in this image. Longtime students loved The Throne, often requesting guidance with this elegant meditation.

Practice this exercise daily in the beginning of your 360-transformation. Remember, what you *feel* from the Soul—you are.

Chapter 3

The Sacred Circle

"The problem with the world is that we draw our family circle too small."

— Mother Teresa

onths before beginning this 360-life work, circles and spheres entered my dreams. I talked my husband into digging a huge, five-foot diameter, two-foot deep hole in our backyard (bless his heart). At first, he thought I was a little nuts. Also, I suspect our elderly neighbor alleged us as weirdoes excavating dirt on those warm summer evenings. I felt a bit loony as well when I saw how gigantic this crater was becoming. Eagerly though, we plodded along mixing cement, then placing red bricks strategically around the circular rim in a pattern important from the Soul-level. Eventually, a handsome fire pit was born featuring the four cardinal directions of a circular symbol called a Zia, of Native Americans from the Zia Pueblo in New Mexico.

Prior to living in the Southwest of the United States, though marginally familiar with Native American culture, I didn't focus my consciousness on this famous, ceremonial motif of the sun. Four groups of four lines represent sunrays pointing out from a circle (four is sacred to the people of Zia). These illustrate the four directions of north, south, east, and west, as in a compass and revered medicine wheel or shield of deep-layered meaning.

The state of New Mexico chose the Zia as its state symbol. Now, here's a dwelling of divinely diversified people that are living harmoniously in sacred space. With this evocative logo gracefully billowing in the breezes high on flagpoles and down on license plates, one consistently receives powerful spirit medicine whether conscious of it or not. Vast and picturesque New Mexico is known as "the land of enchantment."

A few years after that "holey moley" experience I received some fresh, holy, spherical guidance. A whispering inner voice stated that I had been—and would be once more—a "keeper of the ancient circles." It was expressed that Mother Earth sought to honor another healing vortex in my backyard by building upon it a classical style, seven-circuit labyrinth, based on an ancient configuration of these patterned spaces. Purportedly fashioned by the Minoan civilization on the island of Crete 5,000 years ago, the actual earliest reference to the labyrinth seems to be Egyptian, according to researchers hypothesizing that the word "labyrinth" originates from *lapi-ro-hun-t*, or the "Temple on the Mouth of the Sea." Other enthusiasts say the word labyrinth may come from a word *labyrs*, which means double-headed axe, a religious symbol of ancient Crete. In any case, as I discovered, you do not build labyrinths—they build you!

A perfect metaphor for these mystifying times of awakening (and of course perfect for "Doing a 360" work) is the re-emerging, circular tool of walking a labyrinth. I did not know much about the multi-faceted history, benefits, and sacred geometry of this unique, walking meditation journey. So, I began to research this divine path that winds in a circuitous way towards the center of concentric circles… and then out again… exiting where it began. Having mindfully built my own labyrinth, stone-by-stone with joy; along with enchanting walks around the U. S. in recent years as a hobby, I could probably write a book on this subject now. But I won't here; I'll keep this brief, as there are already a dozen good books about this mystical path coaxing a journey to Oneness. I *will* tell you that I highly recommend taking a relaxing labyrinth walk, which offers powerful transformative gifts to higher vibratory frequency. A simple walk can replenish energy and nourish Soul.

Labyrinths are unicursal (single-pathed) so you can't get lost in one like a stressful maze. A labyrinth is an archetype of Oneness, a circular path in which you enter, then walk around in divine contemplation, and walk out, all at your own pace. It's a domain of the Soul, a beautiful connection to an intangible force-field of Great Spirit in the Earth as you walk, step-by-step, navigating the many winding turns.

There is absolutely no right or wrong way to experience walking a labyrinth. When visiting my website, Doinga360.com, there are a few labyrinth information pages with photos to help inspire your heroic voyage to wholeness.

There are at least 4,000 public and private labyrinths in the United States, and the number grows every day. "In an age when many Americans are looking beyond the church pulpit for spiritual experience and solace, a growing number have rediscovered the labyrinth as a path to prayer, introspection, and emotional healing," reports *The New York Times*.[1] We have a charismatic Episcopal Priest, The Reverend Dr. Lauren Artress, to thank for boldly following her Soul's purpose in reviving this lost spiritual tool, lying dormant for centuries. After participating in Jean Houston's Mystery School (as I did in the 1980s), Artress felt passionately called to resurrect the divine labyrinth, now teaching this art tirelessly to thousands. Devotion spills forth in her book, *Walking a Sacred Path*.[2] In 1995, she founded Veriditas to provide training for the healing and meditative powers of the labyrinth. World Labyrinth Day is celebrated globally on the first Saturday in May, inspired by The Labyrinth Society, an international organization founded in 1998, whose mission is to fully support all those who create, maintain, and use labyrinths.[3] [4]

Let's look at other transformative circles in life: There is a Wheel of the Dharma that was turned by the Buddha, with its Tibetan *kyil-khor* (circle of the Five Wisdoms). We have a great symbol of love in the wedding ring; then there are the amazing Whirling Dervishes; the enigmatic crop circles; the round table of King Arthur; a zero in mathematics; and we enjoy a circle of friends. The mystical kiva is round.[5] There is the dazzling, sacred spiral dance of Grouse Medicine; astrologers read a circular chart;

castles are surrounded by water; and of course, Earth is a sphere. We all saw the photo of Earth from space when the astronauts captured that potent image. It evoked a beautiful blue, green, and white, living, breathing cell—only "one" of the entire universe. We witnessed our fragility. Like the 16th Century "Copernican Wounding" (in which we realized that Earth was not the center of the universe, but that it only revolved around a central sun), again we experienced a wounding in our collective psyche. But our planet is lovely, isn't it? What an exquisite home. If we do not act quickly, its life force will dangerously diminish sustainability for future generations.

A circle is so sacred in many, if not all cultures throughout history. Do you know of the mysterious Secret Stone Spheres in the jungles of Palmar Sur, Costa Rico? Until making a turnaround with my life I had not known of these spherical bodies. There are about 300 of these huge, granite orbs scattered around this area. Scientists say these stones are almost perfect spheres (about 96% round), which is amazing considering they weigh tons, dating back many centuries. Why were they made? Were they crafted in honor of the sun or the luminous moon in the sky? We do not know… we can only imagine. Someone long ago chose to work meticulously, chiseling away at hard rock to create these spheres— the shape must have been important.

The circle exists everywhere, doesn't it? Can you possibly think of some more circles? How about the captivating book also presented as a movie trilogy: *The Lord of the Rings?* How about the circular hero's journey monomyth of the great Joe Campbell? How about completely "Doing a 360" with your life?

A full circle consists of three hundred and sixty-degrees. It has no beginning, and no end. "Doing a 360" is completing a daring journey, your own heroic circle in YOUR OWN WAY. A brilliant gentleman, mythologist Joseph Campbell, taught that you have to go full-circle in life to be fulfilled. He thoughtfully said to me in a loving, grandfatherly tone, "You have to go back and be able to embrace your past. Be able to walk into your childhood church, synagogue, etc. and love it, feeling empowered there— and honor it."

The day we met I was attending his cutting-edge workshop, *Mythology Symbols and The Psyche,* at an annual conference of the Association for Humanistic Psychology (AHP) back in the 1970s. Professor Campbell had recently (in 1972) retired from teaching at Sarah Lawrence College in New York. My mentor Joan lovingly said to me before we split up for the day, "I want you to study with the greatest minds of our time. So, learn from Campbell—he is one of the best." I was a little nervous. I had already listened to a dazzling keynote speech from Jean Houston (and briefly met her) so it was a lot for a young adult to absorb.

Not having a clue of what was in store for me, I walked alone down a long hotel corridor to a fairly large room with a big screen. Listening to the scholar speak with alacrity, I watched him very closely, too. He stood erect in a fine, statesman-like stance, sliding hands into his tweed suit-jacket-pockets comfortably to rest, until sprinting them out again in mythic exultation. With bursting, resonate awe I knew I was in the company of greatness.

After a very long day of note-taking from his captivating lectures, elucidating slide after slide (including the hero motif), I finally gathered courage to join the end of a line of enthusiasts waiting to talk with this luminary. When Joseph Campbell spoke with you he contributed a "P and A" (present and available) compassionate presence. He did not speak down at you; he was with you—in *your* sphere. "If you embrace the past," he said kindly to me with elder tenor, "then you know you have gone full-circle. If you have resistance, then there is more work left to do." This was part of a life-altering conversation. Still a teen, I hadn't really *gone anywhere yet* so I did not fully grasp the concept from an adult, seasoned point of view—like I do now. Quite honestly, I probably didn't "get it" for a long time.

Campbell did not mean that you *have* to start going to church every Sunday if you were raised Catholic, or Lutheran, like me. He meant that you should be able to walk into that place of worship freely—whenever you wish to do so with joy in your heart—and *feel* good about the direct "religious" experience. It's your heritage and therefore a part of the journey in life, or your walk on the "good red road." As my personal empowerment coach that unforgettable day, he benevolently said these now famous words: "Well dear, it's like I tell all my students, you have got to 'follow your bliss.' Whatever *that* means to you. You've got to figure it out... and go for it with courage."

I longingly inquired to my new advisor, "Ah... yes. I wish to learn more—much more. How do I stay in touch, sir?" He invited me to join (as student-member) his new Foundation for the Open Eye started with his wife of 48-plus-years, Jean Erdman. Handing me the colorful brochure with a big eye on it, he smiled. Joe and his wife never had children. He saw the sparkle in my eyes. The esteemed mythologist sensed deep yearning of a youngster eager to learn heroic ways. How powerful moments like these can be in life. Do not ever underestimate your ability to affect the life of another. Joe is smiling... Thanks Joe. I know we shall meet again.

360 Knowing: A Sphere of Influence

Consider the space in a circle as a sphere. A sphere is defined as any round body having the surface equally distant from the center at all points.[6] "360 Knowing" is all-encompassing like our equation of $360 = 1$. (The term 360 Knowing is used in this book as a noun and a verb.) So, operate in this universe with confident spherical knowledge. Einstein specified that space—our three-dimensional field—is spherical. This is what he stated during a lecture on Geometry and Experience before the Prussian Academy of Sciences on January 27, 1921:

> "...*From the latest results of the theory of relativity it is probable that our three-dimensional space is also approximately spherical, that is, that the laws of disposition of rigid bodies in it are not given by Euclidean geometry, but approximately by spherical geometry, if only we consider parts of space which are sufficiently extended...*"[7]

360 Knowing, as in circular knowledge or spherical knowing, is a whole way of being that leaves behind linear, limited belief patterns. What does this have to do with changing your life? Everything.

Linear thinking is primarily a left-brain function. 360-degree Knowing is from the right brain *and* also from the left—however, more from the right than the left. Right brain experience is more intuitive and creative in its functioning. The left lobe of the brain controls analytical thought, logic, and performs math functions, etc. There is an excellent book by Daniel Pink called, *A Whole New Mind: Why Right-Brainers Will Rule the Future,* [8] which I suggest you read to further explain this subject (far better than I can). Consider that the brain is only the physical organ of your mind— it does not run the show; the Soul does, in concert with your heart. When you wake up to this realization the ego-mind begins to fade.

One day, my mentor Joan and I lounged dreamily sipping herbal tea on the balcony of her penthouse condo that sits on the Atlantic Ocean. It was unusually clear that morning. The vast sky was bright, and the sea below was very peaceful, extraordinarily blue and rich with a glassy surface allowing me to recognize the Gulf Stream flowing through it. She said thoughtfully, "Look at the horizon line. *Everything in nature has a curve.*" I nodded in silence. No conversation was necessary in that plush moment. The horizon did have a discernable soft curve. It was a lovely intuitive insight, one of those "aha" flashes in life—simple, yet profound.

There are no straight lines in nature. That is a mind-bender for your contemplation. *Seeing* nature as a perfect and reflective creation in all of its glory is a 360 Knowing. This spherical and holographic mindset of Oneness is a fundamental part of being "spiritual." As you voyage into your own nourishing, three-sixty experience, the divine maturation process of cycling through life with this fresh awareness may be exhilarating and empowering. For me, this was as Joseph Campbell termed it—heroic.

A Sacred Spin, the Tibetan Way

In subsequent chapters, you'll explore expanding the vistas of your right brain. For now, here's an interesting spin on it: An ancient monastic Tibetan Yoga practice known as The Five Tibetan Rites. Have you ever noticed that Tibetan monks look youthful?

What's their secret? A retired British army officer Colonel Bradford, seeking the fountain of youth in the "forbidden land," discovered The Five Rites in the 1920s. He was allowed to observe, practice, and share the teachings after spending time with the monks in a lamasery of Tibet. We are not going to cover all of the rites here. If further intrigued, you may study and practice the entire set of yogic movements elsewhere. In the spirit of a 360-re-calibration, I share the apropos First Rite.

The First Rite, or sacred movement of these Five Tibetan Rites is surprisingly unique, especially for a yoga teacher like me because it is not a traditional asana (posture). In fact, its departure is enormous in that you just stand and rotate your body—that's it. Perhaps you may remember as a little kid playing outside in the sunshine with arms outstretched to the world? Spinning around and around in a circle until you got dizzy, falling to the ground, and then giggling in the grass while gazing up to an immense, open sky. I did that a lot.

So, let's look at the purpose of The First Rite: As we age our physical frequency starts to wane. The energy vortexes or centers (chakras) slow down, and then these inner circling motions and energetic vibrations go out of whack—which is not good. It is this secret of circling the body, clockwise, which helps to slow down the aging process, thereby harmonizing the body chi with the energy of surrounded space. Simply stated: The First Rite helps to recharge your battery.

This practice is powerful, and must be approached slowly and carefully with yogic mindfulness. Begin with only one, two, or three turns at-a-time for a while. Then build up week-by-week to a maximum of 21 rotations (not to exceed that amount or the reverse benefits may occur). There is a lovely video (based on the international best-selling book called, *Ancient Secret of the Fountain of Youth*)[9] that I warmly advise you study, first. Of course, learning from a qualified instructor is the best method since there may be a bit of initial dizziness until you become balanced. Be careful! ALWAYS consult your physician before beginning any movement or exercise program, especially if you have health issues with your inner ear, a heart condition, etc.

Exercise: First of the Five Tibetan Rites

Practice Time: 3-10 minutes (as you feel guided).
Practice: Daily, preferably morning, before breakfast.

Read through this script first, and then practice; record and practice, or have someone read aloud this script for you.

To rotate safely now, you'll need a lot of open space. Move furniture if necessary so you don't bump into a coffee table, etc. Usually this exercise is performed with bare feet.

Create a sacred space.

To honor, energize, and balance your chakras for vitality and long life to the body (which is Soul's temple) you practice, The First Rite.

As you stand mindfully in a room of sacred space, feel the stillness. You are barefoot with feet slightly apart. Essentially, this is now a standing meditation, so *feel* the Earth: Meditate in this awareness for a minute or two—as guided. Feel your sphere of influence. Sense your sacred ground.

Feel your breath flowing in and out, rhythmically. Breathe slowly, deeply, and deliberately. Outstretch your arms, shoulder-level, with palms facing down. Now relax your neck area—avoid creating any tension. Focus your mind... *feel* the subtle energies within.

Attempt to turn only once, at first—just for practice. Be patient. Carefully spin clockwise ONLY 1-3 times, very slowly; consciously breathing deeply while staying in place—and not losing your balance. STOP swiftly—and bring palms together at chest-level, gazing at your thumbs (as in the *Namaste mudra*, which means now: I honor this blessed place of my heart within, where the entire universe resides). Initially, you may feel a little dizzy here. Breathe into the feeling of your sacred, spherical space. Feel the presence of the moment. Do not resist. Relax, and let go. Affirm the healing vibrations that you feel.

Patiently return to the awareness of your surroundings until you are ready to lie down on your back in shavasana (pronounced shah- vasana), the yoga pose of deep relaxation. (Please refer to Chapter 8 for detailed instructions on that practice.)

Continue focusing your conscious awareness on what you feel in the moment.

Practice daily, and you will gain speed. This ritual takes only moments to do, but it is so powerful. As the ancient ones taught, eventually (with much practice) a maximum of 21 rotations is performed. Figuratively speaking, that is really "Doing" a 360.

Sacred Space 360

If you are going to make a complete-turnaround in life, you have to learn how to create sacred space. You do not know what I mean by that? It's okay; we all have to start somewhere, don't we? At one point in time I did, too.

How do you *feel* when entering a place of worship? Think about it for a minute. Visualize with me now: There is a sense of the holy, the blessed, the revered, and the sacrosanct—yes? You may feel a need to whisper out of great respect, and move more slowly and deliberately. You might even sense the need to bow. You may feel humbled in the location, sensing an ambiance of holy energy, and a concentration of consecrated "being" in the God Force. Can you relate? That's creating sacred space: Mingling *with* an environment, which you perceive as special, sacred, or holy.

Terrorists rushing into churches—or any place of worship to murder people—don't consider the place to be so sacred or holy, huh? It is *their* dreadful, misguided, and limited perception of separation that directs the action. Those that vandalize a church, or burn it down, do not honor the space, do they? They don't have a sacred space in their heart and mind, which would mingle with that special location.

Wherever you are, you may create sacred space. And now, here is a question: What is the difference between a monk in a cave, and a person in prison? It is the consciousness of the individual(s) that makes their space sacred.

There are sacred spaces on Earth that have special vortexes of powerful energy, such as Sedona, Arizona; Chaco Canyon, New Mexico; and Stonehenge, etc. These locations have been designated by many to be sacred. However, the consciousness of an individual visiting a place is what makes it sacred for them. There are many skeptics. Remember, like attracts like. To repeat: Wherever you are, you may create a sacred space within yourself— on a commuter bus, in a plane, in a waiting-room at the doctor's office, wherever. Even out for a walk in nature you can create a sacred space. Don't assume its obvious sanctity, as there have been atrocious, diabolical happenings in the ostensibly peaceful woods. It's good to be close to nature though because we're part of it. If we don't get quiet, we can miss this spiritual union with Great Spirit: divine winds blowing through trees. If you use iPod headphones to listen to music or talk-radio, or chat on a cell, etc., you may not be fully present to nature's circumstances.

Learn to focus. Do one thing at-a-time. Multi-tasking is not healthy. It astounds me how people go for walks and instead of enjoying the simple view of nature, they are preoccupied on a cell phone totally oblivious of their magnificent surroundings. They are missing quiet time and precious moments communing with nature—Oneness. You *can* be with other people and still create sacred space through consciously raising your vibration. Once during a group-hike, someone said she didn't pay attention to the beautiful mountain terrain because she had been engaged in deep conversation with others. You can still chitchat while remaining in sacred space—it just takes practice. This is what the Buddha called, mindfulness training.

Mindfulness

Mindfulness is a beginning step to the skill of creating a 360 Lifestyle. An old friend (I will call her Zoe) knew how to create the most incredible sacred space in her hotel room during retreats. She covered lamps with beautiful, shear, multi-colored scarves; and lit miniature candles that were sprinkled around this space as stars of an indigo sky. In a glass, she arranged fresh wildflowers mindfully gathered from outside surroundings. On the chest of drawers, Zoe created a shrine using another scarf or material, a little statue of Buddha, and some other pretty objects, like shells, etc. Incense swirled as soft music soothed. Everyone wanted to be in that room. Why? Zoe created sacred space. She mindfully created a divine peace and joy in that typical, plain hotel room.

This is 360 Philosophy: She had inspiration and intention, and then created a mandala (a circular context) for the work that she was there to do on retreat. Creating that sacred space required spherical awareness and her mindfulness in action. Zoe planned ahead, thinking of her upcoming travel, gathering the things that would create the sacredness of her space, once away from home. I thought she was pretty cool. She was definitely skilled in the art of mindfulness, and I learned a lot from watching her.

Once you start being more mindful during daily activities, you may realize how terribly *unmindful* you have been. It takes a lot of courage and practice to go from being unaware… to aware of your (S)elf and surroundings, and then discern how you pass through life. Remember, wherever you go… there you are.

"P and A"

Many years ago I met a kind, gentle, and most sensible man. He said a catchy phrase that I never forgot. In fact, I started using it shortly thereafter. When I teach, lecture or counsel, I usually notice an inquisitive, positive response from folks to this phrase: "P and A" which means, being *present and available*. You might say Zoe (with that awesome hotel room) was "P and A." This means you are mindful; you're present and available to whatever arises. You have leaky margins, which are open to what is happening on the journey to wholeness. In this regard, I had a most affable Aunt. I loved being with her because she was so present and available in our conversations. She was a great listener. When you were with her, she was *with you*. After her funeral (years ago) I was offered a keepsake. I chose a beautiful crystal hanging at her kitchen-sink window, which reminds me today of her crystal clear being, her purity, and clarity of awareness—her "P and A" ness.

Dear reader, have you ever talked with someone and right away you can tell that they are not listening?

Maybe they are busy thinking about what they are going to say next—being a little self-absorbed? Instead of hearing what you say and caring about what you feel, perhaps they are really interested in telling you what *they* know.

How does that make you feel? Can you think of a situation like that? When someone does not acknowledge what you have said, mindlessly rambling on with their own story… they are not "P and A."

For an example, you may be expressing to someone about a recent, untimely, tragic death of a young co-worker. Instead of sympathetically listening to your melancholy, they chide in with a laundry list of people (strangers to you) that *they* know who have died recently. So, without acknowledging your comments and concerns, the conversation shifts to them. You are sympathetic and kindly listen. They probably do not mean to be inconsiderate.

Most folks just do not know about being aware. They do not have the "P and A" skill-set or the developed ability to be present to the moment, which in that aforementioned example would have been, compassionate listening.

When encountering situations as these, allow them to flow through you without getting stuck in the shadow by emotional reaction. Compassionately let the moment arise and dissipate.

This takes practice, and plenty of it. As an objective observer you cannot change them, or anyone else. You may only modify yourself.

If you are "P and A" then you are mindful. If mindful, you know how to consciously create a sacred space. My bighearted Aunt knew how to create sacred space when with me. I enjoyed our time together because it was special and holy.

Do you want that for yourself? Wouldn't you love to have your kids, spouse, family, friends, and co-workers feel that you are present and available to them?

So, perhaps you might be thinking: Okay… I would like some sacred space, mindfulness, and this cool "P and A" stuff. How do I do it?

The Art of Listening

How are you going to hear the musings of your Soul if you do not develop the way to inner stillness? STOP—get quiet to hear the music of the spheres. Listen to the sound of Spirit. That is why it's imperative for you to "Do a 360." It really is a matter of completely shifting your consciousness to see the whole view, the interdependent Oneness of all. Now that you have confident awareness that you *are* a Spirit which creates reality, how about entertaining the idea that if you take action with joyful effort, and get quiet—and I mean *really* quiet—you will turn your life around, entirely.

Listen. Develop your intuition as a valuable skill-set. We all have intuition. Some have this gift more than others, but you will cultivate deep sensitivity. Artists have been born with amazing talent like Picasso and Rembrandt—their abilities were obvious. Yet, someone who seemingly has some marginal talent (like me as a young student at the School of Visual Arts) can study the masters; take classes to learn perspective, light, and shadow, etc. They won't be a Michelangelo, but they sure can produce artistic achievements—many of them quite extraordinary triumphs. It all just takes training and lots of practice.

Quiet—you need quiet. That means, taking walks without talking on your mobile phone. Quiet times of reflection rest your mind from its constant babbling. Sit—you need to sit. Mind needs a vacation and a little "R and R" (rest and relaxation).

People generally whine, "I don't have much time for any meditation or contemplation." It is a cultural thing. Think about this: the United States is only two hundred and thirty-plus-years-old. American culture is young. Compared with other countries America is a toddler, a two-year-old. What do you associate with the second year in a child's life? Yikes—the "terrible-twos!" Try to get them to sit still, huh? It's ingrained in our society to strive, to move, to get ahead, make money, get stuff, and then more stuff... like spoiled children.

Envision one of many fellow beings: Exhausted from the strain of striving, they find themselves in a yoga class at the local fitness center for a hi-tech, stressed-to-the-gizzards, lifestyle fix. After the agony of realizing that they are not very flexible, they collapse on the floor into shavasana, and quite possibly for the first time in life they miraculously taste (S)elf-awareness: A profound connection with their Soul. Then there may be a "knowing in the doing" that this occurred by BEING STILL in a state of yogic radiance. I have always taught shavasana as THE yoga pose for our modern culture. (See Chapter 8.) It is this "uptime" pose that we need more than any other. Mastery of its practice leads to mastery of (S)elf. When people tell me that they do not have time to practice, I kindly say: nonsense. People do what they choose to do in life, and unfortunately that is why we live in a civilization of decadent decay, which is crying out for three hundred and sixty-degrees of change. Quite frankly, our survival depends on it.

When I began teaching yoga in the 1970s it wasn't in vogue like now. Oh, you were definitely on the fringe with the oddballs if you were into "that." During the final relaxation in shavasana, newer students would lift their heads, look at their watches, and then gaze around the room perplexed at the others lying in a deep, relaxed state of consciousness. I smiled at them, motioning my palm down towards the floor, saying telepathically: *"It's okay, you are not missing much out here, just let go now and relax within."* I prayed for them with great compassion in the greatest degree of love that eventually they would listen: To feel the presence of their Soul, and hear their Soul speak. This is an insight of self-realization: An awareness of the creative consciousness living within the context of a physical form. Look at this word: insight. When you go within yourself... you *see* inside: in-sight.

Quiet Your Mind

An essential habit of a 360 Lifestyle is generating quiet time. How are you going to hear God—your inner guidance—if you do not listen? Get quiet. Skills like meditation, *pranayama* (yoga breathing techniques), contemplation, chanting, and prayer (which you will read more of later) effectively reduce incessant thoughts, and therefore quiet your noisy mind. So, less thought equals more spaciousness for your Higher Consciousness. Science shows us that there really is no actual empty space in the universe. There isn't a black hole universe of nothingness—even black holes are filled with energy. Less mental thought allows for more energy, which is additional room for your Spirit.

Visualize a radio playing a song, but there is static interfering because you are not tuned-in exactly on the station. Carefully and slowly turning the dial, you fine-tune to an exact frequency of the radio station. Then you will hear the song clearly. Learn to trust your loving, inner guidance. Tune-in to the divine vibrational frequency, and hear what Soul sings in your heart-of-hearts. (Remember a voice instructing me to build a labyrinth?) It is truth. It is the only truth that matters. What I say does not mean a hill of beans unless you resonate to it as truth. That is all that matters to Soul—YOUR TRUTH—not what someone else tells you. If peaceful, you rest in a state of grace. You do not create peace of mind; it is inherent within the core of being. In quietude, reveal what you naturally are—peaceful.

This is ancient wisdom. However, it may be new to *you*. Just because I have been a meditator for thirty years does not mean you have to become proficient with it. And let's get this straight right now, I am not saying that if you do not sit on the cushion for many years, that you are not going to have your own self-actualization. All of us choose different paths—it doesn't matter. You are going to return to the SOURCE eventually, whether you meditate for decades or not. However, developing a meditation practice is a wonderful, healing pursuit. Like an apple blossom, meditation bears the fruit of enlightenment. So, it helps to have a structure for silence. Just ahead in this book is a meditation practice to work with. For now, just get quiet. Go out and sit in the back yard or on your balcony. If you don't have availability to one of those, how about going to a local park to sit on a bench? Get quiet. It is time for "R and R." Be present and available to the moment: Hear the wind. See the trees sway—stop and smell the flowers.

360 Uptime: "R and R"

I fondly remember when Khenchen Rinpoche's younger brother, Khenpo Tsewang Dongyal Rinpoche—fairly new to America learning the English language with its slang—heard me say the phrase: "R and R." His quick, quizzical, smiling response was, "Nancy, what is this R *and* R? What do you mean by that?" After explaining that it's a shortcut for rest and relaxation, he thoughtfully responded that he liked it very much. Weeks later, during a Dharma lecture translating for his brother from their complex, native Tibetan language, he paused and gazed my way. Smiling widely with amusement he skillfully used the term "R and R" addressing a crowd of students roaring in laughter with him. The Lamas always interject humor in their profound teachings because they exude vast joy and happiness from the core of their being. Now whenever saying, "R and R" peace pervades in my consciousness. It's a fun way to acknowledge uptime—like right now. After reading the following paragraph, put this book (or e-reading tablet) down, and rest with these suggestions:

Create a sacred space.

Be quiet. Close your eyes.

Just be still. Rest and relax your mind in peace. BE in a state of grace. This being is the foundation for doing. Allow your Spirit to consciously *feel* this peaceful presence.

Allow relaxation to be your guide. Experience who and what you are. Breathe... Relax in your divine true nature, which is spontaneously arising and abiding. Truly rest in your primordial essence. Rest in emptiness; rest in your Soul's awareness of this precious moment...........................

Ah... How are you? That was nice, huh? Simply put, be quiet more often, like that—listen to musings of the Higher Self.

Now, if you did "think" during that brief interlude it's okay, those are just the thoughts arising from your vast consciousness. The vastness is the great ocean of emptiness. "Bear in mind" the emptiness discussed here is not blank. It is not dark and blank of nothingness; there is no such thing as blank nothingness in the multi-universe. Our body lives in a dualistic world, so if there is nothingness, then there is also everythingness. If you believe that the purpose of quieting the mind is to go blank then you have misunderstood. Blank is escape. You cannot escape *that, that is;* and *that, that is not*; and *that, that is, in between.* When we meditate we are not trying to go blank or escape. There is no blankness in the Absolute. In our GOD-ness there is only ALL-ness—always and *all* ways.

Perhaps that was a lot to digest? Pause and reflect. Recall that life is just a big playground and now it's recess. Let's take a breath of fresh air… Seriously, right now… breathe deeply. Yes, that's it; take a few slow breaths………. breathe sweetly………. and practice a little "R and R."

Calm Abiding Meditation (Shamatha)

I have so enjoyed teaching meditation for many years. Once you apply sacred space awareness and mindfulness in "P and A" with listening, the art of meditation becomes easier to integrate into daily life.

There are basically two types of meditation: structured and unstructured.

When you are a beginner, it is most beneficial to just use a structured style. For example, if I asked you to keep your eyes slightly open to meditate on the "nature of your mind"—which is an abstract, unstructured method—you would probably feel a bit lost. So you need a simple focus in the beginning of practice with set-up parameters because the local, small ego-mind is so cunning that it will think of anything to sabotage your progress. That's why it is so important to establish a regular time and place to meditate. We are creatures of habit. We are re-calibrating and re-habituating ourselves into empowered, actualized 360-beings with a spherical view of three hundred and sixty-degrees. 360 = One. There are now so many wonderful meditation books and videos available for your perusal. Visit my website also for support at Doinga360.com. Follow your instincts as blossoming intuition.

Observe your Soul making choices when *consciously* selecting a book, Mp3, tape, or video to learn from. Meditation on mindfulness from the Buddhist tradition works really well for many, many aspirants of all paths because it's just fundamentally simple. I did not say it was easy, I said it was simple. We watch our breath in a technique called *"Shyi-ne"* [in Tibetan (pronounced shee-nay), which is sometimes translated as "being undisturbed"—and in Sanskrit this is called *Shamatha* (pronounced sham-ah-tah), meaning "calm abiding"].[10] As part of your 360-action plan ahead in the *3rd Quadrant*, we will look at other meditation styles that you may be suited to. Let's practice a little meditation now:

Exercise: Shamatha Meditation (Calm Abiding)

Practice Time: 5-20 minutes (as you feel guided).
Practice: 1-2x a day, or more, if desired.

You'll need a comfortable, straight-backed chair or a sitting cushion. Read this script first before practice. Record and then practice, or have someone read it aloud for you. Avoid rushing through this meditation practice; pause often between sentences.

Create a sacred space.

Close your eyes. Be in the presence of the moment. Feel the sacred space of your surroundings.

Feel the beautiful, luscious, quiet within. Your spine needs to be relaxed in perfect ease, yet vertical, enhancing the natural position of it, which means "straight"—not to slump forward.

Relax your mind and breathe normally. Just watch the breath at first for a few moments............................ Take deeper breaths and notice the nuances of it. Slow down the breath.......... be mindful... hear the sound it makes and the feeling in your lungs, your chest, and your whole body. Breath is life. Feel your Soul experiencing this physical sensation. The Buddha taught that when you take a deep breath, you should know that it was deep; and when you take a shallow breath, then you should be aware that it was shallow. Be mindful. Breathe deeply, yet very, very gently......... a few more times. Hear the breath flowing in and out, rhythmically. Feel present to this moment—you are so peacefully relaxed. You are "P and A" to your breath. You are "P and A" to yourself. Let the breath soften. Feel a joyful, peaceful sense of calm, arising and abiding, effortlessly. Now, let your breath "be" by itself. In other words, do not attempt to control the breath anymore—just watch it. Let it go...... then maintain your awareness and availability during this state. Continue for a few minutes.

Initially, meditation may be short because you yearn to enjoy it without feeling pressured that somehow the practice did not succeed. Some of my beginning students commented that they had doubt as to whether they could meditate at all. If you set goals too high then you may grow frustrated, creating tension in the mind. This is not what you are attempting to achieve in a meditative state.

Practice only for 3-5 minutes at first, and then expand your meditations later when comfortable, and when you really feel ready. In a group setting, you may be able to sustain shamatha (calm abiding meditation) for much longer. That experience may encompass twenty or thirty minutes, because of the effervescent energy from so many individuals providing abundant, vibratory support in this sphere of influence. You will probably have an instructor or a facilitator leading the group session anyway, so ask for assistance—they will help you.

Your mind is in constant and chaotic chatter. If clinging and grasping to all of these thoughts as you approach meditation, think (metaphorically) of holding something in the open palm of your hand. As an example: let's say, your keys. Imagine turning over your hand, and let them go. Keys instantly fall to the floor, yes? During meditation, when thoughts arise from a vast pool of your consciousness (and trust me, they will)… just let them go.

I shall explain it also in this visual way: Imagine lots of dots and lines configured like this:

    **** _____ *** _____ **** _____ **** _____ *** _____
**** _____ *** _____ **** etc.

Those dots (or star-like symbols) represent your thoughts; and the lines signify the vast expanse of emptiness, the space of your consciousness, between thoughts. This is how your mind operates at first when beginning various meditation techniques. Then, when you are thoroughly training an awakening mind for enlightenment, you will acquire supplementary silence and more stillness; and therefore, additional transcendent space *between* your thoughts during your meditations, like this:

    ****_____ ***_____ ***_____ **_____
_____ *_____ *_____
_____

Quiet the tumultuous mind and your Soul will reveal ITS true nature as tranquil, calm abiding. As you broaden this practice further, realize that true love, wisdom, and peace are not anything you have actually generated. Innately they *are* you—a God Force, a Christ-like Consciousness, or a Buddha Nature, etc. These are energy essences that cannot be created or destroyed. Remember: *It is, as it is.*

Dear reader, as you develop a meditation practice for the sake of all sentient beings, thoughts diminish. Eventually, your ordinary, jumping monkey-mind (which is now in a meditative state of pristine consciousness) produces less discursive thought, and therefore will look more like this:

   *_____
_____
_____
_____ *

2nd QUADRANT of GOING DEEP

Weaving and Healing

2nd QUADRANT of GOING DEEP

Weaving and Healing

Chapter 4

Spider Medicine: Weaving New Patterns

"Occasionally in life there are those moments of unutterable fulfillment which cannot be completely explained by those symbols called words. Their meanings can only be articulated by the audible language of the heart."

— Reverend Dr. Martin Luther King, Jr.

O nce you accept 360-degree Philosophy with a liberated energy of clarity—that you are totally responsible for everything happening in your life because you create reality—then you'll understand how multi-layered and deeply entrenched patterns can shape life experiences. Let us go within, exploring from depths of the heart, operating on a mythic level. This is your mystic, mythic story, a universal life pattern of transformation that Joseph Campbell called the monomyth.[1]

There are large and smaller patterns of display in life. They continuously weave in and out of our lives affected by shifts in consciousness. Personality patterns are mythic arrays, numinous arrangements that form a divine tapestry of who we are, and how we evolve in the world. For example, one of my big life patterns is to teach. I have taught for a long, long time in various, multi-dimensional ways. Most importantly, I am comfortable wearing those distinctive hats. As a natural inclination I know it's a beneficial pattern to nourish because it's part of my Soul's purpose for taking this embodiment. So, I consciously pursue parallel opportunities that will enrich this pattern—like writing this book, and co-hosting a talk-radio program, etc. Here is more Sacred Imagery to assist you in anchoring this awareness of patterned displays:

Visualize within your mind's eye… some concentric circles. This means that these circles are inside of the other. The outer circle, which is of course the largest, is your main pattern or theme for this lifetime (like my example above of teaching). Your essential life work—if you don't already know—is to figure out and "do" what that outer, all-encompassing circle is. There are other large circles, just inside that outer one. These represent other life patterns, which shape, mold, and color your individual personality. Dear reader, no one has ever been you. No one *is* you; and no one will ever, ever, be *you*. I believe an individuated Soul comes in at birth with a spherical blueprint that has circular patterning encoded in the DNA. As colleague Rev. Dr. Bob used to say, "The good news is, there is only good news." The good news is that your patterns may be augmented. Everything can alter. The only thing constant in the universe is change.

Within us are hundreds of patterns of varying types. What may be a small pattern to one person is a big pattern for another. For example, if deathly afraid of riding in an airplane, you may participate in very helpful, desensitization therapy programs to overcome that fear.

You can change. That is what this entire book inspires you to do—change.

When born to the physical realm you build a personality base strongly influenced by your parents. Then around age seven, you develop more of your own decision-making processes, and continue to expand a persona as a young adult affected by peer pressure. Essentially, your personality consists of three things: Soul's blueprint, (which has karmic issues, if you do believe in karma); your parental/family/friends' influences; and your adult lifestyle choices. This model comes from mentor, Reverend Dr. Michelle Lusson, whom I studied with closely during seminary, and also during the launch of her innovative Creative Wellness Program book and teacher training in the 1980s.

360 Spider Medicine

Like the spider, we weave our webs in this life.[2] Our intricate and beautiful patterns with other people are called relationships. Let's examine a typical relational pattern of procrastination as an example to dive deeper into this discussion. A person consistently arrives significantly late to an appointment, event, meeting, class, party, or dinner invitation, etc. Is there someone you may think of in this regard? There may be many reasons why people are always noticeably late. A wonderful and devoted student attended my yoga, meditation, and stress management classes for fifteen years. We shall call her Betty. There was one thing I could always count on with her—God bless Betty—she would appear there faithfully, five-times-a-week. Wow, that is devotion. The caveat: Yes, you guessed it; she was *always* disturbingly late. In fact, Betty's classmate friends would say sympathetically in shades of sarcasm, "She'll be late for her own funeral!"

Some psychologists have theorized that people need to get attention by being late. Well, whatever the case may be it is a lifestyle pattern that can be changed. Why bother? An unbalanced pattern of behavior (like this one) affects others in your sphere of influence, such as your family, friends, co-workers, etc., that are constantly "waiting." From an all-encompassing view, no one is left out of this equation: 360 = One. We know from physics that our individual consciousness affects everything in the universe. That is a huge responsibility. On a practical level, an unbalanced procrastination pattern can make you miss an appointment. An antidote for procrastination and laziness is joyful effort, which was presented to you earlier. In Betty's case, she missed pertinent announcements and some discussion of my class curriculum. Therefore, she felt a little lost during these programs. Puzzled, she always approached with questions afterwards, and I obliged with the answers. Quickly, I realized a pattern emerging in this relationship: Her pay off was additional attention and private time with the teacher. I really appreciated her; so consciously with compassion, I allowed some participation in this pattern while helping her to realize this display of aberrant behavior.

Like our mythic spiders, that's a simple example of *weaving* patterns as we engage people in behaviors that form relationships. After countless times together discussing Betty's tardiness (and foundational worthiness issue) she still could not ground the adjustment. She attempted it a few times. Betty made some noble effort to shift, but it was just too deeply entrenched in her belief system that she was not worthy to be on time.

Remember, you have to "do" the big changes from resilient yearning, inspiration, and intention. The dynamics in this (above mentioned) relationship presented fifteen years of opportunity to practice love, patience, discernment, and compassion—great treasures. ALL of your relationships with functional or even dysfunctional patterns are gifts. Like "tell it like it is" psychologist Dr. Phil always questions us: "What's your pay off?" There are divine benefits to behavior even if ostensibly dysfunctional. When recognizing the shadow (imbalanced) patterns and healing them, you initiate movement from heartbreak to bliss. Avoid judging others though, for we do not know their Soul's plan. Just go deep in discernment, working conscientiously on your own beautiful, mythic (S)elf, the Soul on an excursion to Oneness. Healing the dark shadows takes colossal, heroic effort. It's quite a process. I always say, "ALL in divine timing." How lovely that yogini Betty is finally right on time (here and now) to help illustrate the magic weaving of Spider Medicine.

Doormats and The Armadillo

Do you constantly bring people into life that walk all over you? You do not? Great! If you do—why permit it? Because you create and allow that experience as a life pattern, that's why. Sound familiar? I know there are a few doormats around since it was one of the most prevalent patterns discussed during my stress management classes. This issue has much to do with defining personal space. Do you feel resentful "having to do things" that you really do not want to do? Do you permit people to use you like a doormat because you are afraid that they won't like you if you do not do what they want? Let me introduce an enormous personality pageant called the Doormat Pattern, and its very interesting antidote, Armadillo Medicine.[3] Part of the voyage in "Doing a 360" is developing healthy and sacred boundaries. Learning to creatively say NO without using the actual negative word itself, is weaved into healing and ending this pattern. In this regard, I recommend a book, *The Power of a Positive No: How to Say NO and Still Get to YES*, by William Ury.[4] Most Doormats cannot say no to anyone—ever. It's ridiculously sad, but true. Let's start to mend this imbalance. You may wonder what is all this talk about creepy, skulking spiders and armadillos? Well, an effective healing strategy is the use of powerful wisdom called, Animal Medicine, from our wise, Native American brothers and sisters.[5]

For many years I have honored this ancient wisdom. I take it very seriously with utmost respect for these sacred teachings. Perhaps you will too when *feeling* the mythic power, magic, and beautiful blessings from our fellow creatures of nature: the ones that fly, the four-legged beings, the crawlers, and denizens of the sea. All animals have particular characteristics or strengths, which are viewed (from an all-inclusive, 360-degree perspective) as medicine—healing whatever ails. Sacred Earth creatures show us their exclusive patterns. If you open your heart to mindfully study their natures, they will teach so much about this life. When using Animal Medicine to heal any imbalance such as the Doormat Pattern, you are essentially invoking a 360-medicine shield, or sacred circle of powerful protection. (Recall that circular Zia symbol and logo of the state of New Mexico.)

In this particular example, you call upon divine Armadillo.[6] Focus attention on its medicine power, which is that it wears armor on its back. In a most unusual way it completely rolls itself up into a ball of strong protection. Its predators cannot penetrate its hard shell since it is a sphere of armor. Armadillo teaches the two-legged ones a key wisdom of the art of setting boundaries. What a blessing and divine gift! As part of the medicine or treatment (a strategy in the 360-action plan), envision your sphere of consciousness aligning with the wisdom of this animal.

To assist in this sacred understanding, you will need a piece of paper. You are going to do an exercise to help ground this concept into your new awareness. Draw a circle representing your mythic, personal Armadillo Shield. Write inside of the circle all that you desire to heal in relation to this Doormat Pattern with someone. Armadillo's armor deflects any negative energy or imbalanced, pushy people coming your way. (Remember, you magnetized the energy or vibrational frequency of this unsuitable relationship to your life circumstances.) Here and now in this exercise you will not resist; you pray and affirm the healing in the present moment. Your fresh shield will not be penetrated because you have intentionally created a new pattern, a re-calibrated vibrational field of wisdom around you. What a gift to set healthy boundaries with people in life, and to feel empowered doing it. The little Armadillo is your powerful archetype to invoke this knowledge. Please be patient... this process may take a bit of time, but it really works.

This is a boundless insight of Native American Spirituality: to be at one with Great Spirit, one with *all* things—and animals are no exception. It is similar to the law of vibration or system of radionics, and as mentioned repeatedly, the boomerang principle: What goes around... comes around. When you focus on feeling at one with Armadillo, taking its medicine through the law of attraction in Great Spirit, you augment and foster harmony with its essence. Then you manifest its characteristic strengths, which is discernment of your own sacred space and loving application of boundary setting in relationships. So, if you have a tough, imbalanced Doormat Pattern with someone, humbly request Armadillo to help. Let this fabulous creature aid in your time of need with its potent healing. Be persistent in your practice of Animal Medicine. Remember, all in divine timing. Watch how the pattern shifts as you continually keep the relationship in the light, for the highest good of all.

I take daily doses of Animal Medicine. When seeing a sacred creature—day or night—I feel privileged to be in its presence. Observing an animal, even if just for a fleeting moment, is receiving the gift of its medicine. I share this example: Before I did a three-sixty with my life, I saw hawks—lots of them. They were beautiful, flying around in the morning skies during long commutes to work through the dense traffic of Palm Beach County. I also saw them sitting atop tall light posts lining busy I-95, not exactly a natural location. Let's just say they seemed a bit out of place because I had taken the same route for years, and never saw these majestic birds. I was receiving a divine gift. I respected the tradition of the Elders. Hawk is the messenger. Its medicine helps us to see the bigger picture encircling our lives from a higher perspective. All of those sightings were a guided message to be on guard: To see the BIG "360" picture and change my life… to follow my bliss.

What kind of animals are you drawn to? What creatures tug at your heartstrings? Do you meet specific animals in your surroundings during daily life? What can you learn from those encounters? Many folks love dogs with deep veneration. Most of us absolutely adore them, don't we? That is why we keep them as pets—they become our family. Dog Medicine teaches human beings about loyalty, unconditional love, and service to humanity. All life is precious. Our creatures are part of the fabric of life, the colorful patterns we weave in a great tapestry. Animals are a part of nature that we need to respect and honor. Did you know that even the tiny ant has powerful medicine? Yes, the little ant. Taking a mighty dose of Ant Medicine brings the healing succors of patience and planning. Here is a sacred spin on a story from ancient mythology about Psyche, Aphrodite, and the Ants.[7]

Aphrodite was jealous of the younger, beautiful girl named Psyche. Aphrodite decided to kill Psyche by giving her an impossible task to accomplish. Psyche had to divide up a gigantic mound of mixed grains into separate piles. If not completed by morning—she would be dead! In her fretting and panic she began to pray. Psyche meditated upon the sacred Ants of Mother Nature. She focused her heart on calling the Ants to her side. Millions and millions came that night and effortlessly carried each different grain, one-by-one, to successfully complete this most unreasonable task. The next morning, Aphrodite was furious that the impossible had been accomplished. Metaphoric lessons in this story are to "do the right thing," skillfully prioritize your life, and do not be afraid to ask for help. If all of your clothes were dirty because you are behind with doing the laundry it would not be smart to begin decorating your dining room with a wallpaper border instead. *That* swanky project can be done later. You have got to discern what is the paramount course of action in every moment. As my mentor Joan wisely mentioned after she shared this mythic tale of Psyche's Labor, "Nancy, you do not heal a snakebite with an aspirin."

By the way, if ants annoy you, the universe may be sending a message to be more patient, and to trust in The Great Plan. Once they have done their big job, ants will probably go away. I am serious. My husband and I compassionately remove an occasional ant or spider from our home by sliding paper under them, carefully placing them outside to live in peace. Our friends and relatives think we are kind of kooky. They do not understand why we just shouldn't smash it with a shoe. We know that even the lowly, creepy crawlers carry sacred medicine, and they too, are a part of all life, of interdependent Oneness. We choose to just honor the life. Now, if you are by chance an exterminator, I am sorry to steal a bit of your thunder, but it is the truth. (Well, it is my truth.)

There is more that you can do to heal a Doormat Pattern. Take action to create a new pattern, once you purge an old one. This will attract a balanced energy or good vibes surrounded by your medicine shield. "Bear in mind" that you have to choose to release this dysfunctional pattern deep in your heart-of-hearts. If you do not really *choose* to let it go—it won't be replaced with a new, liberated pattern. Once you do free yourself, remember that nature loves a vacuum, so allow your sacred space to fill and flourish with a new, constructive design. You teach others how to treat you because the teaching is: YOU create reality. They are not "doing it" to you; you are allowing sacred space to be invaded because you have not lovingly established a sacred boundary. (Remember Betty's pattern of procrastination so she could be teacher's pet?) You must choose to honor yourself by consciously identifying undesirable patterns and changing them, if they are not in your greatest degree of love for the benefit of all. Until healed, the universe will deliver to your sphere of influence more people that have the same pattern. Once you have really let it go, they won't come around anymore. Another pattern will surface to work on. There is always the organic grain, that infinite grist for our mill.

360 Spherical Strategies

An effective tool for releasing the Doormat is learning to use a creative and all-encompassing "NO." Practice these following statements (or your own version) when asked to do things that you do not really want to do. (Also refer to your Armadillo Circle drawing.) You will say: "Thanks so much for asking me to do _____." (Fill in these blanks as you feel guided.) "At this time, I don't feel comfortable doing _____." "I really appreciate you thinking of me in this regard." If they persist (they usually do) and say to you, "Oh, but you are so good at doing _____, and we really need your help. Won't you do it?" Take a very conscious, deep breath and calmly stand in your divine power. Repeat what you said before: "Thank you *so* much. I'm just not feeling comfortable doing _____ at this time. Again, thanks for asking. I really appreciate you thinking of me."

This works. Notice that the word "no" is absent from the strategy. We are keeping this positive. With some practice my students exclaimed, "Wow, this is effective—it really worked—and felt so good. I was able to speak my mind so clearly without feeling guilty." Sure it felt very good! They were empowering themselves, being authentic, possibly for the very first time in their awakening lives. They were allowing Soul to take the wheel and consciously respond from a level of divine truth. Copy those sentences right now, or at least mark the page and keep it visible by your iPad, Kindle, computer, phone, or fridge, etc. Practice this strategy like a mantra. Really… you will need to practice. Say the dialog with confidence in front of a mirror.

The next time (and believe me, there will be a next time) that you are asked to volunteer for some project that you totally, completely, absolutely feel is not what your Higher Self wants to do, you are going to smile confidently and say, "Oh, how lovely of you to want to volunteer me. Thank you *so* much. At this time however, I am unavailable to participate." If they persist, lovingly repeat your declaration. *Feel* yourself standing firm in the loving authenticity of Spirit. Eventually, they will stop asking because you broke the pattern with them. You'll feel noble—empowered as the God or Goddess on your honest throne when the doormat vanishes without a trace.

Shout it out to the rooftops! Please write to me about your experiences. I shall be delighted to hear your story of this sacred *no*.

Spiritual Wannabes and Certainty Wisdom

One of the major patterns in life, a numero-uno of all other configurations, is what I call a Desperately-Seeking-Spirit Pattern. People with this are Spiritual Wannabes, which was discussed in depth during the *1st Quadrant*. So many, except living planetary masters and those who have completely awakened to their truth, have some form of this pattern. It's a powerful, magical display to discover and then balance. You have to tweak this one a bit, here and there—honing your skills—like working with the concepts presented in this book. Release this pattern, and then operate in relationships out of a new one: the Certainty Wisdom Pattern.

Focus on Certainty Wisdom to remember who you are. This means that you re-cognize (recognize) or re-know your real self—a true identity of intrinsic awareness in its pure, natural state of Higher Consciousness. When you start living from this spherical vantage point, life flows as a placid river—gracefully, joyfully, and effortlessly. Your exhaustive need to desperately swim against the current of life will diminish. You have probably heard of this old saying: "Go with the flow." All masters know this; they do not react—they do not accept or reject anything that may come their way. They *know with certainty*: It just is, as it is. They wisely go with the flow.

Doing a 360 requires looking at various, fear-based, holding patterns freezing your life, and with honesty and discernment, healing them. Some are relatively small so they will not have as much of an impact as the bigger ones. This entire chapter was named for a powerful healing energy of a very special creature—the Spider. A few days ago, a giant tarantula was sharing our neighborhood hiking path with me. My beautiful gift vanished quietly into a large hole in the ground at the edge of the dirt walkway. Spider Medicine is such a vast teaching. Spider helps us to understand ourselves as fine, mythic, infinite, spiritual beings weaving a magical display of life. The mighty Medicine of Spider teaches that we are changing patterns all of the time as part of God's luminescent array in the web of a divine, spherical matrix of ALL BEING.

Gratitude = Abundance

Let us take a gander at some money issues now. If you are currently broke and even worse, in serious debt, a big messy pattern has already been established. Reflect back on your life. Are you constantly repeating this cycle? Some declare bankruptcy to clear all debts, and then two or three years later they are right back where they were again—in financial ruin. Today, this is a serious problem. So many are suffering. Statistics show that the average credit card debt per American household is almost $14,200, which reflects a widespread and imbalanced pattern.[8] A seasoned desire to change with concerted, spherical action will help to re-calibrate your circumstances. This issue is not really about our funds. Money is only energy. So, money is just like everything else in this universe. Financial expert Suze Orman always says, "It's people first, *then* money." She is savvy.

Debt usually represents an issue of lack that you have, and some generated emotion of unforgiveness and/or resentment weaved in. You may feel that everyone owes you something. You may, therefore, be stuck in a very big pattern called Poverty Consciousness, with its hefty hallmark banner: lack of self-worth. When truly honoring (S)elf as a heavenly Soul-in-charge-driving-the-bus, you will feel abundant. When you affirm and exude self-esteem and self-worth from every cell in your being, then poverty consciousness will diminish.

It will eventually resolve into a new Pattern of Abundance. You can go to all of the counselors that you want, get on their payment plans and all that... blah, blah, blah. You may even read all of those get-rich-quick books and websites that are out there, discovering some clever money tips. Those strategies may help, so please do what you need to do. But I'm telling you that if you don't change your awareness from within to heal this imbalanced pattern, you are going to have money problems, again and again. STOP what you are doing because it isn't working. I am not a professional financial advisor. However, here is what I did: Hit those brake-pedals. STOP and then deeply examine your feelings about money. Face the pattern. Admit you *had* an issue with it. That was then and this is now. You've got to feel abundant. Do not misunderstand the teaching here:

Abundance means
having everything your Soul truly needs
to experience
what it is you came here for.

I know someone (unfortunately, many more than one) who is now, and has always been, broke. They have such a rough time with the stressful bills and consistently groan, "It is *hard* to feel abundant." They create a hardness of life in their mind with those words. Words are energy. Words are power. Life is not a struggle unless you make it so. It may be challenging for them because it is not part of their belief pattern to perceive that abundance is easy.

Abundance is your birthright. When you believe consciously that you *are* prosperous—that all of your needs are met—you will be taking a giant step. Take into account that boomerang: waves of vibrations are sent out—and then come right back. It is an immutable law of the universe. I always advise, "If you desire something, be *very* articulate about what it is. If you are unclear, the universe won't have clarity either." Affirmations that you may use must affirm what you already have. If you *want* something (from the limited, local mind of belief in lack, poverty, and resentment), then you are not going to get it because the universe knows that you do not *have* it, yet—you only *want* it in the future. The boomerang returns exactly what is focused on—the *wanting*. This you already read about in the second chapter. If you are bankrupt, don't put all of your attention on that ominous mass of deficiency. If you feel constant debt and lack, then you will just continue to attract more of it.

Focus with gratitude and gratefulness on what you already have. Make a list of things that you are so grateful for. Create a gratitude journal and then write in it daily. Affirm with gratitude what you already know to be true in Spirit. An effective action tool for abundance may be using the following affirmations of your choice:

> *I am abundant*
> *I am grateful for all I have*
> *All my needs are met*
> *I am blessed*
> *I am prosperous*

Put these on a 'post it' note or a small piece of paper, and place them where you'll see them often: the fridge, phone, wallet, bath mirror, etc. Then let these divine messages merge into your consciousness from your two "eyes" of inspiration and intention. At one point in my long-gone past, I owed so much money that I thought I would never get out of debt. I wish Suze Orman had been around back then. She wasn't, but God was. Today, I am abundant. I have so much to be grateful for.

You have to admit it if you are out of control with your finances. Heal this pattern. Do not borrow money from everyone and from everywhere as a constant bandage solution. You have got to go deep and get to the root, and pull it out. STOP and get quiet. Listen to your heart. That means what you feel, what you intuit—not what you think. Who do you need to forgive? Is it yourself, someone else or both? Calmly sit down and write out an action plan of how you are going to change this poor, miserable pattern. Do you really, truly wish to change? Do not mock this question. Some unconsciously do not. Some people are just quite happy spending money that they don't have, like it was water. Recognizing and replacing a poverty belief system, which is a large lie, can be quite shocking at first—and folks may not like it. Many resist. They may have spoiled themselves like a little child getting whatever they "want"… which results in more and more debt. Have you ever seen a young child sitting in a shopping cart at the grocery store grabbing for everything? They will reach for anything they can: the candy, cereal, pasta, and even the coffee creamer, whatever they see and grasp for—and then they scream bloody hell if they do not get their way.

Abundance means
having everything your Soul truly needs
to experience
what it is you came here for.

Before living in an awareness of abundance through great gratitude, feeling deep in my heart that I had everything Spirit truly needed to fulfill my purpose, I faced the truth and made a specific strategy to get out of a mentally created, financial misery. I wrote out a sensible plan and then focused on saving money. I put the greenbacks in a sacred envelope to build prosperity. One tip is to use smaller bills so that the stacks look really big. Every week these piles grew and grew—I smiled in affirmed abundance. I believed that I had a lot of money. With oceans of healing self-worth I paid myself first. A detailed budget was created as part of the action plan. Do this. It may shock you, but it will help a lot. When you see the numbers on paper it really educates.

Knowledge is power. Get your head out of the sand. You may resist, but remember that what you resist against, draws to you like a large magnet. The saying simply is: "What you resist, persists." You must fake it until you make it: Visualize your (S)elf free; and *feel* in the core essence of being that you are indeed, abundant. Let your Soul take control—hold that wheel calmly with two hands while spinning and make a complete circle—do not stop halfway going in the wrong direction at 180.

Once you have a devoted, sacred strategy set into motion, feel wholeheartedly that God's unlimited prosperity IS manifest. You can do it. If I can do it, you can, too. I live the life I choose. I feel abundant. I have everything needed to experience a life that my Soul is creating.

Some misguidedly believe that you can't be very "spiritual" if you have abundance. Nonsense. Nice things may surround you as long as you are not attached to them. Take into account that all of your stuff is just stuff—it's just energy. I love to use the energy of money because when I do, then I get more. Every time I write a check I pause and focus on feeling abundant. I am happy to pay the bills because my needs are already met. You *can* have the fine "energy" of money. And when you die no one cares how much money you have except the remaining relatives. God does not care! Remember, you already are Spirit incarnate. If you have abundance, it's okay. Great. Money is just energy that helps you to do what you choose. If you are broke, then how are you going to do what you prefer? You cannot, because you are frozen-stuck. Visualize, feel, and know yourself as abundant. If this happens to be your big issue then consider reconciling it now.

Remember The Lemon? Your body does not know the difference between fact and fantasy, so start fantasizing—take action. Dollar bills are not going to fall from the sky. Do not worry about the process of how to manifest things. The "how" resides in the sacred realm of the absolute universe. You can drive yourself crazy pondering how quantum physics works, and how the universe was created. Please let God handle that celestial realm.

Get high up on that sacred 360 Throne. Affirm yourself as the Godlike ruler of (S)elf. Recognize your life experience with seasoned maturity and heal with a dose of medicine—release a pattern that got you enmeshed in dark despair. Create a powerful pattern of divine abundance through massive gratitude. God only provides in concert with your devoted action. Take responsibility with resolute and radical heroism. When adjusting your attitude about material things, life will start to turn around—completely.

24/7—Notes to (S)elf

Here is a strategy that I call "24/7." This means that you are going to make joyful effort to consciously feel your Higher Self: twenty-four hours a day, seven days a week. In the beginning of this practice you may forget a lot, but do not fret, eventually this custom becomes your second nature. When truly realized, it is the first.

When inventory is taken in a store, you know what is left on the shelves. I invite you to take inventory now: What do you want to change, to augment in yourself? Re-invent, starting right now. Create a sacred space. Meditate and contemplate on the following divine affirmations. Write them down in a journal or in a special notebook, as well as here (in the printed form of this book). Also, put them on labels, notepaper or 'post it' pads, and place in strategic places as was mentioned before. Make up your own affirmations based on what you choose. Use these daily—24/7. Remember, any affirmations must be stated in the present tense like these examples:

> I am Abundant
> I am Happy
> I am Healthy
> I am Slender
> I am _____
> I Enjoy Healthy Food
> I Enjoy _____
> I Feel Love
> I Feel Joy
> I Feel _____
> I Love My Body
> I Love Life
> I Love _____

Thank you for My Healing
Thank You for My Beautiful Family
Thank you for My _____
I Feel Grateful
I Feel Grateful for _____
I Appreciate All My Abundance
I Appreciate _____
I am Peace
I am Spirit!

Keep going. Those are just a few samples. Take this a step further as Notes to (S)elf. Here is what we do in classes: I hand out small, paper adhesive labels. Students are then instructed to meditate; and after that experience to write affirmations on these labels (as their Spirit guides them). These go in their wallet or purse—right there in class. At home, they continue the lesson by placing more labels everywhere. I always joyfully anticipate the next session since they are all excited to report good results. These are positive reinforcements reflecting back what you chose to change. What goes around... comes around. They are great reminders of your mythic journey to wholeness.

So, be creative: Do this exercise. Follow these instructions above: put your labels in calculated, visible places. For example, if you are constantly doing laundry every day because you have six young children (God bless you!), then put affirmations near the washing machine so you will be reminded regularly of the Notes to (S)elf. And as behavior re-calibrates, eventually you won't need these reminders as much—or at all. Like being "P and A," Soul's awareness mingles into the heart-space of the new and improved you.

While writing this book, an old hand injury returned after doing some landscaping around our new home. I had mildly hurt the ligaments years ago, incorrectly manipulating two, five-pound barbell weights with only one hand, while placing them in a tote-bag (after teaching class). Though it never required any medical attention then, this time, when the pain re-surfaced it was so severe that I felt actually crippled. Lifting a drink to my lips was absolutely excruciating. I almost dropped many a glass. Passing around a plate of food at a dinner party was intimidating. The pain on a scale of one through ten—was an eight, nine, or a ten.

While watching the torture on my face as I attempted to accomplish the simplest of tasks, a friend said, "Don't you think it's time to go to the doctor and have surgery on that hand?" In that powerful moment I knew that I had to walk my talk. Enough was enough. I decided then to consciously focus on healing this condition. I had to "practice what I preach." The moment that I acknowledged this profound, sacred responsibility, deep healing began. Within a week, most of the pain dissipated. I focused on the thankfulness of my healing—24/7. Using the sacred Medicine of Frog, I cleansed my cells. (You will read about this in the next chapter.) I consistently affirmed in a present tense, "My hand feels great." When lifting something heavy and sensing a bit of pain, soreness, and weakness, I would say silently, "Thank you for my healing. I *am* healed." Within a month I was happily, pain-free.

I still thank God for my little cure. It is interesting to note the play on this dreaded word, incurable: curable from with "in." Perhaps, I manifested this pain because it helped to explain 360 Healing. Obviously, I created re-injuring the hand so I could talk about it in this book. If it wasn't a hand injury, it would have been something else—of *that* I am sure.

Chapter 5

360 Healing

"Be the change you want to see in the world."

— Mahatma Gandhi

ow that you have entered a web-like perception of your world weaving colorful tapestry patterns, the journey deepens. Comprehend your vital constituency in the great, spherical matrix of life—a participatory role *in* and *of* it. Simply put: What you do makes a difference. On this superb playground of life consider it fascinating to see kaleidoscopic patterns manifest in vibrant ways. As Soul drives the bus, watch how you *consciously* create and play in this big game. You create because you are an individuated, divine being—a creator. The game I refer to is the BIG game: Life. In Soul's augmented awareness, you perceive old patterns refreshed while they are enfolding and unfolding with friends, family, co-workers, and neighbors. You will identify "this and that" configuration on a day-to-day basis as a 360 Knowing, which means "certainty wisdom" about what you are experiencing. The further you go on this trip, the more profound realizations will be. It's exhilarating when you get a big *aha* from Soul's consciousness.

While continuing to recognize the various sizes of concentric spherical patterns in your life, a crucial 360 Healing strategy is learning to use discernment. This is very important. Discernment is not the same thing as judgment. You can tell or discern the difference in any situation if there is an emotional charge that you feel, or not. This is the key: Discerning something is a liberated, divine, discriminating consciousness that carries absolutely no energetic or vibratory "charge" in your body. That means, you do not feel anything stirring in your emotional response system; you won't feel a reaction. Judgment always resides in reactiveness. If you get upset, and feel hurt or angry—then you are judging. Judgment lurks in the dark side of the shadows. We all have our shady shadows lurking within. However, if you observe and/or participate in any situation with an objective fascination without "feeling" it and therefore without reacting to it, then you are discerning, which is good—very good. This takes much practice.

A discerning skill-set requires a ground of mindfulness. With respect to the weak links in your life (the imbalanced patterns), God will *always* and *all* ways provide you with some grist for the mill. Why? How else will you hone 360-skills if no one pushes your buttons? The good news is, the deeper you go in the hero's journey slaying the dragons of your ego, the easier this process becomes. Your previously pushed buttons (*chakras*, energy centers) will be shielded with sacred medicine (from whatever methods you choose). From Soul's domain you'll lovingly and mindfully discern whether to strengthen, enhance, or purge (lovingly let go) certain relationships from your immediate sphere of influence. It doesn't mean those individuals are not part of the Oneness of All Being; it just means that they don't have to be around you in an unhealthy way. And you shall wisely choose not to be around them, as well. The loving choice is yours. The 360-detoxification part of healing is not only fundamental on a physical level; it is germane mentally and emotionally, too. So, you are invited to activate clearing all of the weak links with discernment.

A component of doing a complete-turnaround is cultivating divine discrimination with regards to *all* of your relationships. You absolutely have to know if the people in your full-sphere enhance your Earth-walk, or not. If allowing an animated dance with another, crafting discord, angst, and stress, then you have to ask yourself mature questions: Hmm… Why am I creating this trauma-drama? How does this serve my highest purpose? What beautifully wrapped package, what special gift of learning is here for me to receive and open?

At first, your piece of the pie (in this regard) may be a bit disconcerting. The good news is… God will help when you are ready to take action. When wholeheartedly healing a perceived imbalance in any relationship through discernment—and the other party isn't on your wavelength—you won't feel any "vibratory charge" during an exchange of energy (which is usually during a conversation). You won't engage in that friction with them instantly, or as much as you used to do. Dynamics of resistance and conflict ultimately fade. Your necessity to always "take the bait" diminishes into a purity of Oneness. The universe will then co-create circumstances of compassionate healing space between you both. You shall discover that people, not in accord with a "greatest degree of love" in your daily episodes, will ostensibly disappear from your world. They don't really go anywhere. They just won't be where you are at this particular point in time. That is quite okay. Understand this: You are not better than them, and they are not better than you. They are simply not operating on the same vibratory frequency that you are.

Everything in life is energy that vibrates. Vibration is subtle movement and shifts in energy. If you objectively discern strange vibes around someone, then know the frequencies have shifted. It will all "settle" eventually as you progress on this fascinating and full-circle excursion to self-actualization. As I affirmed in the last chapter, it is positively not your business to worry about how all of this is done. The Divine Mother orchestrates it all in her universal, sacred realm of the absolute.

Remember though, you create reality. Toxic relationships are yours, a co-creation with another divine being. Therefore, your responsibility now is the healing. Lovingly work on you—24/7. Ask for help. Pray to your loving Source for guidance and support—I do this every single day, without fail. If I can do it... so can you.

The Frog and Snake

It has been caringly communicated from the beginning that this is a sacred, circular journey to wholeness. So, here is Animal Medicine re-visited to assist with your understanding, and your developing skillfulness in the art of discernment. You will need more paper. Separate the page into three columns. Have fun with this longstanding exercise because it will crystallize your thinking into a liberated energy or medicine of clarity with such powerful, discriminating awareness.

Exercise: The Frog and Snake

Practice Time: 1-2 hours, or more (as you feel guided).

Practice: 4 times a year, or twice annually, as needed.

You will need water to drink (plenty of it).

Create a sacred space.

Relax your mind. Breathe a few times deeply and completely. Feel the presence of divinity in your sacred space. Get in touch instantly with your Soul by being quiet. Soul is quite awake in this present moment. There is only the now. Your Soul is here. Feel Soul in your breath, in your heart, and in your mind.

Invoke the greatest, loving power and the wisdom of God manifested through the animal kingdom with Frog Medicine. The little Frog teaches us to clear away the mud and murk from our shadowed lives. The ancient Medicine of Frog cleanses the Soul. Shamans of various cultures have used this potent creature in their healing rituals for centuries. Frog shows us how to clean up our act. You will shift your energy-field by raising your vibratory frequency. The wisdom of Frog energy uses the element of water—so bathe in the clear, liberated energy that replenishes. Align yourself with this powerful medicine that releases negativity from deep down in the dark night of your Soul. Like the biblical story of Jonah in the belly of the whale—cleanse:[1] Take a break now from reading and pause to drink some delicious pure water. Feel it purifying and nourishing right down into the evolutionary code of your DNA.

Feeling refreshed, we go a bit deeper. According to Tibetan Buddhism, in the cardinal, eastern direction of a circle is a great transcendent wisdom of a liberated energy of clarity (as in the circular mandala of "The Five Wisdoms"). This clarity is known as "mirror-like wisdom." The element of this mirror-like wisdom is water, just like our Frog. Also, in Tibetan Tantric cosmology, west is the direction (in that same circle or mandala) of the transcendent "wisdom of discriminating awareness." Its element is the sacred fire of transmutation.

So, here we have water and fire. The transmuting (fire-like) Medicine of Snake will shed the skin of a new and improved, re-calibrated you. (It is interesting to note that the logo-symbol representing healing in western medicine is the caduceus, which features two entwining snakes. The divine matrix is evidently interconnected in all traditions whether "spiritual" or not.) Focus with clarity (Frog Medicine) and your heavenly, discriminating awareness (Snake Medicine). Within the heart of Frog's wisdom teaching, call upon guidance from its sister, Snake, to transmute any discordant energy in relationships. In this respect, prepare to do the following exercise on paper:

From the depths of your heart, think about, and then write down in the left column, all of the key people in your life. (Please take your time.) In the middle column, discern with great care… writing down whether they empower you, help you, and love you unconditionally, etc. Do you feel really good when around them? Do you feel drained? Do you feel safe? Comfortable? Do you trust them? Are they really "P and A" for you? With discernment (without reactive judgment) write clearly and distinctly what is so important about that relationship.

Then in the third column, patiently compose an action plan to change, shift, or enhance that situation, augmenting it for the good of all sentient (conscious) beings.

Finally, I always dedicate the merit of any practice for the good of all. Learned within many years of deep, devoted Tibetan Buddhist practice, dedication of merit is important to adopt for anyone—of any faith (or none). Therefore, finish with dedication of the merit for the sake of all creation.

1) Name of People in Your Sphere of Influence (left column)

2) Feeling (middle column)

3) Transcendent Frog/Snake Action (right column)

Here is an example:

People in Your Sphere	Feeling	Transcendent Frog/Snake Action
Uncle Fred	not empowered, bad, nervous, scared	I use psychic self-protection techniques before regular family gatherings with him. I make a list of things I like about him: (Uncle Fred tells good jokes, and he loves animals, etc.) I focus on the good things that he does. I feel compassion for him.

Another example:

People in Your Sphere	Feeling	Transcendent Frog/Snake Action
Lucy	empowered, happy, fun, connected	My intention is to ask this friend to coffee every week. (I visualize spending quality time together.) I will lend her my book that she wants to read. I make a list of things I like about her: (Lucy is a very good listener; Lucy is kind, she is very compassionate, etc.) She goes out of her way for me. Lucy makes the effort to be with me by including me in her social plans. Lucy is secure.

Doing this exercise helps to distinguish your core sphere of influence. Since it is comprehensive, it may take at least an hour or two (or more) for completion. Focus on your honest feelings, clarifying awareness with a clean, fresh perspective of liberated energy. Take action—real, concerted action here. Now I wish it were all as easy as making some lists; it's not. You must cultivate joyful effort in this strategy and then *do* your work from the third column. It is worthy of your time because YOU are worthy. You will change relationships because you are shifting consciousness into positive action from the Soul-level. Don't you deserve to be surrounded by wonderful people that respect and love you? How can you feel really happy as a whole new person if you are miserable from the toxic people tugging at your sleeve?

Metaphorically speaking, recall that the law of nature is a boomerang. Once you focus from your heart-of-hearts and take responsible action, imbalanced patterns will begin to change. If folks are not in resonance with your good wishes and luminous light—the vibes that you generate—then they won't be in your reality at this time frame. As already said, God takes care of the "how" job description. I have a friend that calls these "God Jobs."

If people are not in true, peaceful harmony with your Soul's evolutionary plan, then they will not be around—it's that simple. Let them go. Isn't that interesting? It is fascinating to watch it all unfold and enfold. Can you think of any caustic relationships in your life that abruptly ended? They moved away, or you did. They stopped hanging around with the circle of friends that you were in, or vice/versa. You changed jobs or they were mysteriously fired. Remember that they did not "go" anywhere. The scene has just changed. Your script calls for the next act in the play.

There are many sacred scenarios. How about this: Your car broke down unexpectedly, or a family emergency required your last minute attendance. So, you couldn't go to an out-of-town event, discovering later your "ex" (who is not in accord, vibrationally) was at the gathering. Can you think of similar stories?

This all happens in constructive ways for the good of all. When making a 360-transition, our phone rang one night while we were packing boxes. It was a longtime friend who was dearly missed, and we had not spoken to him for quite a while. He and his wife had moved far away many years ago. However, now he said cheerfully, "Oh, I heard through the grapevine that you are moving to New Mexico. Guess what!? My brother-in-law lives there and since we visit him twice a year, we are going to see each other—isn't that great?" I was thrilled, too. Our recent visits with them have been wonderful, so full of joy, good conversation, and loving laughter. The friendship has blossomed in a fresh way because we are *supposed* to be together at this time.

Your action plan will probably include the discerning idea of ending certain challenging relationships. As in a circle, there is no end. If you do not liberate through forgiveness, then you will wind up cycling back into that pattern, again and again—either in this life or another. Focus on genuine, positive characteristics of the person—and then let go.

Once you have done a complete 360 with your life, you may weave (even these thought-provoking) relationships back into being—if it's in your highest good, to do so. Carrying Armadillo, Spider, Frog and Snake Wisdom with you always (as well as other kinds of medicine from any other traditions that you respect and glorify), you shall weave new and healthy patterns. Follow Soul's purpose, which is Thy will for the good of all. God gives us what we can handle. It depends on the individual and the situation. Everyone is different. All fruit does not ripen at the same exact time.

Remember the advice from Joseph Campbell about making a full-circle in the big game of life? You have got to come back to any and all circumstances freely and unfettered without resistance.

A 360 View: Looking at the Whole Picture

Here's another exercise, which is similar to the previous one; however, it includes more general "stuff" affecting your overall energy patterns. Part of Doing a 360 is learning to clear things that are not in accord with your highest good.

You may need two pieces of paper, or just one, divided into two columns. Write at the top: Empowering, Liberating Energy for column one; and Toxic, Distorted Energy for the other column. I've given you a detailed sample below of how to do this 360-degree View Exercise:

Empowering, Liberating Energy

Green 'health drink'

Mary Beth, my co-worker

New organic vitamins

Hybrid car just purchased

Betsy, my friend

360 Mentor _____

Family member _____

_____

_____

_____

_____

_____

Toxic, Distorted Energy

Eating Halloween candy

New employee _____

Current job

Messy attic

Old friend _____ on hard drugs

My brother Elmer

Neighbor's dog barks most nights at 2am

Family member _____

_____

_____

_____

_____

_____

Exercise: 360-degree View: Looking at the Whole Picture

Practice Time: 1-2 hours, or more (as you feel guided).

Practice: 4 times a year, or twice annually (as guided).

You will need pure water to drink.

Create a sacred space.

Relax your mind. Breathe a few times… deeply, and so very completely. Sense your Soul now by being quiet. Feel the divine presence in every cell of your being.

Invoke the presence of sacred Armadillo, Spider, Frog and Snake. Place the names of people, organizations, things, objects, places, activities, etc., in their proper place. Get photos of them, if possible. When looking at and touching all the images, *sense* or intuit these things from your gut, which is the third energy center or chakra. Then put them in the appropriate pile, i.e., liberating or toxic. If you feel constricted in the vibration, then in the toxic pile it goes. Ask for loving guidance. Drink some pure water. Feel a masterful transmutation of these higher vibratory frequencies within your (S)elf.

Write down everything you can (as a reflection of your life). Once completing this entire exercise, look at the toxic column (or entire page) and focus to positively transmute this distorted energy. What would the 360-action plan be for each of the items?

You have to begin to take action, skillfully releasing and healing patterns that you have co-created with people, places or things in your life that don't liberate or empower Soul's purpose. This takes practice. You're not going to telephone everyone today saying, "Hi, it's me. I am calling to say our relationship is over!" Yikes—that would be absurd. And total avoidance doesn't work, either. Another unhealed pattern will be waiting in the wings. What you strongly dislike (reactively *feeling* in judgment) will bang you in the head as a boomerang. Our wise Spiders' know that you must weave a new web by taking responsibility for participation in a pattern wreaking havoc in your life. Remember, you were receiving some kind of payoff, which is why you allowed the pattern. Focus on love and forgiveness—and you won't go astray.

Be patient, this takes time… divine time. All is in divine order. Trust in the Great Plan. Trust in God. Trust in your (S)elf. The universe will align the relationships in the appropriate ways to nurture your Soul's evolutionary journey to Oneness.

Psychic Self-Protection

Back in the Frog and Snake exercise, a categorical term was offered called psychic self-protection techniques, which is in the third column (for Uncle Fred).

All initiates on the path need to know about these and how to use them effectively. In any situation, while inappropriately allowing your body's energy stockpile to drain, visualize the navel area (third energy center, chakra) to be a garden hose, which is gushing water outward. (I imagine holding this hose at my gut, pointing it away from me while the water flows.) Folks usually respond well to this idea of focusing on their third chakra. *Chakra* is a Sanskrit word, meaning wheel.

By the way, actual ancient Sanskrit spelling of the word chakra is "cakra." In Sanskrit the letter "c" is only pronounced with a choppy "ch" sound as in the English word, church. Therefore, the English transliteration has always been spelled correctly as "chakra." Strangely, this popular word has been mispronounced with a soft "sh" sound for many years in western spiritual circles even though the English spelling is a clue to its pronunciation.

Another helpful image is to see light-as-sparks, like American Fourth of July fireworks emanating from that third manipura chakra (*manipura* is Sanskrit, translated as "golden jewel" at the solar plexus or navel area). Keep your awareness focused on this part of the body, which is now flowing the energy *out* freely. This will prevent you from sucking in—like a sponge—any discordant energy. Have you heard of the saying: "I have butterflies in my stomach?" That's a common reactive feeling of nervousness and anxiety from ego-based fear sensed in this power center or energy vortex (chakra).

If someone seems to be pulling energy from you (you feel contracted or drained in their presence), you may wish to attempt another visualization: Imagine you are a beautiful, glistening, giant quartz crystal—or inside of one. Feel protected by it. Clearly see anything reflecting off of it.

Another technique of self-protection is to visualize that you are standing under a scenic waterfall. (I personally enjoy using this.) Feel a cool and showering freshness of water's negative ions cleansing all discord. You *feel* great. Ah, you are definitely in the sacred domain of our little friend, Frog.

There are many effective clearing methods. Popular insight of surrounding yourself with "the white light" or "the light of God" or "a bubble of light" or "the light of Christ" would be fine examples to practice with. I also enjoy visualizing a translucent sphere of white light whirling around my house at night before I go to sleep. You may use this medicine to help protect your home from any discordant energy.

Techniques from other traditions are presented in many books expanding on this topic, which you may choose as well. Doing a 360 is learning to use *your* intuition: Discern what you are guided to for the greatest good of all. And you are *in* the ALL, and the ALL is *in* you.

360 Nourishment

Now, let us move to the physical part of this detoxification plan. Do you love your body? If you do not, then how do you expect it to be healthy?

Contemplate this common phrase: "An attitude of gratitude." Feel throughout your day great gratitude for supreme health, with thankfulness for the temple of your Soul, which is the body. Do not wait until you get sick. Be pro-active—do it now. This is a three-sixty-perspective. In another chapter, you will focus further on the physical action phase of "Doing a 360."

When you physically detox, there is an initial period in which you may feel a tad worse, before you actually feel better. It's like that when you start a vitamin regime, or when you seriously clean up and balance your diet because you are clearing out on many levels—throwing off the toxins. Science tells us that the 50-70 trillion cells in our bodies constantly change. Thank God. We are continually healing ourselves—over and over again.

Whatever you sincerely intuit is good for you—*is* good. Listen to guidance from your Soul. Soul is dying to get out of the dark night that you may have been struggling in. So, dear reader, awaken. When you fully awaken in the presence of divine light you shall inaugurate divine choices from the purity of Oneness. When dining out, for example, take a moment; breathe *consciously* as you scan the enticing menu. Slow down with "P and A." Use this "present and available" strategy from Chapter 3. Words will jump from the page to your awareness—this is Soul's guidance. The trick is to focus *every* moment, as spiritual teacher Eckhart Tolle suggests: There is only "now." [2]

One topic to cover very briefly here is pH balancing. I have worked with this aspect of healing for quite some time. We are too acidic. When balanced in an alkaline nature you cannot get sick. Cancer cells do not thrive in alkaline environments. More alkaline foods enhance a balanced lifestyle. Water is alkaline, and coffee is acidic. Meat is acidic, and vegetables (most of them) are alkaline. When replacing all the toxic stuff with higher vibratory, nourishing, organic food, there is a transitory release-phase (as mentioned before). Some people may break out in hives as all of the toxins are liberated through the skin, which is the largest organ of the body. The rest is freed elsewhere.

This adjustment period is different for everyone. In the spirit of our blessed Frog, bring more high-quality water into your lifecycle. Educate yourself with **Dr.** Masaru Emoto's amazing research that human consciousness has a direct effect on the molecular structure of water, and vice/versa.[3]

Sacred Movement

You have already learned a movement discipline called the 1st of the Five Tibetan Rites. Are you doing it? Give it a spin. Even though I am a huge proponent of yoga, (having taught it for thirty-five years) this is obviously not another yoga book. I *will* say that incorporating this ancient art and science into a 360

Lifestyle is tremendous for your health and well-being. Here is the same advice as before: follow your sensitivity.

What are you guided to do? What interests you? Do not sign up for a yoga class if you are absolutely not resonating to it—experiment with something else. There may be someone at a Nia class, a dance, or on a hike that you *need* to meet right now. You may do some yoga practice later on. Follow the heart-of-hearts, which is your Soul. (Ahead in Chapter 8 you'll read more about 360 Yoga, a style that I created in 2006.)

Moving your body in any way that you can is the balanced key. Brisk walking is just wonderful. I strongly urge you to begin doing that, if at all possible. And have fun in your local library borrowing fitness books and videos—knowledge is power. Notice the ones that summon you to the bookshelves, leaping into your hands—follow your intuition. Put on some beautiful music and move spontaneously from your Soul. Just have fun.

I have long been a fan of healing music. This story goes back again to my teens while beginning a journey to Oneness.

As a novel yoga student, I had traveled into New York City to attend a healing expo. While browsing through hundreds of booths selling cutting-edge wares, I heard an unusual, soothing sound. I stopped and listened to the sweetest, Soul-stirring music ever heard. There was such a profound resonance—a familiar knowing deep within Soul. The tape playing was *Spectrum Suite*, created by the father of healing music, Dr. Steven Halpern.[4]

His jolly mother was behind the table and announced to me emphatically, "This incredible music is my son's. Ya know, he is going to be very famous one day!" Ah... the true love of a mother, is there anything more powerful? I splurged and bought the cassette tape—I just had to have it. I was only eighteen.

Now re-named *Chakra Suite*, this transcendent music of the spheres has been called the most influential healing/new age record of all time by *New Age Voice* magazine.[5] I have used that music (and dozens more CDs of his) all throughout the years. Halpern, the pioneer of sound healing, was the first to investigate the positive effects of music using biofeedback. He undeniably is a music master—a luminary.

Spiritual Stress Management

When I became a certified creative wellness instructor in the early 1980s studying with visionary Michelle Lusson, the term wellness was not defined yet.[6] It was still on the fringe. Today, most everyone understands what wellness is. Every hospital has a wellness center and we all know that it means, living optimally. During my innovative training with mentor Michelle, I learned a metaphoric concept for stress: mis-matched energy. For example, if you approach me for change of a ten dollar bill and I give you a five and only two ones, you would feel a little cheated, a bit short-changed by three bucks—huh? In this same way, you may feel stressed when others do not meet your high expectations. Always lower your expectation of others and raise the bar for your (S)elf.

In these most disconcerting, modern times we've stretched ourselves way too far. "We are stressed-out-of-our-gizzards" as my old friend, said. A 360-stress management approach is an all-encompassing sacred strategy. You don't just turnaround doing a "180," which is just running from problems, you go *all* the way around the circular journey to a new way of being. My husband offers his unique metaphor for explaining 360: Imagine a simple baseball field where there is a home base, 1st, 2nd and 3rd bases. You bravely step up to the plate. Then you hit a homerun, and blissfully walk all the way around until you RETURN to home base. You're victorious. The journey is complete. You are joyfully empowered. 360 = One.

A limited, linear view from false, dualistic notions creates a lot of stress. Yes, of course there are major stressors in the world. Life is what we perceive and then our actions generate reality (like stitches sewn into the tapestry of living). If you feel that life is very stressful, then it will be. If you focus with "P and A ness"— in quiet joy and resonance with all there is (which is God, the God Force), then you'll obviously have less stress. As said earlier: nature is spontaneous; it is free flowing without effort. I also have a saying: "It's against religion to rush; whatever your religion is." It is also essential to know yourself divine—24/7. This is what the new sciences are finally verifying, which the ancient wisdoms of all traditions have always known: *All are One.* Spiritual stress management is 360 = 1.

This book's introduction advocated re-inventing your (S)elf. But you do not have to re-invent the wheel—it already exists. What you urgently need is a new story, a fresh myth. Each one of us needs to assert their vital role in a new mythology of Oneness. What we have to re-invent is MYTH. As Campbell said woefully about myth in modern society: "We've lost it." Yes, what we have all lost is the sacred myth, the monomyth—a universal story of the heroine or hero on a circular journey to wholeness. I believe that we are going to find "it." We are on our way to creating a new, evolutionary myth of Oneness.

Sacred Housecleaning: The Urge to Purge

As you remove the toxins from your life, consider—in the context of a 360 Lifestyle—purging *all* of the clutter. Simplicity is smart. You need a liberated, sacred living space. Stuff is energy just like food and money. If you have too much stuff in your life, how are you going to generate new and cool stuff? You have got to make room.

Now, I am not just talking garage sale strategy here. I am speaking about getting rid of clutter on all levels. Ask yourself: Why am I holding on to junk? Why am I afraid to let go? Let go, and let God. Clean up your act. I am sharing that when you let go—you shall be free, free from fettered and distracting clutter.

When I buy something, perhaps a new outfit, I give away an old one. If I buy two pairs of shoes—two pairs have to go. The study and practice of Feng Shui creates clear, sacred space—getting rid of blockages and obscurations to your energy fields. A strategy to sell a home quickly is purging clutter. Look around your environment with an honest, three hundred and sixty-degree-view. Do you sense a peaceful sacred space? What can you give away right now? Have you ever walked into someone's home that was a cluttered mess? How did you feel?

The issue with most people (in this regard) is multi-faceted, and definitely, multi-layered. A recognized stressful distortion of obsession, fear, and paranoia may be augmented into a sphere of liberating and all-accomplishing, loving action.

When you Do a 360 going full-circle in life, you are waking up with confidence from a dark, deep sleep, to an empowered being of light on track with Soul's purpose. Your Soul is here right now reading these words as a Creator designing a divine life that IT commands. In the upcoming chapter you journey to the underworld, into deep caverns of consciousness. There you will challenge your little "local self" with the treasures of the ancients, encountering the Tao of being. As the *Tao Te Ching* states in the first of its eighty-one chapters: "The tao that can be told, is not the eternal *Tao*." [7]

Chapter 6

Mirror-like Wisdom

"Come now. I invite you to Buddha nature, and, by the way, to Happiness."

— Shantideva

ow that you have cleared space for a fresh view, let us go deeper into the journey. For thought-provoking consideration, you're going to examine consciousness from a courageous, transforming 360-perspective. Consciousness is a divine awareness. There is an individual consciousness, which is your own personal awareness or Soul awareness. And there is also a Collective Consciousness, which is the divine matrix or grand mandala of All Being. Your sacred, individuated consciousness is *in* and *of* the majestic, universal, and multidimensional Collective Consciousness.

Your consciousness and your thoughts are two different things. Please allow me to repeat that because it may be a mind-bender. It's important. Understanding this is a fundamental 360-concept in turning your life around—completely. *Consciousness and thoughts are two different things.* This may shake it up or wake it up, you know, really rock your world. Consciousness isn't a string of wild thoughts running through your mind, just as the brain is certainly not your mind. The brain is only a physical organ of the heart-mind.[1]

I have often used a mirror to teach this concept. So, if you have a mirror nearby, go to it now. If not, imagine this experience in your mind and then please do this effective exercise later—the next time looking into a mirror. It is very beneficial to use a larger mirror rather than a smaller, purse-size variety. Okay, now: As you gaze into the mirror's reflection, you see yourself, yes? Wave at the mirrored image and see your hand moving. Smile and wink at yourself. Play a bit here. Obviously, the mirror is reflecting back to you. Ask yourself this question: Is the mirror, itself—me?

No, it's not. The mirror is definitely not "you." The mirror is just a smooth sheet of reflective glass. It doesn't move. YOU are "doing" the moving, not the mirror. The mirror is just accessible all of the time waiting for you to pass by and look into it. A metaphoric mirror represents the vast and fundamental, infinite consciousness—a universe that reflects back. It also symbolizes individual consciousness. Arising thoughts of your mind are like the reflections moving in a mirror—the waving and winking. What you are thinking about right now isn't your consciousness. Your thoughts are on the move—constantly. Consciousness is the background mirror of sacred stillness that is simply, there.

Consciousness is God. Consciousness is divine energy. We know from science that energy cannot be created or destroyed; it just "is." When looking into a mirror, watching yourself move, you "see" thoughts or the mind-stuff dancing in the reflection. Remember, the movements you make, i.e., the waving, winking, etc., are not the mirror's doing—they're *your* actions. Thus, in the same way, when you think thoughts, they arise and abide in your mind. These routine gazillion thoughts arising and abiding in mind are unattached and different from your vast, mirror-like field of universal consciousness.

Once you realize this, and "get it" right down into your core of being, life changes forever. You shall blossom as a field of colorful flowering awareness, cultivating what is known in ancient

Buddhist teachings as transcendent *mirror-like wisdom.* Knowing the difference between consciousness and your thoughts is quite essential in the awakening process.

The Trinity

Going a bit deeper, consider your consciousness within a universal framework of what is called the trinity: body, mind and Spirit. Most sacred traditions use this three-part structure. To note a few: There is a Christian matrix of Father, Son, and Holy Spirit; in medieval Indian Hinduism the trinity is represented by Brahma, the Creator; Vishnu, the Preserver; and Shiva, the Destroyer. The Trika (triad) philosophical system of Shaivism is categorized as Shiva, Shakti, and Nara, (which represents the human Spirit tainted by karmic influence);[2] and there's The Triple Gem or The Three Jewels: Buddha, Dharma, and Sangha, which are recognized by all the schools of Buddhism.

Within a 360-milieu, comprehend yourself in relation to this omnipresent triad. Revisit the sacred imagery of a juicy lemon to assist with a trinity concept of body, mind, and Spirit.

Imagine having an unconscious body (physical body doing an exercise/lemon visualization, producing saliva); a conscious mind (which thinks about sour, juicy lemons); and also a *Higher Consciousness* (which is your Soul) that divinely understands "fake" or imaginary taste of the fruit. In other words, Soul knows you aren't really eating a lemon but are fantasizing the experience from mind's thoughts. Many struggle through daily life without much, or any conscious awareness of this trinity. If that was you—those days are over. When you go full-circle in this heroic journey joyfully spinning around three hundred and sixty-degrees, you begin living *consciously* from Higher (S)elf. The key word emphasized in the previous sentence is consciously. Therefore you make decisions with pristine awareness from Soul. There is an old saying: "The eyes are the window to the Soul." As you awaken Soul to resplendent blossoming, IT "consciously" sees through the physical eyes of your body. There's no veil. The mists fade. Even if someone is blind they still "see" through those divine eyes.

Higher Consciousness: A 360 Perspective

The term "Higher" Consciousness may be interchanged with Soul. In my humble opinion from what I have learned through decades of dedicated study and practice, Higher Consciousness supersedes the designation of a "subconscious mind." This is a very deep-thinking subject to circumnavigate, so I will explain this newfangled, evolutionary theory as best as possible.

The popular idiom "subconscious mind" has been a common way to describe the mysterious, hidden part of us, indicating a supernatural abyss. Proponents of the word and its philosophy (especially espoused by Hypnotherapists) say the subconscious can be "tapped into" or accessed on occasion. This descent into the realm of the "sub" conscious mind releases from bondage all of the spiritual goodies hidden underneath like treasure buried in the ground. I agree with this concept—well, sort of. I genuinely honor and appreciate the fabulous work done in the field of Hypnotherapy. Some of my friends are leaders in this emerging field of healing. My "sacred spin" is seemingly semantic. I believe that the "sub" in subconscious is really, truly shifting or evolving to "Higher." Your Higher Consciousness is the loving, limitless, boundless essence of GOD: ALL THERE IS, ALL THERE IS NOT and ALL IN BETWEEN.

A 360 Viewpoint is: The subconscious mind is actually re-calibrating through spiritual evolution to Higher Consciousness. The word sub is defined as under or below and usually specifies something "not as good." When Donald Trump was interviewed on CNBC News in December 2006, he was asked his opinion of the state of sub-prime real estate markets. Mr. Trump responded by saying emphatically, "I don't like *anything* with sub in front of it. That indicates it is not good, or it is inferior. I generally don't like that term—it's negative." Frankly, I have to admit that I was really surprised but delighted to hear him say this. What glorious synchronicity since the articulation of this topic had been in my Higher Consciousness during the time that I was outlining this particular chapter of this book. It was amusing to observe this reflected by a prosperous businessman.

Now I know from long-term studies in Dzogchen that duality thinking (high-low, hot-cold, clean-dirty, etc.) is a misconception. The "sub" or "High" really doesn't matter: *It is, as it is.* I get that. However, from an expansive, 360, all-encompassing, and radical perspective, when Soul awakens to a forefront of deliberate living there isn't need anymore for a subconscious mind. Why do I feel this subject is important? My Soul wishes to express a necessity to shift collective consciousness. New ideas aren't typically embraced right away. It takes time to steep in the tea of uncertainty. We are ready to ascend to a next step in collective reasoning. It's part of creating a new story, an enlightened Myth of Oneness. As we move way beyond that great shift of 2012 into an exciting, imminent future of evolutionary consciousness, humanity will re-calibrate. Let's elevate the status of consciousness. A hundred years from now this will already be established in the hearts of many.

Dear reader, by now you know that I love to play around with metaphor and allegory to help explain things.

So imagine: If you walked through some city streets without noticing any entrances to the subways, you would not know there were people scurrying into trains under the ground. In the same way, the boundless, infinite part of our selves has been viewed as though it's always "sub" and therefore doesn't know what's going on above—in reality.

This reductionist concept (of the subconscious mind) began with some constructed theories of the human mind by the noted psychologist, Sigmund Freud.[3] Actually, we may go further back to the nineteenth century for thoughtful, philosophical writings of Schopenhauer (one of Campbell's favorites), Nietsche, Binet, Janet, von Hartman and others, like Dilthey, who wrote of the Hermeneutic circle (which is the recurring movement between the implicit and the explicit, and the particular and the whole).[4] Collectively, they created the philosophy behind this term of a *subconscious mind*, which has obviously survived and thrived into present day. I am certainly not comparing myself in any way to the brilliant acumen of these thinkers. My intent is just to offer a little historical framework and open our minds to explore fresh, new ideas.

The Tree of Life

Let's substantiate the overarching 360 viewpoints further, not as an exegesis, but with another simple metaphor:

Imagine a tall and splendid maple tree bursting with leaves. This tree will represent your body in the trinity. A healer (in a role as your therapist) is symbolized here as a special siphon, which is a tube-like tool that punctures maple tree trunks. Imagine that siphon in the tree with a pail under it, which is used to harvest the dripping maple sap—deep inside the trunk. This delicious syrup represents the domain of your subconscious mind. Now, do not get me wrong here, I love maple syrup. What I'm saying is that the subconscious mind is not some mystical, far out, down below place that can only be tapped into occasionally by someone else. This is your boundless, limitless potential—the essence of your Soul. It is your vast Higher Consciousness awakening to ITS full purpose.

When you make the full-turnaround in consciousness, your Soul is absolutely HERE *and* NOW. It isn't sub or below, it is HIGH, it's GRAND, it's DIVINE—and it's what YOU REALLY ARE. You *are* the sweetness of the maple syrup. In this moment, if it's divine timing, perhaps you'll feel or *recognize* (re-know) what is being said here? When you *feel* something or *intuit* something, it is your Soul expressing ITSELF. Instead of just accepting a generalized old mindset of "sporadically tapping down" into your divine nature using others to get there, feel your own constant flow of sweetness. This divine nectar is unlimited from the tree of life (your physical body)—24/7.

Perhaps you may consider to be (a bit more) open now to a "both and" point of view for this suggested term, trinity of consciousness: the unconscious (body), the conscious (mind) and the Higher Consciousness (Soul in Spirit). Especially, if you work in a healing profession, this is an important consideration. In various healing modalities most have probably been taught to tap into the subconscious mind as the way to help clients heal from whatever ails. This viewpoint assumes that a pristine, intrinsic awareness (divinity) is not instantly manifested AT the surface of their being. And therefore, this belief suggests that our infinite Spirit/Soul with ITS conscious awareness lives only "under" the surface—not around or through us, spherically. The perception is our limitless potential must be retrieved or even rescued—like pulling someone out of a dark hole with a rope. Possibly, we may all (healing professions) consider augmentation of the older view to a spherical, evolutionary awareness of consciousness?

360 Paradigm Shift

When you awaken, the Soul's *modus operandi* or "m.o." is to drive the magic bus. Hand over the keys. You need to step aside and get ego out of the way. You have got to appreciate that your Soul is in control—right here, right now—all around spherically, as well as *in* you. Without a mirror you cannot actually see your face, so you will have to have confidence that you look great. Similarly, if you falsely think that you can't "see" your Soul, then trust that IT is here, awake—front and center. *Feel* IT. *Know* IT. When you turn awareness around fully, three hundred and sixty-degrees to be aligned with IT, you'll join in the ride of your life. You'll be in the passenger seat next to Soul with your feet resting up on the dashboard. Fresh, cool breezes caress your smiling face. Everything you see on this journey is amazing. Life is a trip!

We can shift this awareness if we choose to perceive our Higher Self with a fresh perspective. Even Mr. Trump seems to be aware of this in some unpredicted way. The long-standing theory of subconscious mind feels outdated. Does it serve in the highest good for all? Hmm… it seems like old school to me.

We are in an incredible spiritual revolution during the opening of a new millennium, so I suggest that we evolve our philosophic principles. As mentioned earlier in this discussion, it may seem to be only semantics, huh? Yet, words are powerful energy forms. Words are solid events in the time/space continuum. Language absolutely affects our behavior—doesn't it? If you constantly say: "I hate this and that. I feel low. I feel terrible and I'm miserable." Guess what? You will be! The basic law of attraction applies here, too. It is time to consider shifting the model of consciousness.

I'm sure that there may be others who have pondered the same conversation rendered here. I look now to other brilliant minds in the fields of consciousness to step off the fringe into discussion. Let's kick it up a notch, shall we?

To clarify in review: We have a body that is unconscious. That means it doesn't consciously know stuff (as in The Lemon visualization) but it will do important physical things like: eating (when it's hungry the stomach will growl); going to the bathroom, and sleeping, etc. As far as our physical body is concerned, this level of awareness is definitely "un" conscious. When you are cozy in bed and sound asleep, you don't *know* what is happening in your environment. The Master Buddha used this metaphor in his miraculous teachings more than 2,500 years ago. He taught us to become a Buddha: to "wake up" and see clearly the true nature of ourselves.

Being enlightened means waking up from the dream of life: Remembering the clear luminous light of (S)elf as the no-self of intrinsic awareness, and then creating an evolving identity of that no-(S)elf within the great emptiness. Here dwells the depth of the heart in your contemplative journey to wholeness.

Next in the trinity, you have a conscious mind. It thinks thoughts (such as visualizing your lemon); you take mind (and all it has ever contemplated) with you when the physical body dies. The nature of your conscious mind transcends time and space. However, generally you "think" way too much. You need to quiet your mind as recommended in Chapter 3.

Finally, there is Higher Consciousness, which I refer to as Soul's awareness. Soul ascends when you die.

Within 360 Context, there is also a divine fourth dimension, so-to-speak, encapsulating the other three planes of consciousness. This Supra Conscious State of Being is a mother, orb-like entity patterned *in* and *of* ITS SOURCE. The Supra Conscious State of Being completely packages whom we are in the universe, like a cocoon protecting and nurturing our identity. It's the mother ship. It contains all you ever were multi-dimensionally—all you are—and all you ever will be throughout eternity. This Supra Conscious State continually evolves ITSELF to SOURCE.

To assist understanding these concepts, prepare to draw a tiny circle as a big solid dot. You can do this illustration right here in the white space of the book so you will have it handy for reference. If you are reading this in e-book format, obviously you'll need paper again.

The big dot is your dense body. Around the big dot draw a circle, allowing a little bit of space from the center—this is your mind.

Around that circle draw another, but this time it is really big with a lot of space away from the second circle. This represents the Higher Consciousness of Soul. Now, draw the fourth and last circle. Yes, this outer circle is the mother ship, which isn't that far from the third circle. These concentric circles are the spheres of the divine matrix. They mingle with all energy or God in this spherical patterning.

Most individuals tour through life without much, if any, conscious awareness of the Soul's memory *that is carried* within the Supra Consciousness State of Being. It's interesting to note that in the tradition of Tibetan Buddhism there are the four kayas, or bodies of Buddhahood. The first three kayas are *dharmakaya, sambhogakaya,* and *nirmanakaya.* The supreme fourth, *svabhavikakaya,* is the formless form of the nature of all phenomena. It embodies the holographic indivisibility of the first three. (I was guided to design this entire book or journey into four quadrants of a sphere.) Once you begin to Do a 360, your Soul's memory will be activated... if it hasn't been already. The extent of recognition (re-knowing) of this multi-layered memory has been determined by The Supra Consciousness and your Soul.

The more you put into practice a 360-perception of the great view of luminous clear light, the more *consciously* aware you will be from Soul's memory of ITSELF in daily life situations. What that means is: Soul sees from your two physical eyes. IT remembers. As you live a lifestyle knowing this you shall feel happier, joyful, content, balanced, and peaceful. Your Soul is simply creating the experience we call human life.

That is "Spiritual." Being enlightened means waking up from the dream of life:

Remembering
the clear luminous light of (S)elf
as the no-(S)elf of intrinsic awareness,
and then
creating an evolving identity
of that no-(S)elf within the great emptiness.

Kaleidoscopic Vision

Swiss psychologist Carl Jung, who had been a student of Freud, has written extensively about another term: the collective unconscious.[5] Jung eventually broke away from his teacher's philosophy to describe a new theory of an infinite gathering of consciousnesses and thoughts he said we access spontaneously—whether we *consciously* know it or not. Like many others, I simply call it the Collective Consciousness. I believe we *are* the Collective Consciousness: We are *in* it and *it is in us*—always (which is time), and all ways (which is space). Like cosmic Spiders weaving their lavish webs, we're all interconnected as islands under the sea. And like a thriving maple, sugary syrup flows spontaneously from the great tree of life. We are the trees in an infinite forest of all multi-universes. I call this grand vision, "kaleidoscopic." That means, creatively thinking outside the box, rotating 360-degrees all the way around a colorful circle of divine life.

Now you have progressed through this sacred expedition into a little lighter, charming way to focus on a profound subject of consciousness. So, let's play a cool mind-game. You are now revisiting powerful sacred imagery introduced in Chapter 2. (This will be similar to The Lemon exercise, however, metaphorically-speaking you are going to multiply the view in the vast Collective Consciousness from your own Higher Consciousness—not from your unconscious body.)

Imagine looking into a kaleidoscope now with its spectacular mosaic lens of brilliant dancing colors shifting as patterns of light. Perhaps you may recall as a child playing with one of these dazzling toys? I had one and I loved it. If you're not familiar with the delightful pleasure of a kaleidoscope, it's a long tube (like a telescope) that you look into. Holding it up to a light source, you then turn a dial, which creates amazing, infinite, colorful patterns. Gazing through this looking-glass keep turning the round dial to create gorgeous colors in an array of glittering, whimsical designs. Sense delight in your Soul—feel the childlike wonder. Notice how "light" you feel in this moment of radiant beauty. You are creating the patterns. A kaleidoscope requires rotation of the dial in order for it to work. So, YOU are creator of this experience on many levels. Your Soul sees, and then communicates to your conscious mind that IT desires to *experience* more of this beauty. Mind directs a thought to your hand (physical body) to turn the dial again for the next pattern of radiant color.

Even though you have visualized (just now) seeing through a kaleidoscope, you actually *did* it. Just like The Lemon exercise, it was real. It actually happened. What do I mean? You really felt lovely sensations because Soul saw it CONSCIOUSLY through your mind. What did IT see? Metaphoric Light: The Collective Consciousness of Light. This rainbow-speckled visualization was so delightful—was it not? In order to see fantastic kaleidoscopic patterns of color what do you always need? Light. Without some illumination a kaleidoscope does not work. So, like us as human beings awakening to Soul's purpose, a source of light is necessary for illumination.

What does this have to do with changing your life? A lot— you have to continue turning the colorful dial. If you are "P and A" (present and available) to kaleidoscopic vision, you see with a multi-faceted, spiritual perception of life. You know yourself to be a Creator. The divine beingness is a foundation to the doing. Your Soul (in a physical body) experiences life as YOU ARE CREATING IT.

Every thought that was *ever* thought by anyone, anywhere, at any time throughout the history of our multi-universes is part of the great matrix of life. This is so vast and immeasurable, similar to the mathematical idea of one quadrillion to the one-zillionth degree, and beyond that. (Quadrillion is one, followed by fifteen zeros!) All these thoughts blend with individual and collective consciousness. All resides as immeasurable energy *in* and *of* what we may call, God. Your kaleidoscope visualization is now a part (collectively) of the boundless, consciousness pool of wonder, or as I now spell it: *Oneder*.

Being Centered, Always and All Ways

To recycle here: As your awakening process intensifies, daily activities are orchestrated CONSCIOUSLY from your Soul's blueprint. Though you may not have been fully conscious of that fact until now, this awareness will grow and grow. This is a natural divine inheritance, and part of spiritual evolution to turn your life around completely with kaleidoscopic vision.

When the Supra Conscious State of Being (which harmonically oversees your trinity like a shell) *chooses* to activate Soul's memory, your Soul becomes aware of ITSELF coordinating the mind and physical body. When Soul awakens to remember who you really are, it's like waking from a dream. With a kaleidoscopic memory assemblage, Soul creates *consciously* what IT chooses. The liberated and limitless, inexhaustible part of you has always and *all* ways been—front and center.

Perhaps like me in the not too distant past, you just didn't know it this way. Now, you may affirm it is so, if you feel that it's your truth. Remember—my truth is not yours.

Always and *all* ways feel your truth in your heart-of-hearts. *Always* and *all ways* is an expression I use a lot. I often sign greeting cards this way. Consider the ways as two sides of a coin. Always is a time reference of forever, of the infinite (remember that time is just space that moves, as we perceive it). All ways refers not only to space in all directions—as in the ancient Buddhist tradition reference to the "ten directions" (which are the four cardinal points; the four intermediates of southeast, southwest, northwest, and northeast; and, above and below as in zenith and nadir)—but also to the unobstructed, unfabricated, boundless, and complete view of seeing *everything… as it is*.

I'm sure you may have been to a group session of some kind (to meditate, or a gathering to pray, or whatever), and the host facilitator probably lovingly said, "Let's get centered." That leader was taught to tell you to take deep breaths and center yourself. This is because we are asking our Higher Consciousness (formally labeled the subconscious mind) to "come out" and be front and center in that moment. From this viewpoint we are basically asking Soul to come forward (even though in the realm of the spherical Absolute there are no *real* dualistic directions of up or down; right and left; in and out; and forwards or backwards). As we ascend in the awakening process some of us will not need this ritual of "getting centered" anymore. Why? All present are already "centered." Won't that be fantastic!

I witnessed a taste of this many times during my twenty years of traditional close study with an enlightened master. During Dzogchen retreats my teacher Khenchen Palden would sit down after a tea-break, and instantly BE in a state of the four kayas (mentioned earlier). All of us were still fidgeting with our stuff: getting into a "comfortable" sitting-position, organizing all of our zafu cushions and pillows, meditation shawls, notebooks, water bottles, and blah, blah, blahs... while he was spontaneously resting (within seconds) in his true Buddha nature. Time and time again he demonstrated natural centeredness. He didn't have to "do" anything. He WAS centered.

This of course may not be so easy. Once awakened, it takes dedicated practice to achieve this level of profound focus in your vibrational frequency.

From the realized mind of Dzogchen (which is, atiyoga, in Sanskrit) you already exist and function "front and center." You don't have to do anything complicated or elaborate to achieve the natural state of the great, clear luminosity of being. It is already complete. (Remember, the word Dzogchen translates as "the great completion" in the reflective Tibetan language.) The tricky part—and this is why the Buddha taught us that we need to practice meditation and contemplate the teachings—is to *maintain* this Dzogchen View or "360" Vision. You may have this potent insight often, but sustaining that realization (as the masters have done) is the real work.

We are all works in progress. The 360 Daily Practice ahead in Chapter 8 will assist you in this sacred endeavor, as it has for me.

Radiance

This book has shared some very profound concepts of holy consciousness. You are now finishing the *Second Quadrant*, which represents the deep underbelly of your all-inclusive journey to Oneness. This is the part of Joseph Campbell's hero's journey that encompasses an initiation: Battling your vicious demons and conquering the ordinary, local ego-mind. It takes radiant courage to do this, I know. Ven. Khenchen Rinpoche termed it "Vajra Courage." You *can* and will transform your older, harsh life—completely. Remember, if I can do it... you can, too. Once you rise in victory, having slain the dragons from the depths of your heart, you'll dwell in radiance.

Let us explore radiance: You are up and out of the darkness into the radiant consciousness of light. Consider that it's daytime. Even so, some lights are on in the house to help you to see more efficiently. Presently for me it is afternoon, and I have my office light on (over my desk) to help me type better without straining my eyes. Now, if the lights are already on in your house, then you don't have to ask someone to turn them on—they are already on. Yes? Likewise, as already discussed, you do not have to get centered if already *conscious* from the Soul.

Let's go a little further here with more "light." Even though you turned a lamp on earlier, now you may wish to supplement brightness in the room. Using a three-way lamp with 25, 50, and 75 watts, respectively, you decide to illuminate this view. You adjust to a brighter wattage by consciously changing the setting to a highest glow of light. In this same way, your Spirit is feeling a new experience through raising its vibratory frequency.

All energy vibrates. You raise consciousness. Your Light gets brighter. When suffering tremendous challenges and overcoming them in this journey, you raise the light. You feel wiser, content, compassionate, happy, peaceful, calm, loving, generous, joyful, etc.—in a state of radiance. You shine like the sun in *all* directions. When feeling radiant you divinely manifest what you choose.

As the Professor Campbell taught: You follow your bliss. So, now let us view Soul a bit more consciously. Did you ever forget something and leave it at a restaurant, friend's house, etc. (i.e., your sweater, wallet, reading glasses, book, cell phone, whatever)? Sure you have. You know that you've done this more than once in your life—everyone has. Well, you don't consciously plan to do that (forget) do you? You don't rehearse situations with the following type of internal dialog:

> *"Okay. I'll create an event for myself at this dinner party tonight. Hmm… let's see, I'll purposely leave my favorite expensive scarf and gloves at their house so I will have to drive twenty miles to return to these folks the next day…"*

Or do you? In a way, you do. Your Spirit does. There are no coincidences. Maybe your Soul needs to engage those dinner party hosts again as part of ITS higher purpose. Every decision that we make has a reason behind it, whether you consciously know it or not. Now that you're discerning this as truth, you'll find more meaning in everything you do. The doing is action—radical, concerted action (which you're about to do in the *3rd Quadrant*). Your Soul drives the bus. IT wishes to orchestrate what IT came here to do. You have choice, yes? You may run back to get that forgotten possession right away… if you remember quickly. Or, as in the example above, you may have to call a person to make arrangements to get the thing left behind. You may not even know consciously you "lost" the item until much later on, and then hook up with people at the location again. Are you getting this concept now? I believe there is no happenstance in our lives. You may or may not be consciously aware of this. It really doesn't matter; eventually you will—when you do a 360-turnaround.

If you are responsible for creating reality, then you create ALL of the scenarios with other lovely Souls—whether they are conscious to your mind or not at the time that they occur. Once Soul's energy vibrations quicken during the awakening process, you'll be relatively more mindful of this happening. Day-by-day this awareness expands in your actions. As I have said repeatedly throughout this text: The Soul's sacred ground of being is the foundation for your doing.

When you feel radiant,
manifest what you choose without attachment to it.

Remember this ageless story? Someone attempts to choose whether they should eat a big piece of chocolate cake or be good by not devouring the delicious dessert. Sometimes I have heard this story described with an angel on the right shoulder, and the devil on the left. The angel pleaded, *"Don't eat that—it's not good for you."* And the devil teased, *"Yes, you want to be tempted don't you? Go ahead, indulge—eat it!"* How many times have you thought about doing something (like… uh, let's say bungee cord jumping) but there is this little voice inside telling you, *"You had better not do it. It might not be safe."*

Thoughts arise to mix and mingle in your mind from a vast, cosmic pool of consciousness. When you *Do a 360-turnaround*, you amend perspective to an all-encompassing, divine perception. You totally surrender to Soul, and let IT guide you. Then, and only then, will you know for sure the passionate purpose of Soul, and thereby, your significant life-work. Learn to listen, be "P and A" and IT will show you the way. The way is movement, taking action. That is why your Soul took the human form, so IT can experience life, so IT can "do." All things in the universe move. Even consciousness dynamically moves. Though I often teach about consciousness using a mirror, which is a flat and unmoving object, individual and collective consciousness vibrates. It is energy. Everything in our life vibrates as energy. Energy cannot be created or destroyed. *It is, as it is.*

Brain Waves 101

Let's take a brief look at the physical organ of the mind. I am not a Neuro-scientist or a brain surgeon, so I'm not going to cover the full scope of this topic—far from it. There are lots of excellent books to research further. For now, here is what I call, Brain Wave Technology 101.

Modern science considers brain wave technology to include the four lengths of wave, which are rhythmic electrical impulses.

These result in oscillations of the brain, which are measured in Hertz cycles (please bear in mind some measurements may vary slightly). There is beta rhythm, which is full, waking, active mind at about 13-30 cycles per second; alpha rhythm, which are slower waves of 8-13 cycles per second (and known as the "meditative" altered state of consciousness); theta, measured at a range of 4-8 (considered to be a deep, trance-like state of consciousness); and fourthly, delta rhythm at approximately 0.5-4 cycles per second (the slowest brain waves called the sleep state). When you're sleeping, brain waves are measured in this range. However, when you are dreaming with r.e.m. (rapid eye movement), your brain can be measured also in waves of the alpha rhythm, as in dream yoga or lucid dreaming (that was mentioned earlier).

Within the context of a 360-degree spherical view, look at these four sections as the quadrants of your mind. A quadrant is an arc of 90-degrees. It is one of four, equal parts in the entire circumference of a circle, like the format of this book. Beta, alpha, theta, and delta brain waves form a sort of quadraphonic matrix for mind's quantitative functioning. This synthesis uses four channels or wavelengths to infuse thought through separate states of consciousness as a blend of spherical awareness. It is interesting to note that science has named these oscillations of the brain with words of the Greek alphabet. I find it fascinating that the first wave, beta, is not the first letter of this alphabet—it is the second. Alpha is the first—it means "the beginning of anything." Beta represents (as said before) the waking mind, a general state of awareness I call "everyday life." In terms of basic brain wave technology, here's an example to expand this concept:

Daydreaming. Have you ever gazed out a window to discover yourself daydreaming? Have you ever been on a long road trip, driving mile after mile, and after a while you sort of "spaced out" to realize you don't remember the past few miles at all? Oops... you may have even missed your exit? I've done that. Have you ever been so engrossed in what you were doing that time seemed to fly by? Uptime! You didn't realize how late it was? I know you can relate to these scenarios because we have all experienced this, time and time again. While teaching meditation this topic is always discussed with a unanimous declaration of everyone's daydreams. You dream during the day? Yes, sort of. Your brain waves just slow down—that's all. From beta they flow down into alpha range, which is an *altered* state of consciousness. During meditation you have altered or slowed brain waves measured as alpha waves.

While reading this book you probably floated in and out of beta and alpha waves. When practicing yoga or other wonderful healing modalities, you operate out of alpha and even lower theta, inducing deep states of relaxation for a weary, stressed-out body. This gives your immune system a chance to rest and rejuvenate. Some yoga students during the final relaxation pose (shavasana) go right down into delta—snoring loudly in slumber land—a bit of a nuisance to nearby, fellow yogis and yoginis. Eventually with training, folks stop falling asleep and relax *consciously*. Discursive thoughts of the mind quiet down so the Soul can be heard. The Soul loves to feel this bliss in ITS chosen physical body.

The entire first year that I was practicing yoga at age sixteen, I always fell asleep at the end of class. It was so embarrassing. Classmates were already gone or changing into their street clothes saying their goodbyes to my teacher Joan. There I was still on the floor—just waking up. One time she whispered my name lovingly to my ear. Class was over. She couldn't just leave me down there in her basement! She knew I was stressed-out-of-my-gizzards, a new kid out of balance. Yet, I took to yoga like a fish in water. Three years later, at the age of 19, she benevolently asked me to take over training her students because she was moving away. I did and never looked back. As a young woman though, the other aspects of my life seemed kind of "earthy"—fish don't thrive on land, huh? And I was not very happy. I was hoping to make it in a foreign world like a flapping fish out of water. From deep in my Soul, I wondered: *"What am I supposed to be doing here in this strange land? I just want to go home. Oh God, please let me get back home!"* Recollect that Soul *feels* experience whether you consciously know it or not.

So, when generating the slower alpha range of brain waves (no matter what activity that you are doing), you're altering the mundane mind. You're in the domain of the Soul. You have the capacity to go a little deeper into theta, which is also the realm of the sacred. This is a fine palace of deep, trance-like awareness in which you "get" the solution to a mathematical problem, where you "see" the next painting you are going to create, and where the light bulb goes on brighter in your head to "know" the invention you are going to invent, etc. When you turn yourself around completely in an uninhibited surrender to your divine heritage, you shall resonate more frequently to the alternate alpha and theta rhythms of your brain. With practice on a daily basis this gets easier and easier to discern. In these heavenly states of consciousness you will transcend time and space—always and *all* ways.

3rd QUADRANT of 360 CHANGE

Spirit in Action

Chapter 7

Temple of the Body Beautiful

"The body is your temple. Keep it pure and clean for the Soul to reside in."

— B.K.S. Iyengar

ear reader, you've come so very far in this journey to Oneness. Remember that 360 = One. The last chapter had you venturing into thought-provoking depths of the heart, to regions of deep, supernatural wonder. Now you arise empowered. Victoriously, you embark on the next phase of your journey ready to take radical, passionate action. The doing comes from being. Our physical body gifts the Soul with a vehicle to accomplish ITS great boons for humanity— for the sake of all sentient beings. This is "spirit in action."

According to the New Thought philosophies (new thought, ancient wisdom), Akashic Records (akasha means ether) contain the Collective Consciousness. Therefore, that includes all of the data and information codes of our entire, multi-dimensional, universal history throughout time—past, present, and future. In ancient Egypt six thousand years ago (with some variance in time), diverse temples existed in their very early stages. Many were established after the destruction of the lost continent of Atlantis.

These were centers of high spiritual development in what we might term today, specialty schools of thought. Think of them as similar to our respectable modern universities, whether small or large—each one a place of particular focus for education and development. For example, there is the Cordon Blue in Paris for chefs, M.I.T. for engineers, (SVA) School of Visual Arts in New York City for artists, etc. The Temples, as they were called then, also had different ranges of focus, content, and study within a sacred context of unique, cutting-edge technologies of the day.

The Temple of the Body Beautiful was one of these distinct institutes.[1] It was established during a pre-dynastic period of ancient Egypt (centuries before 3,100 BCE), which is considered by numerous Egyptologists to be the first Dynasty of Menes. Although (as yet) there aren't any discovered records scientifically proving the existence of these various temples, there is a great body of work (based on 1,159 trance readings) compiled by the Edgar Cayce Foundation that helps to support this claim.[2] Other "life" readings sometimes referred to as spiritual attunements channeled by mediums or psychic individuals corroborate these findings.[3] Before the recorded early-Nile-societies, these many Temples were sacred places where the Atlanteans reincarnated. (Atlantis was a very large continental island that sank deep into the ocean because of massive earth change.) Atlanteans had extensive karmas from their gross misuse of power and therefore were born into numerous, subsequent lives with strange, crippled bodies.[4] According to the cosmic Akashic Records, many of these individuals living in Egypt would come to the Temples for the sacred "Higher" psychic surgeries, to correct their physical image of debilitating, beast-like deformities.[5]

Plato's critical works, *Timaes* and *Critias* tell of a lost land, Atlantis.[6] Olaf Rudbeck, a brilliant 17th century Swedish physician who discovered our body's lymphatic system, risked great ridicule devoting thirty years of his life proving that Atlantis existed.[7] There are numerous books to read on the remarkable subject of Atlantis should you desire to do so. One day in the public library I referenced hundreds of them. There is a saying: Where there is smoke, there's fire. What goes around... comes around.

The Temple Today

Today, many individuals that were teaching at the Temple of the Body Beautiful—the High Priests—are living in the West bringing forth many skills from their Soul's collective memory.[8] The clever Atlanteans of advanced culture are now working out their personal, redemptive plans. Just look around: You'll see a peculiar need for lots of plastic surgery (little girls wanting breast augmentation for their sweet-sixteen!); and bizarre, brow-raising "extreme" makeover television shows and an obvious fascination with them, proven by popular ratings. During the decades of the 1970s and 1980s of the last century, our physical fitness had become quite frankly, an obsession. In 1985, I received one of the first certifications in America as a fitness instructor, after passing a challenging, national written exam.[9] The health club where I was teaching (yoga and meditation classes) required this newer and intensified training. Later on in the 1990s, thousands of yoga studios and wellness centers (offering other types of therapeutic healing) were springing up like daisies. These "temples" helped patrons work on their bodies—to make them more beautiful within, as well as without.

When I starting teaching yoga in 1977, you were perceived as a little weird, a bit strange in this genre—definitely "on the fringe." Today, (thank God) 15 million Americans accept and practice yoga daily—it has now unquestionably gone mainstream.[10] All of the wonderful Souls living here right now (consciously or not) are using their extraordinary talents, knowledge, gifts, and skills. Technology is moving at lightening-speed as memories continue to be activated by The Supra Consciousness of Being that you learned about in Chapter 6. In the field of medicine, every year brings exponential growth; what took us years to learn decades ago is now being realized in months. I wholeheartedly wish that I might live to see the full burgeoning of Vibrational Medicine as it now converges with the allopathic healing modalities.[11] [12] In the future, medicine will "Do its own 360" with Vibrational Healing at the forefront of wide-ranging treatment.

360 Ecology: A Whole New You

Discussion of the Temple of the Body Beautiful does not suggest you should aspire to have the body of a Playboy Bunny or The Terminator. If you have an amazingly beautiful physical body that is perfect—just great. And if you don't—that is also great. The 360 spherical view honors the body. Everything in nature has a curve. Whatever your body is this lifetime, *you chose* that vessel. You need to accept what you are—Spirit in Form—and honor it. Your body is a temple—it is sacred. It needs to be swept clean and sanctified, fed, nurtured, and exercised. So, if your body is seriously out of balance—unhealthy, dangerously over or under weight—well, then of course you need to change that condition. You are not going to change your weight if you do not alter some pattern creating the imbalance. Remember back in Chapter 4? Weave a new pattern of supreme health. It is in a divine state of effortless balance that you'll begin to feel at one with all there is. Seek some professional guidance when your intuition tells you to. Honing a skill-set of intuition is ahead in the *4th Quadrant*. What books and videos do you feel drawn to? Listen to your inner voice and take action—now.

Since you have just entered the *3rd Quadrant*, which inspires a tangible action plan of the spherical-turnaround, we'll explore an exercise presenting four rooms of your temple. For this, prepare to creatively draw a huge circle on some paper or another special place, like your journal.

Take a long and passionate, deep, conscious breath. Then, a few more... Feel the presence of this moment (you are now so very "P and A"). Imagine that you are a sphere or a simple circle. Visualize you are lovingly sweeping the sacred, marble temple floors—cleaning the four compartments of your body, mind, emotions, and Spirit. Since you have divided yourself into four sections or four rooms, imagine this "pie-shaped" image. Breathe into it. Please take your time...

Now, which room seems to be bigger than the others? Are they all the same? As you Do a 360 in life, your supreme Spirit (Soul's room as one piece of the pie) naturally becomes larger than the other three. Recollect that you're an eternal, individuated Spirit occupying a lovely body for a fleeting time-period. When you begin to live deliberately, CONSCIOUSLY CREATING life as you move through delicious days and nights, Soul's joy thrives. Soul's passionate memories aflame with divine fire have been triggered in concert with the mother ship of consciousness.

Soul *feels* exuberance to fulfill your destiny. IT may be so robustly zealous in this initial phase of awakening that your physical body may be overlooked. Perceive this as a sign of your passion. You may strangely "forget" to eat or ignore the hunger responses of the body, etc. Initially, you might feel oblivious to basic, important body functions, incorrectly thinking: *Oh... this body is just an unconscious entity that I don't need anymore. I am Spirit... so who cares about this body?* This is just a honeymoon phase, like when you "fell" in love on cloud nine for a while, blinded by the light. Well, I alert you: This is a *real* case of blinded by the light, so please watch out. You may get giddy, dizzy, or light-headed from the higher vibratory frequencies adjusting in your cellular structures. Honor the temple in harmonic balance of physical form. Recall from the detoxification program that your body is precious—so treat it well. Call upon Frog Medicine or whatever treatments help you. I regularly go for acupuncture as a strategy to stay balanced. Find your best methods. Pray. Ask God for help. Always and *all* ways ask.

Temple of the Body Beautiful

Evoked from the last chapter, you traveled deeply through consciousness, bushwhacking old beliefs to a fresh view. In the spirit of action, let's consider the actual physical being that does the undertakings of doing things. Back in my former life (which feels so far away in consciousness), I held a part-time job for fifteen years as an Athletic Director. Along with the basic administrative duties, I taught various fitness and wellness classes to thousands: Classic Hatha Yoga, Chair Yoga, Stress Management, Meditation, Stretch 'n Tone with weights, Stretch 'n Tone without weights, Chair Exercise, Aquacize—you name it, I was probably teaching it.

I even taught Aerobics classes very briefly in the early 1980s. As mentioned earlier, I began practicing yoga at sixteen and then three years later starting teaching, so I have lived a life in touch with the physical. I've been in-tune with some mechanics and the dynamics of this corporeal piece of the pie.

It seems that most people are always interested in losing weight. If you seriously wish to change your body image, you must start from the Soul-level. (Consider the subconscious mind paradigm now shifted to Higher Consciousness.) If you affirm consciously from the depths of the heart, "I am slender"—then eventually, you will be. As you discerned back in Chapter 2, avoid focusing precious time on how fat you think you are, and that you just want to lose weight. You are just going to receive more unwanted *wanting*. Get attention off that. If you perceive that you are heavy and wish to be thinner, don't say or even think, "I don't want to be fat." Please remember, that does not work.

Affirmations are only effective in the present tense—in the now. All you have is NOW. Be "P and A" to the now. If you say "I want to lose weight" especially from an unconscious (body) feeling level, you will not be very successful. Why? Because the God Force is delivering the exact goodies to you, which is that you "want" something. Therefore, it is *not* already established in your vibrational reality.

In order for 360 Strategies (or any strategies that you may read or learn about) to succeed, you must affirm what is *already believed and deeply felt in your Higher Consciousness.* You are a creator because you are patterned in the divine. As explained many times, your body simply does not know the difference between the real and the unreal. So use these types of affirmations: I *am* thin, I *am* slender, I *feel* trim, I *am* healthy, etc. (Refer again to Chapter 4.) The boomerang swirls-around, bringing back what you have affirmed: You *are* slender, thin, and trim. Watch the pounds and inches melt—and stay away.

Approach this wholeheartedly. It can't be a few days or weeks, or on occasion. You can't just try to focus on these techniques. Trying is not going to work. Trying is wimpy. When you are ill, and ask someone to get your medicine at the pharmacy, imagine if they responded, "Well, I'll *try* to get it for you." How does that feel? It's absolutely wimpy! You *need* that medicine; and you need it sooner, rather than later. I have made serious effort to eliminate the word "try" from my vocabulary. (As an author, even writing about that word here is weird for me since I have purged it so well out of my life with concerted willpower and action.) So, dear reader, do not just read this book and then moan and groan to friends and co-workers that you are too unhappy, fat, thin, broke, bored, lonely, or too, whatever. That would severely sabotage all of your positive efforts. You must be consistently conscious and deliberate. Be heroic on this journey to Oneness. Feel courage from the heart-of-hearts, your beautiful, shining, immortal Soul.

Get out of the house and go for a walk. Make joyful effort to commune with nature, which is God manifest on this beautiful Earth plane. Start simply. Take a spin: Practice the 1st Rite (of the 5 Tibetan Rites), which was shared in Chapter 3. As you continue to weave new 360-integral-patterns you shall create scenarios that really help you to self-actualize. Please be patient. All is in divine order. Like Ralph Waldo Emerson sagely said, "Adopt the pace of nature: her secret is patience." People will suddenly appear in your core sphere of influence that are into walking or yoga—or whatever—and will engage you, energizing the Higher Will into action. You will get an exercise video as a gift and/or realize that there are many waiting at the library. (It is unfortunate that so many do not utilize a great treasure in their midst—the local library.) I'm here to prod and nudge you to greatness. As a coach I lovingly say: Get going…

So far throughout this book we've touched upon your Soul, consciousness, mind, and the body. Now you're invited to sweep the floor of all your emotions. What you *feel* is important—very important. Without getting into an in-depth examination of our human emotions, I'm going to present them from a 360 View.

There are excellent books (chock full of extensive research) to study on this fascinating subject. My own journey through the years led me to the works of Harvard psychologist and *New York Times* journalist, Daniel Goleman. He is a science researcher and international best-selling author of *Emotional Intelligence;* and the sequel, *Social Intelligence*.[13] The interdisciplinary field of modern Neuroscience (with its brain imaging studies) has revealed many fascinating facts about our spindle cells and mirror neurons, etc., from which springs emotions, like empathy. If this general topic interests you, then I suggest reading the aforementioned books and others, like: *Blink: The Power of Thinking Without Thinking* by Malcolm Gladwell, author of the bestselling *The Tipping Point;* and, Dan Gardner's compelling books *Future Babble;* and, *The Science of Fear*. These few suggestions provide a panorama of captivating, cutting-edge, and thought-provoking material.[14] And, in the spirit of "voluntary simplicity" (a phrase coined in 1936 by Richard Gregg, an American philosopher and follower of Mahatma Gandhi),[15] I will talk heart-to-heart about our emotions in a simple way from beloved roots of Dzogchen.

The Four Immeasurables

Love, compassion, joy, and equanimity are what I call the essential 360 emotions. They are, in fact, known as The Four Boundless or The Four Immeasurables taught by the Buddha. I learned of this teaching and practice from my dear Dzogchen mentor (that you met already), The Nyingma Master, Venerable Khenchen Palden Sherab Rinpoche.[16]

Though these four are seemingly very simple, The Four Immeasurables: Immeasurable Love, Immeasurable Compassion, Immeasurable Joy, and Immeasurable Equanimity may not be easy emotions to cultivate. As I always say: "It may be simple but not easy." There is a difference between the simplicity of something and the ease of it. Like meditation that is forthcoming in your 360 Daily Practice, meditation practice is so simple, yet doing it daily isn't that easy for many aspirants on the path. Please consider that meditation may *not* be what you think.

The Four Immeasurables is a most cherished meditation that I have used effectively throughout many, many years. These four aspects are the true, ultimate nature of enlightenment. I have taught this potent, heart-centered method in groups as a guided meditation with deep discussion afterward—participants loved it.

This divine practice develops and nurtures the emotions of love, compassion, joy, and peace/equanimity as antidotes (respectively) to the pronounced shadows of fear/anger, apathy/indifference, sadness/depression, and hyper-activity/attachment. Here's a taste of these Four Immeasurables:

Instantly create a sacred space. After creating a sacred space, settle into "P and A"… Focus on softly lengthening your breath. Arouse a deep yearning for love. Contemplate this love as your highest aspiration from the depths of your heart. Envision and expand that awareness in your Higher Consciousness: L-O-V-E. This is not an ordinary love like your profound appreciation for a favorite flavor of tasty ice cream. Now you meditate on the vast, incalculable, immeasurable or boundless LOVE for all sentient beings… and for every part of creation. Essentially, open your sacred heart to *feel* LOVE so great that mere words do not do it justice.

Keep expanding the feeling of great love, which is simply, immeasurable. Breathe in immeasurable L-O-V-E to every cell of your being, right down into your strands of DNA, which are the sacred evolutionary codes of your life. Next, just repeat over and over again these words: incalculable L-O-V-E, and immeasurable L-O-V-E, infinite L-O-V-E, and boundless L-O-V-E, etc. Feel an inner transformation, arising and abiding. Rest in this primordial awareness of pure light, luminescence. Breathe…

Then apply this same exact formula with the other Three Immeasurables that are: compassion, joy, and equanimity (peace). I usually spend about five minutes on each of the four boundless principles, so this practice is basically twenty minutes. Of course, you may wish to make it shorter, or longer, if you have time.

When leading others in The Four Immeasurables as a guided meditation practice, I offer diverse, creative visualizations to assist in broadening a general understanding of the four boundless or nondualistic concepts. For example, when describing the third immeasurable, which is boundless joy, I may reference playing with soft, fluffy puppies; and precious, laughing children; and rejoicing for everyone, including your (S)elf. Then, I may portray detailed, kaleidoscopic scenarios to help meditators *feel* boundless joy radiating out from their heart, like bright rays of the sun—in all directions—360-degrees. I creatively expand this meditation to a vastness of immeasurable joy, beyond measure as a billion galaxies of joy into infinity...............

Feeling emotions of love, compassion, joy, and equanimity are vital to changing your life around—totally. Move your local, ordinary mind into a mythic mind of The Four Immeasurables. In my opinion, training in this heroic way is so worthy. It's not bedazzling in esoteric concepts, it is simply (at this stage in the game), an essential skill-set on the "good red road" to Oneness.[17] Even if not previously exposed to any Buddhist philosophies, if this method helps you, use it often. Follow, as I have, in the glorious footsteps of the heart mystics and great masters. Like a journey around the labyrinth, you won't get lost—you will be found in the sacred beloved.

To re-capitulate, once you initiate the integral process of Doing a 360, affirm confidently 24/7 that your spiritual heritage resides in the Temple of the Body Beautiful. Without a precious form, Soul would not be able to *feel* or experience the life that you are creating. You are still with me on this journey. Now you have entered the courageous action phase of this gallant excursion. It is time to discover the pivotal 360 Daily Practice: the core to changing into a liberated, heart-centered being that knows ITS destiny.

Chapter 8

Spirit in Action

"When you begin to act in the spirit of love, compassion, and wisdom, you are one with the activity of all realized beings."

— His Eminence, Khenchen Palden Sherab Rinpoche

*P*edernal, the celebrated mesa-topped mountain of striated color loomed large in the distance. Its noble stance dominated the landscape into bluer-than-blue skies of God's country. In northern New Mexico, you might say it is Georgia O'Keeffe's country as well, since she made a deal with God years ago to own that beloved mountain shrine. This artist said quite perceptively, "I painted it often enough thinking that, if I did so, God would give it to me." Indeed it is hers (and ours) forever captured by the strokes of her brilliant brush. O'Keeffe was one of America's greatest painters, the only woman to have a museum dedicated exclusively to her work.[1]

Ghost Ranch was just a few miles ahead. The soundless road seemed to go nowhere except up to an immense, enchanted sky over Abiquiu—an endless sanctuary of beauty. The 21,000-acre secluded ranch and retreat was the home of Georgia O'Keeffe during many summers between 1929 and 1949, when she moved there permanently until her death in 1986 at age 98.

She worked incessantly, surrounded by 360-degree views of cherished, painted desert offering a magnificent, rich palette of Southwest color for her well-known masterpieces. It is commonly acknowledged that she seldom spoke with anyone on the grounds, hiking daily with her easel from 7am until 5pm. Georgia communed with nature in God as she walked the wilderness floor collecting barrels of rocks and animal bones, like the renowned, bleached-white horse, cow, and ram skulls waiting to be venerated on canvas.

No doubt, she was quite heroic in following her Soul's passion. Women—or men, for that matter—venturing out to the high desert of 1920s New Mexico with its sparse dirt roads, few lights and weather challenges, were few—very few. This was still the "Wild, Wild West"—certainly not a place for the faint of heart. Only a fragile seventeen years before O'Keeffe arrived and fell in love with this territory did New Mexico become the 47th state of the Union. So vast in expanse with a landscape grandeur echoing 13,000-plus years of human history, this incomparable terrain is ranked the 5th largest state of the U.S. in total square miles.[2]

While my husband and I strolled these ranch grounds in her ghostly, yet palpable footsteps that glorious spring day, cool breezes nudged a set of chimes. Gentle tones in harmonic resonance with some nearby shimmering cottonwoods infused a sacred silence as we entered a large, stone labyrinth. Built in the summer of 1998 by a devoted team of volunteers, the picturesque labyrinth at Ghost Ranch was designed in consultation with Veriditas.

Returning to discussion of the circular journey, that afternoon in Abiquiu we did a walking meditation. We shared this blessed space with the eternal spirit of Georgia O'Keeffe. She lovingly said later in life with measured reflection, "When I got to New Mexico, that was mine. As soon as I saw it, that was my country. I had never seen anything like it before. It's something that's in the air. It's just different. The sky is different; the stars are different; the wind is different."[3] I knew what she meant, having moved there myself to change life completely (as you recall, sight unseen). A kinship bonded that day: I, too, was a woman; I, too, had artist's blood in my veins; and I heard the enchanted call of this land deep in my Soul. Like O'Keeffe, whose ashes are scattered on her beloved Pedernal—I, too, knew I was home.

Creating Your Shrine

Since we humans are creatures of habit, a sacred physical environment helps support a noble journey to self-actualization. A peaceful haven is important to a balanced 360 Lifestyle. Like O'Keeffe's colorful cliffs that she called "curtains," honoring the sacred spaces in your world is essential in a fresh philosophy of all-inclusive Oneness.

My teacher, Rev. Dr. Barbara Hanshaw used to say, "KISS: Keep-It-Simple-Sweetheart!" This now applies to creating a shrine. You don't have to spend much money buying all kinds of ritual objects for a big meditation room. However, you *will* be guided to create what's best for you and your family. If living with others, discuss this tranquil venture with them. It is such a beneficial activity, which gains great merit for all that are involved. Make it a fun project. Be creative. Considering the outside of your home, you do not have to build an elaborate labyrinth in the backyard either (explained in Chapter 3). Just keep it joyfully—simple.

Let the projects spring from your joyful effort. If you are a catalog junky, here is a great excuse to buy some cool stuff for the home. But this is not about collecting more alluring trappings. Creating a sacred space brings more comfort, solace, and silence into your life. Your meditation corner or shrine room will reflect the pure Buddha nature of mind or Christ Consciousness, which is bright as light, vast as space, and open, like the bluer-than-blue skies of New Mexico.

Shifting your environment to sustain the divine, three-sixty-turnaround is, well, fundamental on this journey to wholeness. Here you plant your feet in sacred action from Soul's two "eyes" of inspiration and intention. This will help change your life. As said before: If I can do it, you can, too.

Consider creating a shrine as a visual mandala or vast palace representing all phenomena. According to Buddhism, a shrine embodies the enlightened mind, so you should keep it clean, beautiful, peaceful, and sacred. Designating a separate area for your contemplative practices and meditation, or designing a shrine room—as I have—is an integral aspect of putting spirit into action. Whenever newcomers to our home take a tour, it is delightful to see their reactions to the shrine room, which is the entire sitting-room, adjacent to our master bedroom.

Yours can be a small section of one room; it doesn't have to be fancy (KISS). Perhaps, you may wish to start small. Great—just keep a big vision. Again, if I can do it… so can you. I'm not an interior designer, yet our meditation room is rather lovely. Decorate with exquisite art, photos, and objects of veneration that have special meaning. Use this area as a refuge for Higher Consciousness. Do what Soul guides when creating an auspicious space for your 360 Daily Practice. (Visit my website for assistance at www.Doinga360.com.)

For now, consider going to a location that you may deem as a sacred space, which means, any place that you co-create in fragrant and honeyed, divine consciousness. Mute the phone(s). With a thoughtful intention you may wish to light some candles and/or burn incense, whatever ritual helps you—do it.

Be quiet. Soften the edges of your peripheral vision. Feel the sacredness in this present moment. Be "P and A" to your breath. Feel your Soul resting consciously in the temple of the body. If you have kids, consider telling them now that you need some important, quiet time. Eventually with practice you won't have to be away from children when meditating. You will not reject them in your practices, but flow effortlessly with noise—or anything else that arises. As the renowned Buddhist teacher, Thich Nhat Hanh says most amicably, "You will stay 'flower fresh' during all activities, especially during meditation." [4]

Sri Swami Satchidananda, a great yoga master and student of the 20th Century Saint, His Holiness Sri Swami Sivananda, said, "If you want to be peaceful always, identify yourself as the ever-peaceful witness within." This is a mirror, which reflects wisdom.

As you habitually develop the prudent skill-set of mindfulness, shifts in awareness will be quite tangible. In fact, *everything* shifts. Spinning through this full-circle extravaganza to splendid self-actualization, gradually notice that you are *not* the same person—physically, mentally, emotionally, and spiritually—that you once were. Your awareness of this glorious shift will become more discernible, day-by-day. It is your true birthright and real, sacred evolutionary impulse to move inexorably closer to the Source of All Being. As the mind *consciously rests* in the peace of your Soul's Higher Consciousness, be prepared for the "onederful" changes. This is spirit in action... and it's a game-changer.

Mother of Timeless Time

In the 1990s I was blessed to visit the one and only, Mother India. I have to admit that at times during this pilgrimage I was fluctuating between a love and hate relationship with this startling country. At times, it was exasperating and exhausting traveling within this ancient land. Yet, it was awesome. Most times, I was just utterly flabbergasted by what I experienced.

Our little wooden boat mingled with centuries of tradition as it drifted in the early morning darkness. A sheer, white meditation shawl (adorned with rows of Sanskrit prayer-inscriptions) covered me from head-to-toe. The legendary, sacred Hindu mantra of *Om Namah Shivaya,* held me warm as I sat cross-legged in the breezes.

Gradually, the sun rose over the river Ganges at the Ghats of Benares (Varanasi) bathing us in kaleidoscopic color. As I gazed about, time stood still. Shoreline, ancient funeral pyres smoked dreamily alongside "Laundromats" with piles of wet, dirty clothes being cleaned by men and women slapping them furiously against banks of cement. I learned quickly on this trip that sending white shirts to be laundered in India yields pastels of pink and blue! Standing near us waist-deep in the holy river, an old man was meticulously brushing his teeth with a frayed, green reed of some sort. I watched him as the decaying carrion of a bloated brown cow floated by while being picked at for breakfast by birds. Words do not do justice to this mind-blowing encounter.

In arcane, rural parts of India you *feel* the slower, peaceful pace of life unchanged for thousands of years. It's not evident as much in the bigger cities like Delhi; yet, it's alive deep in the heart of remote villages. "Hills" of strange cow dung disks (diligently pounded into round patties by bare hands of squatting women) were neatly stacked roadside—resting there by the thousands—as mounds of promise. Curious of their ubiquitous presence, I was astonished to learn from our bus driver that this sacred poop is a principal fuel source. Cows are still revered in India. They wander aimlessly on roads, stopping at intersections oblivious to vehicles carefully darting around them. Occasionally, I'd see someone in full-view, squatting in a wide-open field to relieve themselves as people have naturally done for centuries. With the spherical mind in the great view of Dzogchen, these scenes remind us that time is indeed, relative.

Consciousness expands in 360-degree visions. Time doesn't matter when quiescent in a state of grace. Notice how your concept of space-time begins to shift when doing 360 Daily Practices.

Re-calibrating Your Vibes

When meditating on tranquil, calm abiding (as in Shamatha practice at the end of Chapter 3), you nourish stillness. All is calm and clear.

Bear in mind the example shared earlier of "the dots and the lines" representing your constant thoughts (star-like dots) arising in consciousness. As a sojourner to wholeness your aspiration is to create more lines or more space between discursive thoughts. Re-calibrating your vibratory frequency in joyful effort results in more vibrant emptiness. The more relaxed-space there is during meditation—the more you calm the mind. Its constant chatter diminishes. Then you (Soul) spontaneously rest in a natural and peaceful state of beingness.

From being comes the doing. I am talking about radical, passionate, sacred action when I write: "the doing." As Joseph Campbell wisely imparted, "Follow your bliss." And he didn't mean just sitting around all day drinking carrot juice while eating some sprouts. (Although if you really think that *is truly* your Soul's purpose, then do it for the sake of all sentient beings.)

The extensive discussion into a spherical nature of your consciousness from Chapter 6 has offered much to contemplate. When meditating on an object (let's say the focus for practice is a flower), *who* is doing the watching? Thoughts arise in mind about the flower (how pretty it is… the fragrance it exudes, whatever); and then the dialog continues—your chatty mind expands. The original flower "thought" grows into a garden. Then you may think about a particular place, like the huge botanical gardens… and then, blah, blah, and blah. Finally you recognize from *conscious* awareness that mind is thinking way too much! The mirror-like realization arises from consciousness that you are straying from the simple mission of focusing on only one flower. I've had folks bravely share that they re-decorated their entire apartment during meditation.

So, *who* is doing the watching? Who *knew* mind was thinking too much? Our thoughts don't "watch" themselves, do they? You are right; no, they don't. Your divine consciousness observes the thoughts like a lighthouse scanning the world three hundred and sixty-degrees—in all directions. Consciousness is Spirit or Soul. It's a Godlike intelligence—an infinite and unwavering radiance.

Meditation Musings: Style, Elegance and Panache

Dear reader, if you are new to meditation practices, welcome. You will need to gather a few things in your basket for this sacred picnic: an open heart, sacred space, a comfortable position, and commitment with discipline to this blessed ritual. If you already meditate, then please enjoy a refreshing visit.

Many years ago I developed a workshop and class series called the Meditation Sampler. It was a lot of fun. Participants enjoyed learning about, doing, and then discussing very different styles of meditation from various spiritual traditions. Of course, you may intuit by now (from earlier musings) I started this program with that profound mirror metaphor. What a literal mind-blower. How fascinating to observe different perspectives from charming Souls all on an exquisite path to Oneness. I'm so indebted to all of my students throughout the years. Some preferred guided meditation; others didn't. A few liked mantra meditation; a few did not, etc. Walking meditation practices were popular with most, bringing mindfulness into a substantial experience with Mother Earth. My vision is that all religious traditions will one day truly embrace each other, mingling their practices together like weaving a big tapestry of love for all sentient beings. I hope I live to see it fully blossom, but that's another topic for another day, or book.

There are so many distinct kinds of people and personalities in this world. The Buddha always taught in an elegant and most balanced, middle way. It has been said that he would present five totally different answers to the same exact question posed by five aspirants. We are all so inimitable; yet, we each have a gleaming spark of enlightenment. Margaret Meade said, "Always remember that you are absolutely unique. Just like everyone else." Similar to islands seemingly separate, but united underneath the sea, we are suited to different meditation styles.

My heart-teacher Khenchen Rinpoche constantly lectured on this: One must practice according to their capability... flowing spontaneously from their inner nature. As part of a personal, 360 Daily Practice, I still do spherical "sky" meditation that he taught me privately. This is an example of an unstructured method (as you recall from that introductory discussion back in Chapter 3). Meditation relaxes the jumping monkey-mind to help you see a calm and very clear, 360 View. This is the great-uncontrived view of Dzogchen... opening the little, local mind of discursive thought to the vastness of space—the numinous of a phenomenal world of Oneness. 360 = 1.

Meditation is a very beneficial activity that you may wish to undertake on this boundless playground of life. It's the implicit practice (within) that must be balanced with all explicit activity. Explicit means, outside of yourself: with family, in the community, and worldwide. Meditation (including all contemplative practices, in my opinion) is absolutely an essential, integral part of a spiritual stress management matrix. For more information, you may wish to visit my extensive website featuring healing meditation methods.

There are many, many types of meditations that overlap with relaxation techniques and also visualization practices. Within this general framework, here is a sampling for you: Guided Imagery (the lemon, the throne); *Nadam* (natural and continuous sounds: for example, listening to ocean waves); *Shamatha* (calm abiding); *Vipassana* (insight, mindfulness without attachment); Abstract Mantra (*OM*, etc.); TM; Deity; *Chakra*; Music (listening or playing an instrument, like Tibetan singing bowls or gongs); *Dzogchen* (sky-mind, etc.); Koans; Concentration; Candle-gazing (*tratak*); Walking; Labyrinth; Eating; Breathing; *Shi-ne* (as in counting, etc.); Sacred Movement (Sufi dancing, hatha yoga, whirling dervish, etc.); Sensory–awareness (aromas, etc.); *Mandala*; Mirror; Color; *Yoni Mudra (pratyahara)*; Seed Thought (the 'who am I' inquiry, etc.); Contemplative; Prayer; Action (doing the dishes, waxing the car); Art (painting, drawing, etc.); Singing; Writing, etc.

The entire context of this book—as a spherical journey in four quadrants of a sphere—may be contemplated as a *Nirguna* meditation. That means, an expansive circular "seed thought." There are many seed thoughts to use for 360-meditations; for example: A circle has no beginning and no end. Wrap your mind around that one for a while… It has been said, prayer is talking to God and meditation is listening to God. I feel that sums it up quite nicely. Prayer overlaps with chanting. Chanting seamlessly merges into, or arises as a meditation, unto itself. Prayer overlaps meditation. As I chant, I'm praying. As far as I am concerned, it doesn't matter what you label it—just do it. Do it all.

Remember "9-11"—how could you forget? Many witnessed the tragedy live on television—in homes, at our place of business, and in schools. This was a pronounced wounding—individually and collectively. Such terrible earthquakes, tsunamis, hurricanes, tornadoes, storms, etc., also arise in the blink of an eye. Those apocalyptic images can go into your DNA, weaved into the fabric of being. They are a part of the boundless lake of the Collective Consciousness. With an ocean of immeasurable compassion you may practice non-attachment to these awful events.

The luminous mystic and father of Sacred Activism, Andrew Harvey, cautions us in his excellent award-winning book, *The Hope:*

A Guide to Sacred Activism[5] to be careful not to become addicted to transcendence. Balancing all your holy practices with passionate action is the key. Praying fervently for forgiveness to the Divine Mother in sacred heart, remain non-attached in a transcendent way. I do not mean being detached, which can signify aloofness, indifference, and complete withdrawal; the meaning here is the awakened Soul in non-attachment—because as horrible as it all looks—*it is, as it is.* At this stage in the big school of life I call recess, we've got to get in the game, "step up to home plate" and hit it out-of-the-park... then journey back home.

Chapter 5 offered simple, psychic self-protection techniques. Mantras help to protect or envelop your mind with a bit of sacred panache. The etymology of the Sanskrit word *mantra* consists of the root word man–, which means, "to think," and its action-oriented suffix, –tra. Many traditions use chanting as a means to connect with their Source of All Being because like a barrier, they protect consciousness. Mantras are seeded in powerful rapture of God. Amen is a Hebrew word (derived from the Aramaic and Arabic) which means, truth or "may it be so" or "so be it." I sometimes use Amen as a mantra. When concentrating with faith, repeat it again and again. This action affirms what you choose in the moment (for example, healing the body is *already done*). It's truth. And it is interesting to note that Amen is the absolute last word of the Bible (New Testament). So Be It. Truth. AMEN. In my personal 360 Daily Practice, I chant primarily in Tibetan and Sanskrit, since these particular mantras and prayers resonate to Soul's preference. I also feel sacred affinity to the power of the ancient, Hawaiian shamanic tradition of *Ho'oponopono*, reciting a shortened version: I LOVE YOU. THANK YOU. All of my correspondence ends in some expressions of gratitude and love. Follow *your* heart with supplication to elegance in grace.

Breath of Fresh Air

Imagine in this heroic journey to an empowered, conscious life that you are standing at the top of a mountain, seeing in all directions—three hundred and sixty-degrees. Breathe fresh, clean air into a re-calibrated, new you. Breathe in a lush, magnanimous beauty of Oneness. Purify and nourish all your cells with oxygen. Inside of every sacred, passionate breath that you absorb is a shimmering, golden, liquid light or energy known as *prana*.

Prana is a Sanskrit word meaning, vital life or life force. In English, this vital life force is referenced as "energy." Egyptians called it "ka"; Chinese term it "chi"; and it is known as "ki" in Japanese. During a fast you can live for weeks without food; people have survived many days without water; but without air, you die in minutes. Prana is the life force of all creation. The air that you breathe is not prana—prana is *in* the air. Prana is *within* everything. Therefore your breath is not prana—prana is *inside* and *all around* your breath. Prana is everywhere as an eternal field of energy. According to yogic science, *pranayamas* (the drawing out or the extension of this life force) are breathing disciplines to harvest the mind of enlightenment. This is part of your 360 Daily Practice. As mentioned before, *Doing a 360: Turning Your Life Around to Follow Soul's Purpose* is not another yoga book. There are many wonderful publications already available for your perusal. My inspiration and intention is to provide a brief overview for your deliberation.

Breath is the connection between the physical body (the functioning of the lungs) and your Soul's conscious awareness. With the proper breathing techniques you will establish vibrant health and vitality, and deepen your sense of (S)elf on the circular journey to wholeness. Start practicing a simple exercise of *conscious breathing* to set you on the path. This is not just about moving air; conscious breathing rests in the domain of Soul, helping Higher Consciousness sweep the temple—nice and clean. As a former asthmatic, I know the desperate feeling of gasping for breath. It's scary to speculate if you are going to suffocate, but that is how millions live daily with this affliction.

Conscious breathing is learning to "catch your breath" so-to-speak. Being very "P and A" right now—focus on your breathing pattern. Is it smooth, hurried, labored, slow, shallow, deep, or erratic? Most people are unaware that they breathe poorly. Take a minute now... and just breathe consciously. Breathe in and out...

and in and out. Focus, and be calm and clear. Watch your breath from pure consciousness (the mirror-like wisdom). Do not alter it right now—not yet. Just watch it; witness it the way you did in Shamatha, a calm abiding meditation practice. After a minute or two, begin slowing down the process of your breathing. Be in the presence of the now, or as Ram Dass succinctly wrote: "Be Here Now." *Consciously* feel your divine breath deepen, while it softens; let the belly—your core—rise and fall. Listen to the inhalation and the exhalation... and the pauses... sacred spaces in between.

The action of breathing comes from our autonomic nervous system. So, obviously breathing occurs to sustain life. In other words, we do not *have* to make ourselves breathe; we just do it automatically, anyway. *Conscious* breathing, as a preliminary yogic pranayama, is an activity we "do" from Higher Consciousness. Our Spirit wishes to experience it. As noted here, again and again: the doing comes from the ground of being.

From the 360 View, before diving into the varied, intense practices of yoga's pranayama, one needs to establish a beginner's baseline. I highly suggest starting with *conscious* breathing. Do not let its simplicity fool you. Recall that something may seem simple but that doesn't mean it's easy. This practice (especially on a daily basis) may not be as easy as you think it would be. Many get so impatient. Especially in the West, we are a crazy culture of go, go, go, strive, and let's go-some-more. Yikes, the faster we go... we think, the better. You have got to really slow down.

So... S-L-O-W... D-O-W-N.

For example, as you are reading these sentences right now... what happened to your breath? Did you forget about it already? Remember that breathing is automatic. However, are you still *consciously* breathing like you were in the last few paragraphs? You are? Great! If not, okay. You just forgot.

Like being "P and A," *conscious* breathing is being present and available to your breath. That is why your mindfulness is so very important to changing your entire life. Work on it. As part of a 360 Daily Practice, breathe consciously—more often.

The next training step in *conscious* breathing: Inhale slowly while counting to five. Hold that breath for five counts, and then exhale slowly for the same, five counts. If this is way too easy for you—good. Increase to the count of six.

If inhaling, retaining, and exhaling to the gentle count of six is easy—great. Then... increase to seven.[6]

Please be vigilant now, as it is more challenging than it may seem. Avoid strain at all costs. Sacred awareness generates oceans of prana. Your life force strengthens. Peace settles in as you re-calibrate your vibratory frequency to a much finer, higher level. Set up a time for this actual practice, but also use it spontaneously during daily activities. If you're very busy with a full schedule, let mindfulness guide you to a healing power of *conscious* breathing.

Take a full breath of fresh air into a free, deliberate life. Just ahead, you will move into some yoga, the sacred union of being, which is so very dear to my heart-of-hearts. What is the "heart-of-hearts" I refer to? Why, dear reader, it's your *Soul.*

360 Yoga

"A mind free from disturbance is Yoga." This is a general and classical definition from Patanjali, who codified the timeless, pragmatic science of self-realization more than two thousand years ago in his treatise of the *Yoga Sutras.*[7] He called this, *ashtanga* yoga—the eight stages, or limbs of yoga: *yama, niyama, asana, pranayama, pratyahara, dharana, dhyana,* and *samadhi.* In 2006, I was guided to create a style of yoga called 360 Yoga (three-sixty). 360 Yoga emphasizes attunement to the Soul through the practice of hatha yoga asanas. To learn more, you are invited to visit the website, Doinga360.com.[8]

360 Yoga is a method developed from decades of teaching... in thousands of classes with wonderful students from all walks of life. Whether just beginning or a seasoned practitioner, it focuses on a healing, sacred attunement of the temple to the Soul. It is an all-encompassing, intuitive, and compassionate approach to this ancient art and science—honoring all sacred traditions.

The 360 Yoga style blends the best essence of various yoga schools within a matrix or mandala of the Tibetan Buddhist vehicle of Dzogchen. 360 Yoga is for everyone: How could it not be since the philosophy is "spherical"—three hundred and sixty-degrees. No one is left out. Not even the sick, the frail elderly, the obese, the mentally and physically challenged, or the strongest of body-builders. All are guided to their divine heritage through a sacred movement system developing keen awareness FROM the Soul. Vibratory frequency is raised to very fine levels. The asanas provide a template or portal for connecting with SOURCE. Soul feels ITSELF in the temple that IT has chosen for this lifetime.

The first two stages of ashtangha yoga, the *yamas* and *niyamas,* are rudimentary, ethical precepts to 360 Yoga, or any style. They are foundational guidelines of restraint and observance, which means, discernment to "do the right thing." Essentially, yamas tell us to: do no harm, to be tolerant, to speak the truth, not to steal, or be greedy. They also advise us to practice sexual responsibility. Niyamas are cleanliness and modesty, including a moderation in diet; contentment; austerity; self-study with discernment; and the surrender with devotion to the truth—to God. As you awaken to the truth of *your* inherent divine nature, then naturally all these insights are espoused.

Did you know that a little bit of yoga could be secretly practiced in public? Can you imagine doing an asana (pose) while standing in line at the grocery store, the bank, or even waiting for a table at your favorite restaurant? The "portable pose" as I call it, is the mountain posture, *tadasana* (tada means, mountain in Sanskrit); it's also known as *samasthiti*. (In Sanskrit: sama, upright, straight; sthiti, standing still.) Yoga master Iyengar teaches this pose as the foundation of all others.[9] Its lesson is in the art and science of standing—that's right... just standing. You may mock this because obviously you already know how to stand on your own two feet. In yoga class, one may spend quite some time developing this pose. It will help you also in your practice of the 1st Tibetan Rite, which was discussed in Chapter 3.

During the mountain posture, stand firm and erect, evenly distributing weight of your body on both feet, which are hips width apart or together, with arms at the sides. Then, elongate the spine naturally while feeling an essence of Earth beneath your feet. Once established, close your eyes to imagine standing steady and strong at a mountaintop, observing a 360-degree View: the splendor of landscape with its breathtaking vistas. Visualize an enormous feat of climbing to reach the top of the world feeling a sense of awe and wonder at the omniscience of life. This is the essence of tadasana—uplifted in the clouds, yet grounded with both feet on the floor. As Iyengar says in his classic text, *Light on Yoga*, it is essential to master the art of standing.[10]

Though not a very portable posture like its aforementioned brother, shavasana is the most essential asana. This relaxation pose completes any yoga session (the Sanskrit word "sava" means corpse, and it is pronounced, shava). With an honest and mature understanding, approach the dead man's pose without getting upset that you are morbidly thinking of death. (I don't believe we die anyway, but that is another topic.) In alignment with a healing medicine of animals, consider shavasana as the pose of a little opossum. Opossum plays dead, rolling over, belly-up to save its life from predators. There is great wisdom in Opossum Medicine. I have suggested this compassionate theme to students, especially if they have recently experienced the devastating death of a loved one. This is a simple example of blending the ancient wisdom of one tradition with another: Merging the Yogic Philosophy with Native American Spirituality. The purpose of this posture is to pretend that you are dead like our marsupial furry friend. You lay down flat on the floor, or in the grass, or bed if necessary, in a supine position. Stay still—very still—like a corpse. By remaining motionless, yet conscious (not falling asleep), you learn to relax.

Most people don't know how to relax. I'm not talking about sitting in your recliner chair to watch television. This is not that practice you learned earlier, "R and R." Shavasana is profound, unfettered relaxation of the body through sensory withdrawal, which leads to a deeper *conscious* awareness from the Soul. This rejuvenating and easy posture is the most challenging to master. That's not my exclusive opinion. All the yogis and yoginis that I have studied with have shared this realization. If so difficult, then why do I have students habitually practice: Simply because of the noble, multi-dimensional benefits. Remember my old buddy who said people today are stressed-out-of-their-gizzards? Well, I agree.

Mastery of yogic relaxation can quite literally be a lifesaver. This was evident during a class I taught at a Buddhist wellness center every Monday night for five years. Think about this: How do *you* feel after work on Mondays? Fatigued folks arrived with one big collective sigh of the Monday blues, having just started another workweek. Immediately, they would just plop down in shavasana (some of them arriving very early to practice this pose). Usually yoga practitioners warm-up instead by doing stretches and other preliminary asanas. So, an instinctive need for shavasana seems to be tremendous—even crucial to our well-being. The power of it to reduce stress is incredible, as it leaves the mind refreshed and re-calibrated. Once the skill has been attained through regular practice, use this pose to enhance a luminous gateway or portal to Soul's *experience*. ITS Akashic memories are activated during 360 Yoga. Here is a basic instruction for shavasana; and then you may expand to an all-encompassing 360-presentation:

Shavasana

Exercise: Shavasana
Practice Time: 10-30 minutes (as you feel guided).
Practice: Daily, or twice a day.

Read through this slowly with long pauses,
and practice; record and practice; or have someone read
the script aloud for you.

Create a sacred space.

During shavasana, avoid becoming uncomfortably cold, so make sure the room temperature is good for you, and that you are not directly under an air vent, etc.

Prepare to lie down flat on your back with hands away from your thighs, palms up with fingers, softly curled.
Eyes are closed during this practice. I teach this pose with

feet apart the width of the hips, however, as you eventually become more proficient and flexible, you will keep your heels together—toes nice and soft.

Make sure that your neck is comfortable without the chin tilting up. Use a folded towel or pillow under your head to keep the cervical spine (neck) relaxed—not contracted. Experiment with the best position for you and then continue to make other adjustments, tweaking a bit here and there, as needed.

Once you are "set" in this asana, do not move. If you are still fidgeting, it's okay; those are just your frayed nerves... playing themselves out. Eventually, you will eagerly approach this yoga pose quickly and efficiently without any squirming. But once you decide that this pose is fixed—do not move again. Next time in shavasana you will adjust with more refined awareness, making corrections noted from the prior practice.

To begin... breathe *consciously* for a few minutes... stay aware, mindful, and of course, "P and A." Allow the breath to smoothly "breathe by itself" in sacred space. Bring your focus to scan the entire body.

Observe any sensations without judging them, such as your stomach growling or gurgling, etc. Relax your entire head and face, especially the jaw area, tongue, and eyes, etc. Rest the mind. Allow your true nature to spontaneously arise and abide. Relax into delicious inner peace, the silence of this present moment.

Feel the glorious essence of this pose as hyper-nerves begin to mellow. Let go. Be relaxed. The doing of this pose comes from being.

Your body feels nice and long as you sense Mother Earth underneath, supporting you with her loving surface. Stay in this altered state of consciousness; alpha and theta brain rhythms harmoniously flow—from head-to-toe.

Feel that you are coming home now... returning from a long journey. Remember the feeling deep in your Soul and experience comfort, safety, and joyful familiarity when you turn the corner and see—home, sweet home.

If you do fall asleep, then just let go (eventually you will train yourself to stay *consciously* aware). Maintain this beautiful pose of deep relaxation. It is your birthright...

When feeling finished, do not jump up quickly. Deepen your breath. Move slowly and gracefully from Soul's awareness. Just roll very gently now onto your right side, so as not to infringe upon the heart.

Wait a few moments... and then, mindfully, and very slowly, sit up; meditate for a while. Dedicate the merit of this sacred experience for all sentient beings.

Like the lovely Buddhist practice of the Four Immeasurables, shavasana is an immeasurable antidote to stressful living. This is spiritual stress management at its finest: an effectual way to sooth ragged nerves and calm your entire being. If you haven't been drawn to doing yoga, there isn't any rationale that would prevent a smart individual from undertaking this practice. Don't let any limiting beliefs ever get in the way. Almost all religions are finally incorporating some yoga into their curriculums.

Let's look at this pose now with an enlarged spherical view:

Exercise: Shavasana (expanded with visualization)

Practice Time: 10-30 minutes (as you feel guided).

Practice: Daily, or twice a day.

Read through this slowly with very long pauses,
and practice; record and practice; or have someone read
the script aloud for you.

Create a sacred space.

Assume shavasana.

After the initial breathing phase... (for a few minutes...)
begin to practice visualization.

Imagine your consciousness is rising up to the ceiling of the room. Visualize that you are looking down at your body, which is lying in this pose...

Looking down now, see clearly what you are wearing, and what the surrounding materials are: such as a carpet, your mat, bamboo floor, or your bedspread, etc.

Distinguish the color of those things, including your clothes. Image your entire body in great detail: your hair, any jewelry, etc.

Feel your Soul looking down at the temple of you, and then develop great compassion and loving kindness towards this fine Temple of the Body Beautiful. Honor the (S)elf that lies below.

Expand the 360 View... Remain in this relaxed, conscious state as you are guided, allowing the breath to be natural. When finished with shavasana, exit gracefully in ease; and contemplate the experience with meditation practice.

Dedicate the merit. Write about it in your journal.

The 360 Daily Practice

An ounce of practice is worth a ton of theory.

The core of this inspirational book, *Doing a 360: Turning Your Life Around to Follow Soul's Purpose*, is developing a sacred, daily practice. You must practice diligently to affect complete change in your life. Then always dedicate the merit of all you do for the sake of all sentient beings. Remember... according to Dzogchen, we are already perfect beings of luminous light. Now, reveal your perfect, divine nature and *maintain* this 360 View.

Here is another trinity matrix to help you sustain this view—24/7: study, contemplate, and practice. Words, written or uttered, are limiting—language is not transcendent. Your realizations will come from direct experience, which are *consciously* created, not just from intellectual knowing.

Study: 360 Philosophy

Contemplate: Refine 360

Practice: Take Action in the 360 Daily Practice

The 360 Daily Practice is performed 24/7. Its design is all-encompassing—on *and* off the cushion, so-to-speak. Within the sacred space of stillness while developing "P and A" (presence and availability), your quiet mind yields to illuminating musings of your Soul. Meditate; breathe in deeply the inner peace of your newly created world. You *are* Spirit. So, celebrate that good news with immeasurable joy. Rest in your true nature.

Even though you'll set aside specific clock-time for practice, move through mundane daily activities deliberately. The mundane is now divine because you live in the great, unfabricated view of Oneness from three hundred and sixty-degrees. You commune with nature because you *are a part of* nature. You commune with God because you *are* divine. A constant flow of primordial energy (prana) permeates your entire being—no matter what you DO.

Consider this imagery:

First, breathe *consciously* for a few minutes... (Stop reading for a minute or two, and really focus on your breathing.)

Now...

Visualize a vast, white, translucent sphere surrounding you. As your image becomes clear with regular practice, you may also be able to articulate a divine matrix of four concentric spheres: Your body, mind, Soul, and the fourth, a surrounding glowing orb of magnificent Supra Consciousness.

It may help you to use the following metaphoric comparison: Sizes of concentric, celestial spheres, which are planets.

Imagine your dense body is like the tiny planet of Mercury. Earth (that is larger) represents your mind, as it surrounds that smaller, solid sphere of Mercury. Envisage the huge planet of Jupiter to represent your Soul. The other two planets or spheres of Mercury and Earth are inside of Jupiter, concentrically.

Lastly, but not least, contemplate our brilliant, golden sun containing the other three spheres (planets) within it. Obviously, without the radiance of the sun we would perish.

Rest in the natural state of this "spheroid knowing" merging your awareness with all phenomena. Then, dissolve your (S)elf into the great universal emptiness and dedicate the merit.

The 360 Daily Practice comprises these general activities:

Your 360 Daily Practice:

- o   Affirm I AM Spirit… I AM Divine

- o   Maintain the 360 Spherical View—24/7 "360 = One"

- o   Mindfully create sacred space (wherever I am)

- o   "P and A"—be present and available… *always*, *all* ways

- o   Take a dose of Animal Medicine—weave healthy patterns

- o   Integrate Uptime

- o   Nourish the Temple: drink water, rest, etc.

- o   Commune with nature: walking, etc.

- o   Practice *conscious* breathing—24/7

- o   Practice meditation, prayer, etc. (dedicate the merit)

- o   Do sacred movement: 1st Tibetan Rite, 360 Yoga, etc.

- o   Listen to Soul's passion and purpose—devote my life to it

- o   Expand Higher Consciousness: sphere visualizations, etc.

- o   Follow my bliss, which is "Spirit in Action"

challenging yoga practices when they love it enough. That is the key: Your passion, your love for what you "do" in life. Students are the greatest of teachers. Divine webs weaved together are so very priceless in this journey.

I was with Lila during the final days at Hospice as she made a peaceful transition home. She was so very brave. Having lived marvelously during two centuries—the entire 20th and early 21st— she was ready. I knew deep in my heart-of-hearts that when she passed from this relative world, my "work" would be finished at the facility where I was employed. Once she turned the milestone of age 100, it was a gut feeling that the next few months, (which blossomed into four more lovely years together) would be the signal from Spirit to re-calibrate my life. As shared earlier, when she passed, the hawks came. One-by-one, their sacred medicine encircled my life.

About eight months before she died, Lila flatly stated at the close of one of our private sessions:

"A few ladies have requested me to teach them yoga here in the apartment."

Stunned, I responded enthusiastically but with a little bit of questioning in my voice, "Really? Uh… wow Lila, starting a new career at 103? You are an amazing woman!"

Then she asked candidly, "Would you teach me 'how' to teach?"

I was both delighted and dumbfounded by this question, but of course agreed to help. Later on, after her initial experience I asked Lila, "So, how was it teaching your very first yoga class?"

"Well," she said with some consternation, "it was good. The only problem was getting those old ladies on the floor with me."

"Well, how old are they?" I chuckled, respectfully.

"Oh… two are in their late-nineties, and the other two, well, younger, in their eighties," she matter-of-factly replied. I had to remember that her son, whom I also taught privately when he visited the community periodically, was around eighty-years-old.

"Lila, you are just so amazing and inspiring," I said, hugging her with a wide smile on my face. When I suggested to her, and then demonstrated how to teach some modified yoga postures using a chair, she listened quite attentively, but scoffed at the idea, preferring to tough it out on the floor like the rest of us.

Her courage and commitment was a rare gift. She gracefully floated into class early, quietly setting up her mat—front and center. She promptly assumed shavasana before sessions began. Her classmates whispered in admiration from the back of the room to newer participants: "There's that lady who is a hundred years old." This radiant yogini was skilled in the art of creating sacred space. She was "P and A"—always and *all* ways. Lila loved yoga. She absolutely knew how to align herself with divine love. She was heroic.

When I write, occasionally my gaze turns up at her framed photo resting on a bookcase shelf. In prayerful grace she greets me with the traditional *Namaste*. I smile in quiet ease and comfort knowing she watches over me. We meet here often at the corner of easy street and love. Now that you've met one of my beloved allies, let's move along in *your* journey to alignment with divine love.

Align Yourself with Divine Love

Here's the car metaphor again, this time with a shift in gears. The Temple of your Body Beautiful is a vehicle. If your car veers or pulls too much to the right, or to the left, it needs to have an alignment to drive straight. For safe operation tires must wear evenly. They have to be rotated periodically, too. With cars, as in your body, it's about balance. Being "P and A" and then taking responsibility for its maintenance conveys loving care—that's balance. If the vehicle needs an alignment, but you don't get one, all kinds of things go wrong. With tires badly worn or even bald, you can imagine how much trickier it will be to safely spin around in a three-sixty. Think about it: Two cars on the same icy road lose control and slide. One badly needs a front-end alignment; the other is well maintained with new tires, etc. Which one will probably handle better when you firmly grab the wheel and hit the brakes? Brakes—did I need to mention brakes? They must be maintained, too. Of course it's all up to the driver, isn't it?

Let your Soul drive the bus. Surrender your life to alignment with divine love. *"What else is there to do in this life except be aligned with divine love?"* This is a maxim I use quite often. You may quote me on it as you wish. So it is with the process of "Doing a 360" in life. You change to a fresh perspective. You re-calibrate in total responsibility and maintain a "360" View—the complete view. You love your life. Your sacred spin takes you full-circle, in the *right* direction ready to travel on to your next destination, which is to bliss: Divine bliss in radical, passionate action for the sake of all sentient beings.

Someone questioned me once, "What do you mean by 'true' love?" True love is unconditional. It is divine, eternal pure light. You know it when you feel it—for it is your truth. Like the truth, true love resides deep in your heart-of-hearts, which is Soul. You resonate to it because of its inherent presence in all beings. This is part and parcel with the concept of Oneness. Like your practice earlier with The Four Immeasurables, true love is boundless.

With a core, seasoned understanding of love in the "greatest degree" consider that this is not the love you may have for a particular flavor of ice cream (which was asserted earlier). That love may change next year when the hottest, new outrageous flavor arrives: intergalactic fudge-swirl with toasted almonds, crunchy ice-cream-cone-pieces melded with caramel candy, dark chocolate, and toasted coconut macaroons. Oh, did I mention it is also organic? Hmm... I would like to taste that one. Divine love is a pure, unfabricated energy that cannot be created or destroyed. It dwells in the realm of the absolute. Feel the greatest degree of love in all of your surroundings. Be authentic in life. Be happy and content, to whatever degree that is for you.

Lifespan on Earth is smaller than a nanosecond. It goes by so fast that you need to awaken now—wake up and realize who you really are. Life is precious. Sometimes when we are too close to things we just can't see them. Like the old adage says: Don't miss the forest for the trees. Seizing this fortunate opportunity to experience The Oneness of Being is truly heroic. 360 Philosophy teaches an unconditional and integral true love of the (S)elf. Love yourself first? *You may think... isn't that egotistical... isn't that wrong?*

Not in this book. Love yourself to the greatest degree. Why? God created you therefore *you are* divine. There are religions that still teach this view to be preposterous—even blasphemous. This is certainly not a 360-perspective. If we are patterned in the image of God how could we not be divine? Some don't really have the core belief that they are divine love incarnate. As you rightfully place The Source "first" don't forget the humble, true love for (S)elf as a divine, worthy being. It's like the two sides of a coin discussed in the next chapter.

As a teacher, coach, and mentor, I have observed that some people really don't like themselves. Some loathe their life. They have no mythology of being. "Doing a 360" inspires a heroic realization that loving oneself—truly and completely—is quite paramount to the mind of enlightenment. If you are one with all there is, then how could "you" not be a part of this equation: 360 = 1? You are certainly a part of all there is. That is "Oneness." Separation is an illusion.

Here is a metaphor to assist in this understanding, which I acquired years ago flying coast-to-coast. I have shared it often to quick, unanimous head-nods—people seem to easily "get" this: After boarding an airplane and then settling into your seat, the attendants provide instructions. While demonstrating emergency procedures, they adamantly instruct that if the yellow oxygen mask drops down... you put it on FIRST—*before* helping a child with theirs. If you fumble to put it on them first, you may pass out from lack of oxygen before getting it adjusted over your face. (You know that small children will fight the uncomfortable, scary mask and strap, struggling to pull it off in panic.) Take care of your (S)elf first, and then you may effectively aid others. How are you going to help those around you if you don't love yourself? This is not selfish love. I am not discussing the illusory "me" vs. "them." This is aligning "you" with divine love in a state of grace—always and *all* ways.

Lovingly accept yourself with all faults and foibles as a devoted work in progress. You aspire to greatness and enlightenment. Dear reader, love yourself unconditionally. Every human being has a twinkling spark of the divine in his or her heart no matter what wrinkles, fat, or ugly imperfections they falsely see. Please love your body, too. It is the great temple of Spirit, the vehicle for this miraculous journey we call life.

Mentors and Allies 360

An ally and a mentor are different. You'll usually have more allies than mentors in life. Consider yourself very blessed if you have had, or have presently, more than a handful of real mentors. Though a sacred mentor is an ally, an ally is not necessarily your 360 mentor. An ally is any particular spirit being, person, or even an animal (as in the power totem of their medicine mentioned before), in which you have a very deep connection or alliance.

It is important to have 360 mentors and to know your allies. Scripted in unison with your Soul before taking a human birth, mentors and allies have *your* best interest in their heart-of-hearts. You met one of my sweet allies, Lila. I've also been blessed with cherished mentors throughout my entire life.

One of these mentors sadly passed away many years prior to publishing this book. She was a significant and influential force in my life. As my longtime, superb acupuncturist, I could ask any question about Oriental Medicine and she would then answer thoughtfully in unrestrained detail. I learned so much from our discussions swathed in her unconditional love that this great, ancient, Chinese healing discipline became my serious hobby.

She even named me her "moxa queen" as I needed long moxa-burning treatments until I got balanced. During hundreds of sessions she offered me so much extra time. Whenever I had a subsequent commitment right after our appointment, she had to be gently reminded of my necessity to leave early. She genuinely loved her craft. If my well being required two hours of treatment that day, then two hours it was. She was so "P and A." Some practitioners may just "go by the clock." Like many allopathic treatment facilities, you are in and out—real quick. My mentor's successful, burgeoning practice exuded a quality of uptime. She did not overbook patients. I never had to wait. Her inspiration and intention in divine gratitude was to heal, not to rake in more money than needed. She operated so beautifully in abundance. Remember from Chapter 4:

Abundance means
having everything your Spirit truly needs
to experience
what it is you came here for.

Do you have 360 mentors? Think of the unique people in life that inspire you with a deep passion for their craft—whatever it is. Most importantly, they support you. This is key. These are the individuals that empower you—unconditionally—because they align with true love in your divine presence. This is a demonstration of the greatest degree of love: they offer advice needed for your journey to wholeness. Mentors co-creatively help you stretch and grow beyond the limits of your ordinary mind. When explaining to another dear heart-friend and mentor that I was moving away most unexpectedly, she wholeheartedly replied, "Good, now take this opportunity to re-invent yourself." I was so relieved and comforted by her empathy. She totally understood a spherical view of life. During the move to start fresh, I wasn't sure exactly what she meant in a practical sense, but now that I've done the full-circle 360-degrees, I know. And I'm grateful.

Remember my Aunt who was "present and available?" She was an ally. I have discovered teaching this process that people generally do not recognize their allies. With discernment, during chunks of sufficient time allowing your relationships to unfold and enfold, you may come to realize that someone is not an ally as previously assumed. It's relative—there are strong allies and weaker relations. Like the Spider, weave a sacred web through life. A regular dose of medicine from "spirit mentors" and true allies will help to sort this out.

Observe patterns with all-encompassing vision: People who do not support your bliss in spiritual growth are not allies, and certainly not your mentors. Consider that your friends may, or may not, be allies—and that is fine. Just know with a mature responsibility what sphere of influence you have created, and may be altered from Higher Consciousness. In that regard, here is an exercise to help: List your mentors and allies below in this simple template. If reading in digital format you will need paper again, or a journal. Use honest discernment, not judgment, when making the lists. When I do this practice periodically (at least every year around my birthday), it takes about two hours. As recommended earlier, drink lots of water and breathe *consciously* into a spacious and calm, complete view. Like all of your 360 Daily Practices, approach this exercise with mindfulness in an open heart for the sake of all sentient beings. Then, dedicate the merit.

Meditate and/or contemplate these few questions for each person considered: Who are my allies? Who are my strongest allies at this time? Who backs my crazy ideas, projects, and whims? Is there unconditional support from them? Can I confide in them with trust? Are they generous with time and energy? Are they "P and A?" Do I intuit from Higher Consciousness that they help me in a "greatest degree" of love? Am I truly aligned with them? Would I consider calling them right now to joyfully share that I desire a new life—to "Do a 360?"

Mentors

_____

_____

_____

_____

_____

_____

_____

_____

Allies

_____

_____

_____

_____

_____

_____

_____

_____

_____

Your lists may surprise you, huh? An old adage is true: When the student is ready, a teacher will manifest. These are important, sacred relationships. If you don't have anyone in life as a mentor then pray humbly for divine guidance. Who inspires you? Who are you drawn to? What is your passion? Is there a minister you may talk with? Seek people that are doing what you desire to do. Take a workshop, learn from them, and read their books; take some classes. A mentor will arise in your spheres of awareness. Listen—pay attention as your heart guides you to mentors and allies. You don't have to spend a lot of money, either. Go to local clubs and organizations to volunteer—as it feels appropriate. Respect the elderly. Like dear Lila, their wisdom is immeasurable. These charming, sacred buddies may help cultivate a new you.

Sangha of Oneness

Align with divine love. Surround (S)elf with uplifting people that cheerfully support a 360 Lifestyle. As Buddha taught, sangha is one of the Three Jewels—therefore it is precious. (_Sangha_ is a Sanskrit word meaning "assembly" "company" or "community.")

Noble sangha is so important especially in the earlier stages of awakening. Sangha fosters a deep communal sense of Oneness with all. There is a global sangha or family of Oneness that is growing and getting stronger every day. As humanity shifts into a global community, the focus changes to a philosophy of "we" rather than "me."

At times you may need to retreat, working alone on a quest for wholeness. As in the Hero's Journey of Joseph Campbell, you go this route alone. Fight demons with great courage to conquer your fears. And conquer, you must. As Campbell wrote, "the adventurer still must return with his life-transmuting trophy." [3] Your Soul will guide you—so listen up! Great Buddha left a luxurious, princely-life, separating himself from all of his worldly goods. After six years as a wandering, starving, ascetic yogi, he meditated alone under a giant fig tree—the famous Bodhi Tree. The key here is that he returned from his journey with an enlightened mind. This experience is called a sensible, balanced "Middle Path" which is now known as Buddhism. If he had not compassionately re-surfaced to reveal his teachings to us, which is known as "turning the wheel of Dharma"—all would have been lost. That would have been a travesty to humankind.

The whole point of a Mythology of Oneness is *to come back and serve others*, bestowing *your* gift to the world—whatever the treasure is. Bring to mind what scholar Campbell said to me as a youngster, "To go full-circle the hero *has* to return." You also should consider his mentoring advice. Bring back your golden nuggets from the deep, dark sphere of rebirth. That dark night of the Soul is sometimes symbolized by an image of being in the belly of a whale. To paraphrase author Campbell: "After you are swallowed up by the great mystery—arise, born again. You only die to "time" in this life-renewing act." [4] Once your heroic self arises from a 360-journey, the sangha will continue to inspire and support your noble efforts. A sacred community of friendly allies appreciates your road traveled, surrounding life with goodness in purpose. Within a community of Oneness you will discover allies, and maybe a mentor, or two, waiting to help. Follow your heart to happiness in the company of others.

Changing Your Scenery

Like Georgia O'Keeffe finding new life in a painted land of enchantment, you too, may change your scenery. When I turned my life around completely to follow Soul's purpose, a divine panorama embraced. With strong faith I stepped aside to let Soul drive the magic bus. Soul knew the scenic byways and rustic back roads much better than I did, anyway. Going from coastal sea level up to 6,000 feet in the foothills was a drastic change. From flat terrain to mountainous vistas; from humidity to dry desert air; from the clamoring east to the hushed southwest—it was quite a "trip." You may not feel inspired to move far away, but you will have some type of change in scenery—a new, 360-perspective.

How will you change the scenery without moving far away? Look in your backyard like Dorothy did in *The Wizard of Oz*. She took a heroine's journey, didn't she? Dorothy left home, took the rites of initiation, fought the trials and tribulations on her yellow brick road, and then returned (even though she had never really left) with the self-realized message for us all: There's no place like home. *Wherever you go… there you are.*

So, as suggested much earlier in this book, you do not have to leave your location unless you are guided to. Expect some type of change in scenery or "a separation" as it is a dimension of the journey: Whether it is quitting a job that is lackluster and you are floundering in it, or quitting a cruel, dysfunctional relationship—whatever it is—you will change it. Then, eventually when ready… you may return to it joyfully without any resistance. All in divine timing. Basically, the new scenery reflects your true nature on the path. You have *always* been on a path—possibly just sleepwalking through much of it.

The 360 Daily Practice has birthed self-realizations in your blessed turnaround: You've accepted the fact—*as your own truth*—that you are a Spirit 24/7 and therefore create ALL reality. As daunting as it may sound, you now know you are courageously responsible for EVERYTHING happening. You have cleaned up your act, and know about weaving authentic, empowered, and balanced patterns into a sacred space, or core sphere of influence.

You take awesomely brave, comprehensive, radical, and resolute action: Creatively loving your body from Higher Consciousness while quieting the local or ordinary mind.

You are primed now to enter the *4ᵗʰ Quadrant of Actualization* completing the heroic sphere of 360 Transformation. Having absorbed a lot of information, concepts, and ideas, I trust you are digesting them well like a delicious meal of blended flavors and textures. On this awesome journey to Oneness, you are "seeing" spherically—three hundred and sixty-degrees. Therefore, you are more open, flexible, and clear. You honor the concentric circles of all consciousness. Walking through life, eyes open to Soul's passionate direction. You are aligned with divine love—24/7. No one can stop you now because Soul drives the rainbow bus— hosting the loving sangha of mentors and allies. This is a magical mystery tour, and all you need is love. Love is all you need. Align yourself with it. Meet me at the corner of easy street and love. I am waiting there… to play in this great game of life.

Remember in THIS moment: You are in and of the One Source. In the entire history of the universe, no one has ever been YOU; no one is like YOU, and no one will ever, ever be as *onederful* as YOU.

4th QUADRANT of ACTUALIZATION

Transformation 360

Chapter 10

360 Faith and The Invisibles

"And when they were come to the multitude, there came to him a certain man, kneeling down to him, and saying, Lord, have mercy on my son: for he is lunatic, and sore vexed: for ofttimes he falleth into the fire, and oft into the water. And I brought him to thy disciples, and they could not cure him. Then Jesus answered and said, 'O faithless and perverse generation, how long shall I be with you? How long shall I suffer you? Bring him hither to me.' And Jesus rebuked the devil; and he departed out of him: and the child was cured from that very hour. Then came the disciples to Jesus apart, and said, 'Why could not we cast him out?' And Jesus said unto them, 'Because of your unbelief: for verily I say unto you, If ye have faith as a grain of mustard seed, ye shall say unto this mountain: Remove hence to yonder place: and it shall remove; and nothing shall be impossible unto you."

— The Bible, Book of St. Matthew, 17: 14-20[1]

*G*azing out the car window to a big sky of painted scenery, the sun had just dipped below the mesa, casting a rich salmon color in vigorous, rouge hues onto the Sandia Crest at 10,678 feet.[2] Called "Turtle Mountain" by Native Americans living peacefully on the land for thousands of years, it got its other colorful nickname "sandia" by European colonizers of the sixteenth century. In Spanish, "sandia" means watermelon and during our rosy sunsets there is some likeness to this enormous, delicious fruit. Yet, when driving southward from the state capital of Santa Fe, the Sandia mountain range (which is separate from the Rockies to the north) resembles a gargantuan turtle, more so, than a melon.

As you recall in the *2nd Quadrant*, I fondly discussed Animal Medicine of our Native American brothers and sisters. In this tradition, they see the *entire* world as sacred—and a mountain is certainly no exception. Carrying in your heart-space the feminine principle of Turtle Medicine means that you are aligned with the oldest energy of our planet, Mother Earth—and are therefore, grounded. When I was in the process of Doing a 360, providence faithfully guided my relocation to this area. It wasn't a question—it was a knowing. Settling into our home in the foothills of this huge turtle, I remember the very weighty, profound sensation of picking up a granite stone in the backyard—knowing it was one billion years old. This was sacred ground.[3]

Traveling through landscape awash in a great mystery of the ancient ones, I looked up to father sky surrounding this palette of sunset color. Kaleidoscopic twilight was now upon us. Mountain vistas greeted in comfort with silence. Their powerful presence restates beauty of the land with a subtle, invisible *knowing* like the Master Jesus taught in his parable of the little mustard seed: We can move mountains if we choose to.[4]

So there I was, encircled by majestic peaks just a few, fragile weeks into writing this book. As I road on southward getting closer to this mama turtle, some doubt crept into my small, local mind that many writers get:

> *I am here to serve… but is this book any good? Am I wasting my time? Will it wind up in the trashcan? Are my musings going to help anybody? Is this 360-stuff awful or full of awe?*

That night a wondrous thing happened. Well, it's not really "wondrous" since I have been (from the time as a small child) acquainted with the numinous of our phenomenal world. I had a sign…

Dancing with the Angel

A glistening, golden bronze angel of heaven's "most high" appeared to me, not just in a dream, but a lucid dream. (Lucid is from the Latin word *lux*, meaning light, which was mentioned in dream yoga practices.) This androgynous angel had overtones of decidedly feminine features, though more of a male-looking face and body with a smooth, bare chest and gorgeous head of thick, black hair. Words are a finite, limiting way of communicating, so it's challenging to describe an indescribably shimmering, heavenly being. Have you ever tried expressing what a banana really tastes like? Good luck! You might say, "Well, it is sweet and yellow; it's soft and good." You will need a taste to discern the difference between a banana and an orange.

My angelic host did not speak or even seem to smile. In fact, there was no human expression whatsoever, which later was confirmed to be "normal" in the realm of God's messengers after reading *Life on the Other Side,* by Sylvia Browne. There was however, a strong telepathic communication: What entered my Higher Consciousness was transference of power. You see, I had never witnessed an angel before. Lots of people see them—I *knew* that—but I wasn't one of this fated crowd. In fact, as a skeptic, I never read angel books like many friends and colleagues. There was a time in the 1990s when a flood of angel stuff flourished and everyone was collecting angelic figurines, pictures, divination cards, etc.—I didn't. As a serious student of Tibetan Vajrayana Buddhism, if anything was going to appear to me (I thought from the limiting "conceptual" local mind) it's going to be a dakini or Tara, the female Buddha of great compassion; or some sacred formless form, like *that.*

An aura of intensely, radiant gold, dust-like particles of light swirled around this divine messenger's body, which was a beautifully illumined, extremely tall (8-10 feet) human-like shape. IT was the most significant vision I'd ever seen. Even considering the ultimate, alarming and unusual array of both (wrathful and peaceful) deities depicted in Tibetan Buddhist iconographical art, (which I'm quite familiar with), this appearance was AWESOME.

Obviously, I did not use that word lightly. I was humbled by this divine visitation and feel inept putting into coherent words what this Spirit looked or felt like. As said before, words are limiting—they do not dwell in the blessed realm of transcendence.

I will disclose to you: This angel was *real*. It was the most commanding lucid dream ever experienced, and this being was divine—of that, I have no doubt. There was incredible POWER and in *feeling* it, I sensed the magnanimousness and benevolence of God. My angel of the most high "directed" me to dance (it was more like floating a few feet above the floor) in a circle with our arms upraised towards each other and the heavens. Around and around we went like two whirling dervishes in unison, effortlessly circling my family room in front of our kiva-style fireplace. Initial apprehension grabbed me because this celestial being did not smile when IT looked directly into my eyes—but I *felt* the holy authority—*that* was incredible. Unwavering telepathy was: THIS IS THE POWER OF GOD. LET GO and TRUST—so I did.

The next morning when I told my husband (my greatest ally) about the nocturnal visitation, he was intrigued and supportive. A great blessing had been bestowed—and it was monumental. I pondered the clockwise emphasis of floating in circular dance. *I got it.* Faith and confidence with certainty wisdom: I was "doing the right thing" writing a book called *Doing a 360*. The metaphor delivered made sense—I was on the right track. My messenger made it clear that I was not to give up.

Feeling empowered, I continued writing with faithful fervor that "360" was in some way anointed. Spirit had sent a message, and I was listening. It had magic with palpable energy. So, I typed feverishly, knowing these writings would help someone discover a heroic path to self-actualization.

Though I had an affinity for writing, I had never published a book. Now I knew confidently God would take care of *that* part of the journey—the "how" it was going to get into the hands of readers, essential seekers of Oneness, like you. I had a convincing sign; God wanted it—that was for sure. This was a "God Job." Nothing could shake my conviction. "Certainty Wisdom," which the Buddha gave as pith instruction—was alive and well on the computer keyboard.

Still a bit perplexed about this whole angel thing, I grappled with the label obsession. What would my hardcore Buddhist friends think? I did not realize until the book began to take shape that it was meant for ALL—any tradition or no tradition. God loving or Atheist. Anyone. This was not to be another yoga book urged by my students to write; or another Dharma book, since authentic masters had eloquently presented so many.

Just days after this angelic revelation, intuition took me to visit the library. On the shelf were a couple of books by Sylvia Browne I was strongly guided to. Reluctantly, I borrowed these as well as other publications. Once home, hers beckoned me from out of a large and juicy pile of classic Yoga and Buddhist texts stacked on the coffee table. This world-renowned psychic and prolific bestselling author of thirty-plus books examines levels of angels, including their imageries. She says "gold" angels are the eighth of eight-levels, the "highest level of breathtaking power" known on the other side as, The Principalities. There in print was a perfect description of my heavenly being.[5]

Years back while shopping I remember a girlfriend inquiring incredulously, "You haven't read any of Sylvia Browne's books?" "No," I said matter-of-factly, "You know me, I don't usually read a lot of that psychic or new age stuff." "Oooohh," she responded with that little word drawn out s-l-o-w-l-y in a tone nuanced with tiny sarcasm. Yet, as we stood together in that pleasant bookstore she smiled lovingly with compassion through a minuscule speck of disappointment at my foolish judgment... as if she saw my future golden messenger, hovering—right there. *It is, as it is.*

Two Sides of a Coin

Gold angel? You may be ruminating: How is this going to help me? Well, it is simple at the core. You must have faith in the invisibles. Bear in mind it is only a limited perception that makes them invisible, anyway. There really is no other side, as in two sides of the same, shiny coin (that limited concept comes from your ego, duality thinking). There is only the ONE SOURCE OF BEING in the realm of the Absolute, which is also here and now in the space-time continuum. In the ostensibly relative reality of life, we erroneously think (from that old subconscious paradigm) of an "other side" where the beings—angels, spirit-guides, fairies, dakas and dakinis—whatever you wish to call them, exist separate from our side.

My earliest childhood memories recall that I enjoyed a rock collection that included crystals. Also as I got older, I loved to burn incense much to the chagrin of my mother, who would yell up the stairs, "What is that smell!? Are you burning that stuff again!?" Holding séances with the Ouija board (at age ten) were enigmatically fun, especially one time when my bedroom window shade mysteriously snapped, and then rolled up in a scary, loud bang. I was keenly aware of the invisible world. With the benefit of hindsight in these vivid memories, it is astonishing that my devout Lutheran mother even allowed me to have a Ouija board in her house.

Continually bewildered, I did not belong to these good folks who gave me precious life. I don't mean that in any negative way, it was just youthful intuition to know that I (my Soul) chose parents without a culture of fairylike magic. Of course, as a child I did not fully get the nuances of that perception, but I knew I didn't fit into their scheme of life. Everything seemed so harsh and hard. Life was *supposed* to be a struggle in their world.

So, I communed with my animal friends, the trees, and the big sky—especially the moon when exceedingly full—what a glowing delight. Around age eleven, I got my wish-fulfilling jewel in a little telescope. I was ecstatic! Other girls desired Barbie dolls and such—not me. I wished to escape in the big view, craving visitations with celestial hosts. It felt so good to fantasize where I came from. How nice to seem closer to twinkling stars of the universe—my home. I connected with the invisibles to help bide time, setting my life in perspective as I got older. Like so many of us on the journey, I just had to figure out my resolve to stay in this wonderfully weird place.

Developing Your "Lighter" Side

Having entered this last *4ᵗʰ Quadrant*—preparing for what Joseph Campbell called "the return," which is completing the journey as a hero ready to bestow boons on his fellow man—we are going to sightsee into a lighter side. Your "lighter" side is intuition or spheroid knowing. As you live a heroic, empowered life, intuition naturally integrates as a hefty and practical part of it.

Intuition is not something unusual or far-out that happens to just a few "spiritual" types. You are Spirit. You will learn to trust intuition because you step aside and surrender to divine, Higher Consciousness. This is the hallmark of creating and living a 360 Lifestyle. What you feel—as a deep sense of peace—is your true nature. Intuition is a signpost on a trail in the woods helping you find the correct way. Your way is Soul's mission, a noble quest for enlightenment through service. In the sacred ground of being-ness, you will know what to do for the good of all. The good of all is Oneness.

Guidance amplifies in a quiet mind. Listen to Soul steering the magic bus wheel on this journey to wholeness. Coincidences or miracles will be so common; they won't marvel you anymore because they just "are what they are." Expect them. They are part and parcel with Soul's experience as a divine being. Operating from a lighter side, you will manifest (more quickly) what you think. That means, you must be careful of thoughts—they have such power. Why? Because dear reader, you are a Creator. With a fresh view from three hundred and sixty-degrees, you'll see the omniscience of a much lighter side of life. You'll discern through a plush, intuitive nature your unique importance *in* and *of* this divine, spherical matrix. With this knowing firmly grounded in your heart-of-hearts you will bring forth gifts to humanity.

Re-calibrating life to bestow boons and blessings on your fellow humankind is a hero's pledge. As a channel of the lighter side, offer a whole, sacred being. This is a real, heroic ministry. And you don't have to be a minister (like me) to have a ministry. Following your bliss will be how you minister to others.

Chapter 11

Creating a 360 Lifestyle

"Every artist dips his brush in his own soul, and paints his own nature into his own picture."

— Henri Matisse

t seems a lifetime ago I received mantra initiation from the inimitable, Swami Vishnudevananda. A great yoga master of the twentieth century, he founded one of the largest schools of yoga— Sivananda Yoga.[1] My treasured heart-friend and mentor, Chandra Shekhar, was a senior disciple of Swamiji. That is how I met this world-renowned yogi of limitless energy and inspiration. Years ago, when Swami Vishnu visited our area, Chandra requested that I be responsible for greeting him at the airport; and then driving Swamiji to a friend's home-yoga studio where he was giving a lecture and then staying overnight.

Living on the Lotus

After the customary protocol of *Namaste* with prostrations, smiles, and flowers, a cheerful crowd of Swami Vishnu's devotees scattered to their cars. My husband was driving (thank goodness) so I had the perfect opportunity to chat with Swamiji. After initial fun, small talk, I wished to know the deeper meaning of a name that he had given me. The previous year at his New York ashram, Swami Vishnu conferred ancient blessings of mantra initiation during a private, transcendent ceremony (with two other friends). Along with that sacred tradition was the bestowal of my spiritual name, Nalini. (*Nalini* is Sanskrit for a name generally meaning, lovely lotus-plant.)

Now I asked him to explain it, in-depth. In his heavy Indian accent—which seemed to dart dynamically as sparks through the air—Swami Vishnu explained that *nali* is water, and that *ini* (as I already knew) meant the female aspect of it. (All Sanskrit words that end in "ini" signify the feminine, such as kundalini, dakini, yogini, etc.)

"However," he affirmed so intriguingly, "this name for *you* means that, you, Nalini, are like a perfectly round drop of water that rolls on a lotus petal." There was a very long pause. He was waiting to see if I would react in some way—I did not. I was stunned by the magic of the moment.

"You are IN the world," he continued cleverly in broken English through his playful trademark smile, "but you are not OF this world. Do you understand me?"

"Uh... uh... I think so. Uh... would you tell me more, Swamiji?" I replied hesitantly to the master, almost speechless.

"A lotus represents spiritual awakening, as it has risen quite miraculously and beautifully from very long roots out of thick, dark mud. The little water droplet *is* made of water, yes?" He questioned me seriously this time in piercing eye contact from his comfortable back seat of our car.

"Yes." I nodded thoughtfully with my head turned to the yogi (cloaked in traditional orange robes with a saffron shawl).

"Ah... so you see, *Nalini*... you are like the water drop

moving around on the soft lotus... yes? You are flowing through life as a part of it... but you are really not in it—not attached. Like the little droplet, you have left the pond, yet, you are still the essence of that element—water."

After a pause, the legendary yogi asserted with compassion and wisdom: "Do you understand this now?"

"Yes, Swamiji, yes, I think I do," I replied enthusiastically in astonishment.

We drove on in silence for a while.

Carrying this precious being, our priceless cargo, I attempted to focus on the busy highway traffic so we wouldn't miss our exit. He sensed this teaching would sink in eventually. I was a young yogini—in my twenties—but I *got* it. It was one of those very special "aha" moments in life that are so incredibly powerful, they can literally define who you are.

When heroically spiraling up from deep, underworld regions of heartache and then transformed into beauty as a lotus, you have done a 360 with your life. As in our evolution—you can never go back. Fluidity and flexibility are leaky margins in day-to-day living. You create and live a heavenly lifestyle, like the little water droplet effortlessly rolling along... aligning with divine love. You move to the corner of easy street and love. Living on the lotus—peace, love, and joy inspire heroic reality: knowing you are in this material world, but not really of it.

Walk the Talk

Sustaining a 360 Lifestyle springs forth from an overarching application of the 360 Philosophy of Oneness, and a 360 Daily Practice. Your individuated Soul spins around to a renovated, re-calibrated life.

As a creative being you design and polish a practice that filters through your own expression of light. For example, if you are a Buddhist monk, you chant, meditate, and say prayers for all sentient beings—that is your "practice." If you are an attorney, a law practice is how you describe what you "do." A doctor has a practice. Similarly, develop a practice suited to your needs—this is a 360 Daily Practice. Having died to your former self, engage the world with a new, unaffected identity. Like an exquisite lotus plant, your fresh persona is authentic because it sprang forth genuinely from your Soul. Radiance rules from the core of your being. The throne is yours. You rest in the recliner chair of a heroic life. You walk the talk. As said numerous times, you are here in human form for Soul to experience the gift of life, as IT is being lived—moment-by-moment. You ascend. And you evolve to the next spiraling, spherical experience. The fourth and fifth dimensional realities begin to blend with 3D living.

Integration of higher, universal vibratory frequencies during this stage of your total-turnaround will vary, rolling back and forth like the water droplet. Sensitivity to the denser energies (as well as some finer ones) is to be expected. The relative world of programmed functionality is now over for you. Robotic phases of time-segmented sequences, such as minutes, hours, mornings, afternoons, evenings, and night, fade into fifty shades of material world obscurity. Time shifts. *You* shall shift like the round, fluid drop living on the lotus. Earlier, you were introduced to uptime and the desperate need for it—as a poet's muse. Uptime is now your cherished companion to wholeness.

Balance is the key as you reflectively merge day-to-day stuff with Higher Consciousness and The Collective. A 360 Daily Practice keeps you grounded in the world. Remember that this world—like your temple—is sacred. It's not something to escape from. Wherever you go... there you are. That is true Oneness. 360 = One. In total heroic surrender to the mystery of life in the great void, open-mindedness and compassion develop as you re-calibrate the nuances of living.

Do not compare yourself to anyone.

And—patience *is* a virtue. Remember the young child in a grocery store cart that wanted it all, immediately? God does not perform this way. You need faith and common sense. You shall manifest as Soul directs. What may be perceived as a "long time" is always appropriate in divine timing. Uptime is in the domain of your Soul. Use that sacred time wisely as you yearn for a full flowering of the life that you are creating.

Peaks and Valleys

Do not make the mistake of going around town preaching the gospel—driving your family and friends, nuts. Do your own thing in your own way. People may not understand these changes that you are going through. Each has their own spiritual blueprint with a huge house to build and decorate, so please do not judge. Practice discernment in weaving the patterns of living. Work on you—the *one* and only you—not the dualistic two of you (Higher Consciousness and fear-based, ego-mind), but the one true being of wholeness. Your mirror reflects the divine.

Use skillful means, like Psyche, who summoned Ants to help divide the many piles of grain. Gather allies and mentors to your side. Focus on your 360 Daily Practice—24/7. Contemplate and meditate upon great gifts you have for the world. When you are ready—gift us. We wait patiently… If you hear some undesirable comments, brush them off—and move on. Be brave; know that there are others like you growing in the army of Oneness.[2] You are not alone in the world during these challenging times. Practice the strategies and exercises offered here to magnetize (like a boomerang) balanced choices, enacted with grace and gratitude. Use warmhearted Animal Medicine to heal patterns. Focus on virtuous qualities from the lighter side. Let shadows of negativity flow through because you are porous, light, and free. You are "P and A" and therefore, know how to mindfully follow your bliss.

Walk the talk. That means every journey starts with one step. So, put one foot in front of the other and get going. Do the work presented. Keep the faith during times of great heartache when it seems your re-calibrated frequency has been washed-away down an arroyo of imbalance. It hasn't. Each experience is orchestrated from divine providence. Step aside, and see your life as a series of "God Jobs." Remember the peaks and valleys: they are a natural part of any mountainous landscape. As The Christ Consciousness taught through Jesus: Have faith to move mountains. Apply the tools shared here—they work.

Do not talk, yet. Walk. Walk the talk. You can do it. Be still in this present moment. All that exists is now. When deliberate, life is deliberate with you. Your Soul aspires to fulfill ITS mission. Remember the mission. However you joyfully spend time is a clue to Soul's passion. When I compose, hours slide by in uptime. When engrossed in sacred impulses an entire morning may pass to twilight without "realizing" it. If you are focused in ebullient rapture during projects, then look to those as your passion. What brings immeasurable joy? How can you serve in joyful effort? Will you establish a sacred ground by acting upon these passions? However you choose to do it, in whatever way guided by Higher Consciousness—do it.

Ah, now months pass… Know with great determination and certainty wisdom that you *have* established a more balanced life. Do not let yourself fall back into those old destructive patterns. Keep in mind that we are creatures of habit, and therefore, must re-habituate into a new philosophy. There are peaks and valleys because everything in nature has a curve. Re-calibration depends on your particular situation. Focus on the present moment with joyful appreciation of a wonderful opportunity—life. The past is gone and the future is only speculation. Perception is always a key to salvation—which is in this "present and available" moment. Use this book as a reference and do the exercises—24/7. Keep steadfast in your daily practice.

Doubt: A Robber of the Mind

Attending a party one chilly winter evening, a few gathered near warmth of the glowing kiva-fire. A younger, well-educated man asked me what category or type of nonfiction book I was writing. Enthusiastically, I regaled that *Doing a 360: Turning Your Life Around to Follow Soul's Purpose,* was about changing lives—totally. He countered with a doubtful squint on an intelligent face, "I don't know if people can change. Do you *really* think that people can transform their life? I mean… is it possible for people to change themselves *totally?* I don't know… I doubt it."

My heart sank hearing this sincere questioning, for I *knew* in a heart-of-hearts that he was referencing, himself. When using the phrase "my heart sank" it means, energy or vibratory frequency has shifted down from the heart-center to the manipura (a lower chakra residing in the solar plexus area, as mentioned earlier). Consciously knowing this I raised it back to the heart, replying with deep compassion, "Oh yes, yes, I absolutely believe we *all* will change—the survival of our planet depends on it."

My Soul felt his yearning. I heard the cry and sensed a Soul-to-Soul conscious connection in that powerful moment. Whether he intuited that or not doesn't matter because his Soul helped me to help you, right now. Everyone we meet (anywhere we go) has purpose, a reason—there are no coincidences in the excursion to enlightenment. All are interconnected as islands under the sea. We know with confidence that the bottom of the ocean, though seemingly an endless abyss, is indeed, down under the surface. If God sucked all of the water off the planet in one, great, big gulp, then all you would see remaining would be the ground of brown Earth. "Islands" would no longer have water isolating them from the other island masses. Separation *is* really an illusion, isn't it? Oceans only "cover" the land deep below. In this same way, Soul is here. You *know* because Soul's memory has been activated—you remember—you *feel* it. These stirrings infuse the heart. You were *supposed* to read this, so there is resonance.

The Buddha called doubt, a robber of the mind. Khenchen Rinpoche gave this essential dharma teaching because he knew that the dark shadows of doubt and fear could creep in and steal our clear light luminosity. There are times that you may doubt the brilliance of your being. As you make a 360-turnaround, those times will become few and far between. If doubt arises… let it go in a nanosecond or just as quickly as you can. Call upon The Wise Ones to help in your darkest hour. Ask. Always ask, and they will assist. Pray. Always pray in *your* way. Because we are Spirit Beings of free will, you must request help. And know you aren't alone on this journey. Though you walk the "good red road" as a solitary hero traversing a steep and narrow path, your mentors and allies (on both sides of the coin) walk lovingly ahead, and just behind. Have faith in the invisibles as you live spherically on the massive playground of life. Be patient. All emerges in divine timing.

Chapter 12

Following Your Bliss

*"Follow Your Bliss. Find where it is, and don't be afraid
to follow it."*

— Joseph Campbell

rising from bed early one morning, my eager feet touched the Earth with great joy, excitement, and thrilling, childlike wonder as if it was Christmas. However, this morning was a crisp, kaleidoscopic, wind-blown cascade of colored leaves type-of-day in the month of October—October 24th. Was this my birthday? Nope. Was I receiving an award? Not at all. Was I going on a well-deserved long vacation to the Island of Fiji? Ah... no. Why then, such a special date, you might ask? Well, it was Global Oneness Day, modeled after the festivities of Earth Day, successfully produced forty-plus years ago.

Global Oneness Day was launched in 2010 as a worldwide celebration of the sacred Oneness of all life. Humanity's Team, a large, not-for-profit organization with volunteers or "teammates" in 150 countries, is shepherding this "grassroots movement for the Soul," vowing to inspire and uplift humanity to a thriving consciousness of Oneness, in one generation.[1]

The Oneness Revolution

Look around with fresh 360 Vision: Our world is in the midst of revolution—a spiritual evolutionary revolt. Like that adage mentioned earlier: "Do not miss the forest for the trees," we are in so very deep that some people may not know. This worldwide spiritual revolution has been fought on numerous battlefields of consciousness, playing out in cultures everywhere like the "Arab Spring" and "OWS" (Occupy Wall Street), etc. These sacred combats (and others to come) are in full-view when opening your eyes to the truth. Remember, this is my truth, yet I implore a consideration to open your heart in a truth of Global Oneness. This is a "Oneness Revolution" whether you are aware of it or not (until now). You are a major player in this divine affair. Me? Yes, YOU. We are midwives (men and women) at this glorious birth to the united and peaceful world of seven billion living in harmony. I may not be here to see its full, vibrant flowering in this embodiment, but I have fervent hope for a sustainable future beating as one global heart. This may sound a bit Pollyanna, but I don't mind because I have conviction of the heart—a global heart. *Doing a 360* helps you awaken to Soul's specific purpose and commitment when joining this heroic army for planetary enlightenment. Early on it was said that this is your clarion call to a renewed, divine life. Yes, re-calibrated deliberate living may be yours—if you choose to accept it, right now. If you already have then I salute you, dear reader, in this sacred endeavor.

At the turn of the 20th Century, industry—with its massive factories and machines—infused The Industrial Revolution. Next came a mind-blowing Technology Revolution: The Nuclear Age had arrived with the first explosion at Trinity White Sands, New Mexico. We literally (and of course figuratively) dropped the bomb on consciousness. Then, the global blast of computer technology accelerated our already chaotic lives in crazy, yet fascinating ways

never before imagined. We've evolved into a r
frontier" is not space, and it's undeniably
Consciousness. Humanity has emerged at the ev..
of the door to heroic Oneness. We celebrate this ...
phase of the great spiritual revolution, or as I see it with spher..
knowing, The Oneness Revolution. 360 = 1.

Jumping Off the Fringe

As shared previously, when teaching yoga back in the 1970s
it was considered "on the fringe." Yoga is so popular now that
this open shift in consciousness stretches me into great hope and
encouragement. Now, even the most conservatively stodgy and
rigid person says, matter-of-factly, "Oh yes, I've done yoga; It's
good for you." Here in the 21st Century, I pray I'm not hanging
out on the edge. Honestly, individually and collectively, we can't
wait much longer as a species co-inhabiting a sick, abused planet.

This is the eleventh hour. Or, as a colleague tweaked it, "It is
11:59." Modern-day messenger and spiritual teacher (Humanity's
Team founder) Neale Donald Walsch, advises that we are in the
"storm before the calm." [2] My fervent belief is that this book,
Doing a 360: Turning Your Life Around to Follow Soul's Purpose, is not
dangling out there on the ledge. I've already joyfully jumped off
the cliff into mainstream integration of consciousness. May this
"three-sixty" be wholeheartedly embraced and assimilated into
our modern lexicon as a sacred and sensible, all-encompassing
way of expressing: "I am getting my act together—totally, for my
Soul, family, friends, community and world—for the sake of
serving all sentient beings in heroic ways."

Mythology of Oneness: 360 = 1

As a global community of heart (sangha) we've lost our way.
We must re-invent the metaphoric wheel to a mythic platform with
structures, or spheres of Oneness. Each exquisite being needs to
live his or her own monomyth, which is a radical, passionate, and
heroic journey to wholeness. Now is the time. It may be storming
with lightning and thunder, but now you need to step up to home

plate in a seasoned, spiritual understanding with an umbrella of courage—and hit a home run.

Our individual achievements in life are just that—individual. No one has ever been you, no one *is* you, and no one will *ever, ever be* YOU. This is an awesome truth. Your magnificence, which is an individuated, creative potentiality of a Soul living today, is part and parcel to the entire sphere of creation. You've got to sing your song, write your own book, draw your pictures, and "be" you. Walk your poetic talk, which is spirit in action. No one in the complete multi-verse will ever be able to produce the exact lovely creations that you can. Like The Buddha, who brought his own realizations to the world from an inner journey, you must bring forth your light. And—your virtuosity is sorely needed. It is precious. We are all counting on you—so please "do" it.

That is what revolution does: First, it brings mayhem and turmoil. It springs uprising and upheaval; then, it yields freedom and change—three hundred and sixty-degrees of it. If each one of us awakened splendidly to a grand realization of an actualized (S)elf, imagine how incredibly superb life would be? Since we have drifted away mindlessly from a healthy relationship with the cosmos, the heroic philosophy of a new, spherical, all-quadrant mandala of pure consciousness is now quite vital to a sustainable future. We've become devoid of a personal, meaningful life—a thriving mythology—living in a dismal, default society that is not presently aware and grounded in 360 or spheroid knowing. May the wisdom and therapeutic value of the universal Mythology of Oneness be our children's future.

If you embrace these principles to do a complete-turnaround, then I believe we all have a gallant chance. Our planet has been dying; our rivers and streams are so polluted you can't even wade in them, let alone drink the water. It makes me sick just thinking about it. You have heard this before—it's nothing new. We are destroying the collective temple, which is our lovely home of Earth. But nature can turn itself around, completely. Have respect: Do not fool with Mother Nature—she is capable of "Doing her own 360!" Like the well meaning, but helpless, hasty doctor who tells his patient with "incurable" cancer, "There is simply nothing we can do. I will give you just six weeks to live." And then, this patient miraculously heals and survives month after month, year after year in remission, thriving to a heroic life from Soul's purpose to do so. The physician is in complete awe to the miracle cure: not understanding *how* it happens… but it does.

With its kindhearted medicine, Frog is crying, shedding his sacred tears like fresh, nourishing spring rains to wash away our cloak of ignorance. We can heal, too. With humanity raising its personal and planetary consciousness the world will mend. Every long journey starts with one step. You don't train for a marathon by running 26 miles the first day. You begin with one or two. In subsequent days and weeks, you train harder—run more. You build muscles and get stronger; then you run, ten miles… and five more, as endurance strengthens. Eventually, you run like the wind, and perhaps complete an entire race—maybe win.

Our story—as individuals—is the genuine planetary story. 360 = One. I pray this spherical philosophy penetrates present-day consciousness, living and breathing in the hearts of all—and the sooner, the better. If you adopt and affirm awareness that separation (from all there is) is an imposing illusion, then I know—beyond a shadow of doubt—humanity will thrive. If you take one step, avowing conscious life to the awe of ALL, then there's hope—BIG hope. Each one of us evolves every moment of every day, whether *conscious* or not. Through written material like this and many others, words beckon an awe-inspiring quality of being. So, use 360 as a conscious spherical matrix and change will joyfully be embraced. Authentic living from a heroic Soul is your legacy. Some may call this enlightenment. Others term it waking-up or self-actualization; it does not matter exactly because words are limiting. Language is not transcendent, only experience transcends. This is what counts now—the "doing."

Your Turnaround: "I Did a 360"

The fun begins on the playground of consciously creating life. During recess there are so many cool games to play. We are all children of God, patterned in the SOURCE's creation as Souls experiencing form. Like a character cosmic bag lady pushing her cart, here is some advice in twilight linguistics: Please do not squander this opportunity. Whatever you choose to do, know this: It doesn't matter what you do—you are loved. You do not have to write a book, you can drive a truck; you don't have to join an ashram, you can sell fine cigars; you don't have to live in a cave, you may sail a yacht; you do not have to go to church, instead, you may walk the woods; and, you do not have to act spiritual—you *are* a spiritual being—24/7.

Like Swami Vishnu's little water droplet rolling on the lotus of life, being in the world is only temporary. Earlier, I alleged that it might be scary to change. As in death, we fear the unknown. I think it was comedian Woody Allen who once said, "It's not that I'm afraid to die. I just don't want to be there when it happens." Life is precious. Live consciously, remembering confidently who you are at all times in the great game. Hit your home runs. Go for a "grand slam." Be mindful and "P and A" in sacred space. Listen joyfully to angelic music of the spheres—celestial sounds of your Soul rejoicing in the creativity of ITS being, which is a divine reflection of ITSELF. As genius Joseph Campbell wholeheartedly encouraged: *Follow your bliss.* Find out what that means, precisely and most importantly, uniquely to you. Feel aligned with a greatest degree of love in situations, which bears fruit for all concerned. You are a living, breathing body of bone and flesh with a Higher Consciousness. Live deliberately in every moment. All is given in gratitude and grace when you affirm abundant blessings.

It is envisaged that after reading, practicing the exercises, and conscientiously undertaking the 360 Daily Practice in this book, you'll say "I Did a 360" with my life. This sacred spin harvests a newer you, re-calibrated to higher vibratory frequency. Today, you may imagine your attendance at some future gathering: During a conversation someone announces in heroic assurance, *"Hey, I am doin' a three-sixty with my life."* You'll respond considerately, "how wonderful" because *you* have also done a 360-degree-turnaround to follow Soul's purpose. You applaud them as a new sangha member of Global Oneness, congratulating their sacred journey to heroic wholeness.

As my mentor, the late Reverend Dr. Barbara Hanshaw used to say, "We are only as strong as our weakest link." Eventually, in the shifting years to come, all are going to "Do a 360" in their own inimitable way—our human species depends on it. Soul depends on it, too, whether it happens in this lifetime or the next. In divine time we'll spin around to a fresh, sacred perception of Oneness because it is the inexorable, evolutionary nature of consciousness to do so. This is an exciting period of boundless change for the entire galaxy and beyond. We evolve swiftly in the ascension process. Thank God our planetary consciousness is shifting. Incarnating Souls are exponentially more complex than in the previous generations. The human team in The Collective Consciousness is becoming aware of itself, like a very young child looking in a mirror to recognize itself for the very first time.

John Lennon's legendary lyrics from his song, Imagine: "I hope some day you'll join us and the world will live as one" is so apropos. He was a true visionary. Yes, I hope I don't have to wait another thirty-plus years to see a world grounded in Oneness. I rejoice in the revelation of millions changing lives by following their heroic heartbreaks to bliss. Nothing would please me more than to see this Oneness Revolution explode like a sacred fire igniting the passion of sacred action. I see it happening—I *know* it will. This "certainty wisdom" feels good.

Like my revered furry friend emerging from a long and dark winter hibernation in her cave of consciousness, please "Bear in mind" what you focus on, manifests. The Clear Light Luminosity will deliver. So, get ready. "Do" what you came here to do.

I jumped off the fringe, and stepped up to home plate. The sold-out crowd is cheering. Will you join in the game? Come with me. Like a circle, it is only the end... of the beginning...

360 Epilogue

"Stop the words now. Open the window in the center of your
chest, and let the spirits fly in and out."

— Rumi

n your heart-space and mind—through reading with visualizations—you have gone, full-circle. It is time to fashion a 360 Lifestyle of sustainability. As you take each step in this heroic journey to self-actualization, realize you leave footprints on the "good red road." Others walk *with* you, but no one will walk *for* you. Stroll deliberately, knowing who you are: A Soul fulfilling ITS purpose. Carl Jung coined the term, synchronicity; from now on observe an enchanting acceleration of it. Synchronistic life experiences will be the norm. If they have been already, then just watch their augmentation escalate to greater vistas of vibratory reverberation. You won't be surprised because deep in your heart-of-hearts you *know* it's a magical display of phenomena. In spherical knowing there are no coincidences. It is, as it is. Miracles are the makings of God; and you, my friend, *are* divine. Expect them—24/7.

During your delectable uptimes of "P and A ness" within deep, contemplative practices and profound meditations, you will discern purpose behind every moment of a re-calibrated life. Your life default button has been deleted. In a liberating way you die to your former self. Similar to a common belief by those of the Christian faith: You are re-born. Re-birth or re-calibration is Soul's collective memory activated so IT can proceed to build from the blueprint of ITS divine existence, which is moving inexorably to the Source of All Being.

Perceiving a setback or lapse of any kind, have confidence it is just a required re-set or adjustment to your frequency. Every occasion is a golden opportunity for weaving a better you. When I look back on life, all experience was perfect, though at times I incorrectly thought it was not. Remember that grist for the mill? While in your spheres of influence during (what I call) recess, all actions, like: surfing the web, stuff you read, watching television, going to the movies, places you go, what you eat, who you hang around with, etc., will be what Soul needs. Be "P and A" (present and available) to enigmatic choices (of it all) as you make friends with the mystery. Even seemingly mundane activity affords you incalculable prospects for uptime "spirit in action."

There is much to do, so many awesome games to play on the sacred playground of life. It's recess. And this is a beautiful thing! Your Soul rests in the cocoon-like Supra Conscious State of The Collective Consciousness. Your Soul is here to accomplish ITS supreme tasks. That's the only reason you've chosen this precious birth. Your body is so priceless—honor it well. During extremely challenging times of prodigious awakening, be still and listen to celestial music of the spheres. It's your heroic birthright. You are spiritual.

Remember dear reader: No one in the history of our entire universe has ever been as magnificent as you. No light shines like you; and no one will ever, ever, *ever be* as inconceivably Godly as you. Do not squander this divine gift. Not now—it's too late for that. Once Soul's memories are triggered you can *never* go back. With love as inherent energy, evolve yourself to the next spiraling level of Oneness. What else is there to do in life except align your (S)elf with divine love? As a heroic mathematician of the highest order, your new equation is: $360 = 1$.

Congratulations… you "Did a 360."

Oneness

is the energy of love
that lies within and connects all of life,
enabling us to recognize ourselves in everything.
The universe is one being and we are its cells,
all essential and responsible
for the wellbeing of the whole.[1]

Luminaries

nother metaphor: As warm glowing lights from the desert Southwest winter *luminarias,* (which are celebratory candles illuminating the path from darkness), contemplate these spiritual evolutionary leaders and visionaries in your quest for wholeness. This list is by no means complete. It is a very brief compilation of great voices speaking for global change. I know you'll add to this list—good. Though some have departed this plane, please learn about these brilliant light-beings, their philosophy and life-works. Google and YouTube to your hearts content, and then consider supporting the various projects of these Luminaries, as you feel so inspired:

Esteemed Mythologist, Joseph Campbell (1904 - 1987)
The Joseph Campbell Foundation, http://www.jcf.org
Finding Joe, the movie, 2011

(In alphabetical order)
Maya Angelou
Sri Aurobindo
Thomas Berry
Gregg Braden
Joseph Campbell
Deepak Chopra
Andrew Cohen
His Holiness The Dalai Lama
Wayne Dyer
Masaru Emoto
Mahatma Gandhi
Steven Halpern
Andrew Harvey

Louise Hay
Jean Houston
Barbara Marx Hubbard
B. K. S. Iyengar
Khenchen Palden Sherab Rinpoche
Rev. Dr. Martin Luther King, Jr.
Krishnamurti
Nelson Mandela
Mother Teresa
Padmasambhava
Ram Dass
Don Miguel Ruiz
Sai Baba
HH Sri Swami Sivananda
Huston Smith
Pierre Teilhard de Chardin
Thich Nhat Hanh
Eckhart Tolle
Archbishop Desmond Tutu
Iyanla Vanzant
Swami Vishnudevananda
Neale Donald Walsch
Alan Watts
Ken Wilber
Marianne Williamson
Paramahansa Yogananda

... and so many, many more beautiful Souls.

About the Author

*R*everend Dr. Nancy Ash, E-RYT is a heart-centered mystic celebrating 35 years as a teacher of the ancient sacred ways with an all-encompassing "360" message of Oneness. Born in New York, she studied art for three years at the School of Visual Arts in Manhattan before receiving a B.A. in Creative-Expressive Therapies from the University of Maryland. Ordained in 1985, Rev. Nancy is presently a trans-denominational senior minister with a federally recognized ministry, The Alliance of Divine Love. She was awarded a doctorate in Metaphysics and Spirituality, and is actively teaching, ordaining, and mentoring to those called to serve humanity.

Nancy works passionately as a sacred activist, yoga therapist, counselor, vibrational energy healer, author, and radio co-host and producer of the spiritual talk-radio show *Consider This...* on Blogtalkradio.com, assisting individuals to "Do a 360" with their lives as they fully awaken to Soul's purpose. She mingles a life of service with her best friend and husband of 30-plus years, nestled in the solitude of their home in the foothills of New Mexico. Her favorite "uptime" activities are listening to rolling winds of the canyon, gazing up at stars, walking the woods, and communing with ravens, hummingbirds, and other sacred creatures that visit their home.

Reverend Dr. Nancy Ash invites you to browse through her comprehensive site: www.Doinga360.com (scan the QR code at the bottom of the back cover). An electronic version (e-book) of this publication is distributed worldwide by Smashwords.com and is available now to download on most reading devices. Consider "Liking" this work on Facebook: Doing a 360: Turning Your Life Around to Follow Soul's Purpose. Heartfelt blessings with great gratitude and love for your support.

Nancy is available for interviews, lectures, workshops and classes, as well as one-on-one spiritual direction and mentoring.

End Notes

Gratitude in Grace

[1] Joseph Campbell, *Hero with a Thousand Faces*, (Princeton, Bollingen), 1941, p. 30. This is an essential book for any library.

[2] Padmasambhava Buddhist Centers International; Nyingma Tradition of Tibetan Buddhism; Please visit http://www.padmasambhava.org.

[3] CCWH, Community Chapel for Wholistic Healing, Virginia, USA; founded in 1977 by Reverend Dr. Michelle Lusson.

[4] "The ADL" Alliance of Divine Love International Ministry, www.allianceofdivinelove.org.

[5] *Consider This... with Linda Marie and Nancy*, online talk-radio show, The Art of Living Well Network (TAO) of Blogtalkradio.com (link to author's archived radio program) http://www.blogtalkradio.com/artoflivingwell/2012/06/25/consider-thiswith-linda-marie-and-nancy.

[6] Generally, the Tibetan phrase *lha gyalo!* translates to, "May the Deities Prevail in Victory!" It is a joyful shout one may hear in the Himalayas when a traveler has arrived at the top of a mountain peak, or has reached his or her destination after an arduous journey. The author's teacher, Ven. Khenchen Palden Sherab Rinpoche would customarily jump up in the air at the end of long Dzogchen retreats and joyfully shout, *lha gyalo!*

Preface

[1] Please visit and support The Joseph Campbell Foundation online at this comprehensive and beautiful website: www.jcf.org [Joseph Campbell (1904 - 1987)]

[2] *Autopoeisis*: A word used by Eric Jantsch of Stanford University (*The Self-Organizing Universe, Scientific and Human Implications of the Emerging Paradigm of Evolution*, Pergamon Press, Oxford, New York, Toronto, Sydney, Paris, Frankfurt); and Ilya Prigogine, the 1978 Nobel Prize-winner for his work on Dissipative Structures. Joan Kaye, Ph.D., doctoral thesis, *Healing: A New Paradigm Based on the Teachings of Ilya Prigogine as Presented by Erich Jantsch in The Self-Organizing Universe*, 1986. Auto means, self; poeisis means, producing, forming; also having beauty, imagination, and creativity. Autopoeisis means, self-healing, self-correcting or re-calibrating the self to the (S)elf.

[3] Mythologist and prolific author, Professor Joseph Campbell explains a 'circling' or full-circle experience of a hero's journey in his seminal work: *The Hero with a Thousand Faces*, (Princeton, Bollingen), 1941, p. 30.

[4] Initially the word *monomyth* was written by James Joyce in *Finnegan's Wake,* (New York: Viking Press, Inc.), 1939, p. 581. In the text, *The Hero with a Thousand Faces*, scholar Joseph Campbell elucidated the term as one's universal, mythic journey to wholeness.

[5] Maya Angelou, online interview by Linda Wolf, *"The Teen Talking Project,"* 2004. http://www.daughters-sisters.org/8_interviews/maya/Angelou.htm.

[6] The Five Wisdoms of Tibetan Vajrayana Buddhism are: Mirror-like Wisdom, Equanimity Wisdom, Discriminating Awareness Wisdom, All-Accomplishing Action Wisdom, and All-Encompassing Space Wisdom. The Five Wisdoms are known as the element and color symbols positioned in a circle, *mandala,* or palace of liberated rainbow energy. The reader is asked to envision a circle with the four cardinal directions and a center. To the east is Mirror-like Wisdom; to the south, Equanimity Wisdom; Discriminating Awareness Wisdom is to the west; at the top of the circle or to the north is the Wisdom of All-Accomplishing Action; and in the center is the Wisdom of All-Encompassing Space.

Introduction

[1] Joseph Campbell, *The Hero with a Thousand Faces*, (Princeton, Bollingen), 1941, p. 30.

[2] Ibid.

[3] The word *mandala* from the classical Indian language of Sanskrit is loosely translated as "circle." It is a circular structure, pattern or framework that represents cosmic wholeness. A mandala is a structure organized around a unifying center. The author considers that a labyrinth is a close cousin to the mandala.

[4] *Dzogchen*, a Tibetan word translated as "The Great Completion" or "The Great Perfection." Dzogchen is the highest yoga *(atiyoga* in Sanskrit), the ninth *yana* or vehicle of Mahayana and Vajrayana Buddhism. "Great" is the natural aspect of all phenomena, it is effortless; "Completion" means that the nature of mind perfectly rests in its natural state of consciousness: pristine awareness within emptiness, *always* (time) and *all* ways (space).

[5] Joseph Campbell taught Comparative Literature/Mythology at Sarah Lawrence College in New York for 38 years, at which The Joseph Campbell Chair in the Humanities was endowed in 1986. He posthumously achieved fame from the popular *Power of Myth* PBS television series hosted by Bill Moyers. A master storyteller, Campbell would weave tales of the

world into spellbinding narratives. Joseph Campbell taught that the great scriptures of the world's religions were metaphors for transformation. He is now known best for his saying: "Follow your bliss."

[6] His Holiness The Dalai Lama, *An Open Heart: Practicing Compassion in Everyday Life*, Edited by Nicolas Vreeland (Little, Brown and Company), 2001, p. 30. Tenzin Gyatso, The Fourteenth Dalai Lama received the Nobel Peace Prize in 1989; he has been the beloved spiritual and temporal leader of Tibet.

[7] His Holiness The Dalai Lama and Howard C. Cutler, M.D., *The Art of Happiness: A Handbook for Living* (Riverhead Books, N.Y., 1998), p. 13.

Chapter 1

[1] Mythologist and prolific author, Professor Joseph Campbell, explains the 'circling' or full-circle experience of a hero's journey in his seminal work: *The Hero with a Thousand Faces*, (Princeton, Bollingen), 1941, p. 30.

[2] John Lennon, *"Beautiful Boy (Darling Boy),"* Double Fantasy Album, 1980.

[3] Cyndi Lauper, *Girls Just Wanna Have Fun*, song composed by Robert Hazard.

[4] *Ho'oponopono* is an ancient Hawaiian Shamanic practice, which according to this author, is aligned with "360" forgiveness: *"I love you. I am sorry. Please forgive me. Thank you."* The technique has been popularized in the book, *Zero Limits: The Secret Hawaiian System for Wealth, Health, Peace, and More* by Joe Vitale, (Wiley; 1st Edition), 2008.

[5] Padmasambhava means, The Lotus Born (8th Century Tibet). Padmasambhava is considered the father and founder of Tibetan Buddhism.

[6] Guru Rinpoche is the honorific name lovingly used by Tibetan Buddhists for Saint Padmasambhava. Padmasambhava is Sanskrit for "the lotus born." Guru Rinpoche (at the urging of the Tibetan King, Trisong Deutsen) brought the profound teachings of the Buddha into Tibet from India towards the end of the eighth century AD. Please visit my teacher's website, www.padmasambhava.org.

[7] The dichotomy between local and Higher Self: local is the everyday mind of ego; Higher Self is divine mind of Higher Consciousness within the limitless sphere of Supra Consciousness. The author considers the Soul as Higher Self, as well as the Spirit, which are all used interchangeably throughout this text. The word Soul has been intentionally capitalized throughout this book emphasizing the essential importance of "IT."

[8] Stuart Wilde, *Audio Recording, Visions of Destiny Conference* (Denver, CO), 1987.

---

[9] The Three Times according to Tibetan Buddhism, the space-time continuum.

[10] *Shavasana* is a word in the Sanskrit language, which means corpse or dead man. Pronounced "shah-vasana" it is an *asana* or yoga pose that usually follows a series of other yoga asanas, however it is a powerful, restful posture with its own merit. It is crucial for western culture to master shavasana because it teaches the connection to a portal of deep Soul relaxation helping one to be in the present moment (P and A).

[11] Professor Joseph Campbell is most famous for his quote, "Follow your bliss." The author met the renowned mythologist during a conference for (AHP) Association for Humanistic Psychology in the 1970s. She was (at that time) too young to fully grasp the encouraging message that he personally gave her – until now with a circular journey of "Doing a 360."

[12] The *khandro* in the Tibetan Tantric language means literally, "sky-going lady." The sky walker, or sky dancer is an important female deity of Tibetan Buddhism. (In Sanskrit, the word is *dakini.*)

Chapter 2

[1] Relative Level vs. Absolute Level: This philosophic comparison is used according to Vajrayana Buddhism. Relative is the popular and common understanding of reality having subjects and objects: the ego, the "I" and "Them," which are based on dualistic thinking. The Absolute is non-dual. The author compares relative reality with the "local, little self" and its functionality from the unconscious, unrealized ego-mind.

[2] Venerable Khenchen Palden Sherab Rinpoche, translated by Venerable Khenpo Tsewang Dongyal Rinpoche, *Prajnaparamita: The Six Perfections,* (Sky Dancer Press), 1990. Mahayana Buddhism teaches that the *Prajnaparamita,* or The Six Perfections are the transcendental aspects of generosity, discipline, patience, joyful effort, concentration and wisdom – in that order of development. *Paramita,* a Sanskrit word, is usually translated as perfection. The author, Reverend Dr. Ash, designed and assisted in the publishing of this book, which is still available at www.skydancerpress.com

[3] *Bodhichitta,* a Sanskrit word roughly translated as "enlightenment mind" with the intention to help all sentient beings, cultivating an attitude of compassion and loving-kindness. Developing *Bodhichitta* is very important in the Vajrayana tradition of Tibetan Buddhism. (Oral teachings from Ven. Khenchen Palden Sherab Rinpoche to the author.)

[4] Stephen LaBerge, Ph.D., *Lucid Dreaming*, (Ballantine Books), 1985, pp. 23-25, 117,127, 144-45, 194, 261-64. This is one of the best, simple books on the subject for the reader interested to learn more about lucid dreaming.

[5] Padmasambhava (of India) was invited to visit Tibet by the King Trisong Deutsen in the 8th Century AD to bring the precious Dharma (teachings of the Buddha) to this remote country. Tibet was practicing the ancient Bon religion at that time.

[6] Stuart Wilde, *Audio Recording, Visions of Destiny Conference* (Denver, CO), 1987.

[7] Dzogchen is the profound ancient Tibetan Vajrayana Buddhist practice of The Great Completion. *"It is, as it is"* means, seeing life without duality: life isn't bad or good... it just is, as it is, no matter how tragic or fantastic. The "Complete" View is lovingly non-attached.

[8] Tibetan Saint Padmasambhava said sometime in the late 8th Century, AD: *"When the iron bird flies and horses run on wheels, the Tibetan people will be scattered like ants across the face of the earth, and the Dharma will come to the land of the red man."*

[9] Khenpo Tsewang Dongyal Rinpoche, *Praise to the Lotus Born: A Verse Garland of Waves of Devotion* (Dharma Samudra, The Padmasambhava Buddhist Center), 2004, pp. 13-14; and, Khenchen Palden Sherab Rinpoche, Khenpo Tsewang Dongyal Rinpoche, *The Light of the Three Jewels* (Dharma Samudra), 1998, Editor's Introduction, Michael White, pp. ii-iii.

[10] To learn more about premature birth, please go online to visit and support www.marchofdimes.com

[11] To learn more about Adam Walsh please go to: *The Milwaukee Journal: Life/Style 2* (Online Article), April 30, 1985; and *The Pittsburgh Press* (Online Article), May 1, 1985.

[12] Please visit and support the Institute of HeartMath (Connecting Hearts and Minds) www.heartmath.org

[13] "Bear in mind." It is interesting how play with words is so very powerful. Bear Medicine from the Native American Spirituality Tradition is a great ancient healing medicine of introspection and of deep, inner knowing. Notice the usage of the phrase "bear in mind" when referring to something that we want to "take into account" or "remember." The wisdom of Bear teaches us to go within our cave, deep into our innate true nature, which is at *One* with all things and all life. With Bear we wisely attune ourselves to The Great Spirit... to God... to ALL.

Chapter 3

[1] Labyrinths: Laurie Goodstein, *"Reviving Labyrinths, Paths to Inner Peace,"* New York Times (May 10, 1998).

[2] Reverend Dr. Lauren Artress, *Walking A Sacred Path: Rediscovering the Labyrinth as a Spiritual Tool*, (Riverhead Books), 1995.

[3] Labyrinth info online: Veriditas: http://www.veriditas.org

[4] Visit The Labyrinth Society: http://www.labyrinthsociety.org

[5] Kivas are ancient circular structures. These huge sacred holes were dug into the ground and used for ceremonial purposes by The Ancient Ones (*Anasazi* people) of the United States Southwest, (as well as other indigenous people).

[6] *Webster's New World Dictionary*, (Simon and Schuster), 1982.

[7] Albert Einstein, *Ideas and Opinions* (New York, Bonanza Books), 1954. Based on *Mein Weltbild*, Edited by Carl Seelig, p. 243.

[8] Daniel H. Pink, *A Whole New Mind: Why Right-Brainers Will Rule the Future,* (The Berkeley Publishing Group), 2005.

[9] Jille' Gleason & Rory Reich, *Ancient Secrets of the Fountain of Youth—The Video* (Harbor Press, Inc.), 1999.

[10] *Shamatha*, a Sanskrit word meaning, tranquil, calm abiding that is usually considered a first step in meditation according to Buddhist teachings. (Ven. Khenchen Palden Sherab Rinpoche, oral teachings to the author over a span of twenty years.)

Chapter 4

[1] Initially the word *monomyth* was written by James Joyce in *Finnegan's Wake,* (New York: Viking Press, Inc.), 1939, p. 581. In his text, *The Hero with a Thousand Faces*, scholar Joseph Campbell taught the term as one's universal, mythic and heroic journey to wholeness.

[2] Spider Medicine from the Native American Spirituality Tradition; Ted Andrews, *Animal Speak: The Spiritual & Magical Powers of Creatures Great & Small*, (Llewellyn Publications), 2000; Jamie Sams & David Carson, *Medicine Cards, The Discovery of Power Through the Ways of Animals,* (Bear & Company), 1988. These are wonderful and essential books for any library.

[3] Jamie Sams & David Carson, *Medicine Cards, The Discovery of Power Through the Ways of Animals*, (Bear & Company), 1988. Armadillo Medicine: Ted Andrews, *Animal Speak: The Spiritual & Magical Powers of Creatures Great & Small*, (Llewellyn Publications), 2000.

[4] William Ury, *The Power of A Positive No: How to Say NO and Still Get to YES*, (Bantam Books), 2007.

[5] Ted Andrews, *Animal Speak: The Spiritual & Magical Powers of Creatures Great & Small*, (Llewellyn Publications), 2000.

[6] Jamie Sams & David Carson, *Medicine Cards, The Discovery of Power Through the Ways of Animals*, (Bear & Company), 1988. Armadillo Medicine: Ted Andrews, *Animal Speak: The Spiritual & Magical Powers of Creatures Great & Small*, (Llewellyn Publications), 2000.

---

[7] Jean Houston tells this ancient tale as "Sorting the Seeds," the first of "The Four Labors" of Psyche, in her book, *The Search for The Beloved: Journeys in Sacred Psychology*, (Jeremy Tarcher, Inc.), 1987, p. 162.
[8] *Federal Reserve Survey*, (Online) February 2012. Based on two cards per cardholding household.

Chapter 5
[1] The Bible, Book of St. Matthew, 12:40, (Authorized King James Version Public Domain), 1611. *"For as Jonas was three days and three nights in the whale's belly; so shall the Son of man be three days and three nights in the heart of the earth."*
[2] Eckhart Tolle, *The Power of Now*, (Namaste Publishing and New World Library), 1999.
[3] Dr. Masaru Emoto, *The Hidden Messages in Water*, (Beyond Words Publishing), 2004.
[4] Steven Halpern, Ph.D., *Spectrum Suite,* music CD; the book, *Tuning the Human Instrument*: *Keeping Yourself In "Sound Health,"* (Halpern Sounds, Update edition), 1980. www.innerpeacemusic.com
[5] *New Age Voice* Magazine, February 1999.
[6] Michelle Lusson, *Creative Wellness: A Stress-Management Guide to Total Health and Happiness*, (Warner Books), 1987. The author, Rev. Dr. Ash is featured throughout this publication demonstrating yoga postures; and assisted her mentor Lusson as a yoga consultant for that book. CWProgram founder, Michelle Lusson, certified Rev. Dr. Ash in the *Creative Wellness Programs* as a Wellness Instructor in 1984.
[7] Stephen Mitchell, *Tao Te Ching*, (Perennial Classics, Harper & Row), 1988, p. 1.

Chapter 6
[1] Institute of HeartMath, please visit http://www.heartmath.org/
[2] Georg Feuerstein, Ph.D., *The Shambhala Encyclopedia of Yoga*, (Shambhala Publications, Inc.), 1997, p. 309.
[3] Sigmund Freud (1856 -1939), *The Ego and the Id*, (Pacific Publishing Studio), 2010, original text in German; *The Interpretation of Dreams*, translated and edited by James Strachey, 1955, (Basic Books), 2010, Chapter VII, pp. 513-616; Sigmund Freud, *Group Psychology and the Analysis of the Ego*, (Empire Books), 2012, p. 55.
[4] Philosopher Schopenhauer (a particular favorite of Joseph Campbell), Nietsche, Heidegger, Binet, Janet, von Hartman and others like Dilthey, discussed "the Hermeneutic circle" (the recurring movement between the implicit and the explicit, the particular and the whole).

[5] "The Collective Unconscious," has been written about extensively by Carl Jung, see *Memories, Dreams, Reflections* by C.G. Jung, recorded and edited by Aniela Jaffé, (Vintage Books, Random House), 1965.

Chapter 7
[1] Mark Lehner, *The Egyptian Heritage, Based on the Edgar Cayce Readings* (Virginia Beach, A.R.E. Press), 1974.
[2] Ibid.
[3] Rev. Michelle L. Sycalik and Dorothee L. Mella, *The Future's Blueprint* (McLean, Virginia, Great Adventure Press), 1980; The Lusson Twins, *The Beginning or The End*, (Virginia Beach, The Donning Company/Publishers, Inc.), 1975; information from private life-readings or spiritual attunements; ministerial program and oral instruction from Rev. Dr. Michelle Lusson.
[4] Ibid. *(Future's Blueprint)*
[5] Ibid. p. 8 *(Future's Blueprint)*
[6] Plato's *Timaeus, Critias* Dialogues, 360 BCE. *Timaeus* briefly references and describes Atlantis as only a preface. *Critias* provides much more of a detailed description of the lost continent of Atlantis. For more information visit the website of Bernard Suzanne, http://plato-dialogues.org/plato.htm
[7] Frank Joseph, *Atlantis and Other Lost Worlds*, (Chartwell Books), 2008, (Olaus Rudbeck aka Olaf Rudbeck, the Elder), pp. 35-36. You may also enjoy reading *The Atlantis Encyclopedia*, (New Page Books, The Career Press, Inc.) 2005, by the same author.
[8] Rev. Michelle L. Sycalik and Dorothee L. Mella, *The Future's Blueprint* (McLean, Virginia, Great Adventure Press), 1980; The Lusson Twins, *The Beginning or The End*, (Virginia Beach, The Donning Company/Publishers, Inc.), 1975; and spiritual attunement "life" readings with the author's mentor, Rev. Dr. Michelle Lusson.
[9] ACE is the American Council on Exercise, a nonprofit organization originally founded in 1985 as IDEA, the International Dance Exercise Association. www.acefitness.org
[10] *Yogi Times*, online magazine, 2007.
[11] Richard Gerber, M.D., *Vibrational Medicine*, Third Edition, (Bear & Company), 2001.
[12] Joy Gardner, *Vibrational Healing through the Chakras*, (The Crossing Press), 2006.
[13] Daniel Golemen, *Emotional Intelligence*, (Bantam Books), 1995; and *Social Intelligence: The New Science of Social Relationships*, (Bantam Books), 2006. (See Chapter 4.)
[14] Gladwell, Malcolm, *The Tipping Point: How Little Things Make a Big Difference,* (Little Brown), 2000; and also by Gladwell, *Blink, The Power of*

Thinking Without Thinking, (Black Bay Books), 2005. (Featuring the topic Gladwell calls "thin-slicing.")

[15] Gregg, Richard, *The Value of Voluntary Simplicity* (Wallingford, PA: Pendle Hill), 1936. This is a good philosophical essay on the need and benefits of living more simply.

[16] Ven. Khenchen Palden Sherab Rinpoche and his brother, Ven. Khenpo Tsewang Dongyal Rinpoche, (oral Dzogchen teachings during the 1990s in Florida, New York, Moscow, Russia and India).

[17] Used often in this text, the saying "walking the good red road" is the poetic term for a "balanced" human life on Earth according to the ancient teachings of Native American Spirituality. According to Black Elk from *The Sacred Pipe*: "The red road is that which runs north and south, and is the good or straight way… thus similar to the Christian 'straight and narrow way,'" (University of Oklahoma Press), 1953, p. 7.

Chapter 8

[1] In her own words from a video of her life, *Georgia O'Keeffe in New Mexico*, Georgia O'Keeffe Museum in Santa Fe, New Mexico; www.okeeffemuseum.org, 217 Johnson Street, Santa Fe, New Mexico 87501. Georgia Totto O'Keeffe (1887 – 1986).

[2] Paleo-Indian Period: The Clovis Culture of New Mexico, appearing around 11,500 BCE. Archaeologists now suggest that human settlements were established in this area of the Southwest USA much earlier than previously thought – possibly 30,000 BCE.

[3] In her own words from a video of her life, *Georgia O'Keeffe in New Mexico*, Georgia O'Keeffe Museum in Santa Fe, New Mexico; www.okeeffemuseum.org, 217 Johnson Street, Santa Fe, New Mexico 87501.

[4] Thich Nhat Hanh, *"Flower Fresh"* from an Audio Cassette of *The Miracle of Mindfulness, A Manual on Meditation*, 1994.

[5] Andrew Harvey, *The Hope: A Guide to Sacred Activism*, (Hay House, Inc.), 2009, p. 188. Radio interview with Andrew Harvey (with the author and her co-host) on *"Consider This…" with Linda Marie and Nancy*, Art of Living Well Radio Network, February 20, 2012. Listen here at this archived link: http://www.blogtalkradio.com/artoflivingwell/2012/02/20/consider-thiswith-linda-marie-and-nancy

[6] Majid Fotuhi, M.D., Ph.D., *The Memory Cure: How to Protect Your Brain Against Loss and Alzheimer's Disease*, (McGraw-Hill), 2003. Though not a yoga or pranayama book, this is a great resource for any library. Harvard trained Dr. Fotuhi, a neurology consultant at Johns Hopkins Hospital, has dedicated his entire life to healing the brain. He has found that

ancient yogic pranayama is a key factor in reducing stress and enhancing brain function, particularly in the left and right brain hippocampus. He teaches the 7-count breathing exercise as part of his integral program to improve the brain.

[7] Sri Swami Satchidananda, *The Yoga Sutras of Patanjali*, (Integral Yoga Productions), 1978, p. 3: Sutra #2: *"The restraint of the modifications of the mind-stuff is Yoga."*

[8] Doinga360.com: http://www.Doinga360.com/Hatha-Yoga-Poses.html is the author's extensive website. Click on the Yoga Site-map tab for more information on 360 Yoga. Enjoy!

[9] B.K.S. Iyengar, *Light on Yoga*, (Schocken Books, New York), 1966, pp. 61-62.

[10] Ibid.

Chapter 9

[1] Rev. Dr. Nancy's (the author) yoga towel, which she designed and illustrated in 1992, *Yoga: practice makes perfect,* was featured on the cover of *Pyramid Books and the New-Age Collection Catalog*, Spring/Summer 1994. This graphic design logo, *Yoga: practice makes perfect* was also printed on t-shirts, mugs and tote-bags, which were sold worldwide in the 1990s to yoga centers, healing centers, stores, etc.

[2] Suzanne Snyder Jacobson, *Too Busy to Count the Years*, (Andrews McMeel Publishing), 2002; and, William F. Powers, *Alive and Well: The Emergence of the Active Nonagenarian*, (Rutledge Books, Inc.), 1996.

[3] Joseph Campbell, *The Hero with a Thousand Faces* (Princeton University Press), 1949, 1968, p. 193.

[4] Ibid, pp. 90-92.

Chapter 10

[1] The Bible, *Parable of the Mustard Seed spoken by Jesus, the Christ*, Authorized King James Version Public Domain, 1611, Book of St. Matthew, 17: 14-20.

[2] Robert Julyan and Mary Stuever, Editors, *Field Guide to the Sandia Mountains* (University of New Mexico Press), 2005, p. 21.

[3] Ibid, pp. 22-23.

[4] The Bible, *Parable of the Mustard Seed spoken by Jesus, the Christ*, Authorized King James Version Public Domain, 1611, Book of St. Matthew, 17: 14-20.

[5] Sylvia Browne with Lindsay Harrison, *Life on the Other Side: A Psychic's Tour of the Afterlife*, (New American Library), 2000, pp. 155-158.

Chapter 11

[1] Known as "Swami Vishnu" and "Swamiji," Swami Vishnudevananda authored the classic text, *The Complete Illustrated Book of Yoga,* as well as other yoga books. He is considered a 20th Century Master of Hatha Yoga. His guru was the Indian Saint, medical doctor, and prolific author of more than two hundred books, His Holiness, Sri Swami Sivananda Saraswati. In honor of his teacher, Swami Vishnu founded the International Sivananda Yoga Vedanta Centers, which you may visit online at sivananda.org. More than 26,000 individuals have graduated from the Sivananda Teacher Training Program, the first Yoga Course of its kind. The author, Reverend Dr. Nancy Ash, successfully completed this training in 1985 with Swami Vishnu's senior devotee, Chandra Shekhar Robinson, who resides and teaches in Maryland.

[2] http://www.humanitysteam.org (Humanity's Team)

Chapter 12

[1] For your consideration: Please visit and support the grassroots organization, Humanity's Team at humanitysteam.org. Global Oneness Day is the annual celebration of the unity of all life, which was started in 2010 by Humanity's Team, a worldwide nonprofit organization now in 150 countries. G1Day is celebrated on October 24th of each year. Please consider signing the Declaration of Oneness at another Humanity's Team website: www.global-oneness-day.org

[2] Neale Donald Walsch, *The Storm Before the Calm: Book 1 in the Conversations with Humanity Series*, (Emmin Books, Oregon), 2011. Walsch is the bestselling author of the *Conversations with God* materials, and founder of Humanity's Team. Visit The GlobalConservation.com and nealedonaldwalsch.com

360 Epilogue

[1] Definition of *Oneness* created by humanitysteam.org from the 2011 Humanity's Team Global Council Meeting in Greece.